DICTIONARY OF COMMERCE AND MANAGEMENT

K.C.S. RANGANAYAKULU

ATLANTIC
PUBLISHERS & DISTRIBUTORS

Published by
ATLANTIC PUBLISHERS AND DISTRIBUTORS
B-2, Vishal Enclave, Opp. Rajouri Garden, New Delhi-110027
Phones : 25413460, 25429987, 25466842

Sales Office
7/22, Ansari Road, Darya Ganj, New Delhi-110002
Phones : 23273880, 23275880, 23280451
Fax : 91-11-23285873
web : www.atlanticbooks.com
e-mail : info@atlanticbooks.com

ISBN 81-269-0312-0

Printed in India at
Mehra Offset Press, Delhi

PREFACE

The Dictionary has been carefully compiled and edited to provide all important words, terms, concepts, institutions and principles commonly used in commerce and found in standard books on commerce and management or commercial sections of magazines and newspapers.

Every effort has been made to write the entries in a simple and lucid style to give both straight forward meaning and useful background information and explanation.

The Dictionary would be useful for students of Commerce and Management and candidates preparing for examinations of professional institutions like Institute of Chartered Accountants, Institute of Cost and Works Accountants, Institute of Company Secretaries etc. It would serve as a ready reference source for professional and practising managers, functional executives, management consultants, professional accountants etc. The Dictionary would also be found useful by general readers who may be interested in understanding terms commonly used in commercial news.

I am thankful to my wife Lakshmi and my children Kittu and Subbu. I am also indebted to my colleagues and students who have helped me in this endeavour. I am highly thankful to M/s Atlantic Publishers and Distributors, New Delhi for publishing it.

Suggestions, if any, for improvement of the Dictionary in the next edition are solicited from the readers.

K.C.S. RANGANAYAKULU

A

ABOVE PAR. The par value of a share is its face value. When the share price is above its face value it is said to be above par.

ABSENTEE OWNERSHIP. Exists when the owners of a business firm do not take active part in its operation.

ABSOLUTE ADVANTAGE. A theory first presented by Adam Smith, which holds that because certain countries can produce some goods more efficiently than other countries can, they should specialize in and export those things they can produce more efficiently and trade for other things they need.

ABSOLUTE CHANGE. A theory first prescribed by Adam Smith, which holds that because certain can produce some goods more efficiently than other countries can, they should specialize in and export those things they can produce more efficiently and trade for other things they need.

ABSOLUTENESS OF RESPONSIBILITY. *See* Responsibility.

ABSORPTION COSTING. That type of product costing that assigns fixed manufacturing overhead to the units produced as a product cost. Contrast with direct costing.

ACCELERATED COST RECOVERY SYSTEM. A system of the internal revenue service that requires depreciation deductions to be based on arbitrary 'recovery periods' instead of useful lives.

ACCELERATED DEPRECIATION. Any pattern of depreciation that systematically writes of depreciable costs more quickly than the ordinary straight-line method based on expected useful life.

ACCELERATED DEPRECIATION. *See* Depreciation.

ACCEPTABLE QUALITY LEVEL. A concept of quality control whereby managers are willing to accept a certain level of production defects, which are dealt with through repair facilities and service centres.

ACCEPTANCE. The paying of the first call on a rights issue, thereby accepting the allotment.

ACCOUNT DAY. (*See* settlement day.)

ACCOUNT STATEMENT. When an account with a broker is active, he periodically issues a statement to his client, featuring all transactions, including long and short positions.

ACCOUNT. Summary of the changes in a particular asset or equity.

ACCOUNT. A stock exchange's dealing period is usually two weeks. All deals done for the account during the period are due for settlement on the settlement day relating to that account.

ACCOUNTING. The process of identifying, recording and interpreting economic events.

ACCOUNTING METHOD. *See* accounting rate of return.

ACCOUNTING PRINCIPLES BOARD. The top private sector regulatory body, which existed from 1953 to 1973, when it was succeeded by the financial accounting standards board.

ACCOUNTING RATE OF RETURN. An expression of the utility of a given project as the ratio of the increase in future average annual net income the initial increase in required investment, also called book value rate and unadjusted rate.

ACCOUNTS PAYABLE. Debts that are owed to others and payable within a short period.

ACCOUNTS PAYABLE. The debts shown on the buyer's balance sheet when the buyer has bought goods or services on open account. Usually a current liability.

ACCOUNTS PAYABLE. It represents the current liability towards supplies from whom the firm has purchased raw materials on credit.

ACCOUNTS RECEIVABLE. Debts that others owe the firm due within a year's time.

ACCOUNTS RECEIVABLE. The claims against debtors generally arising from sales of goods or services on open account, usually a current asset.

ACCOUNTS RECEIVABLE TURNOVER RATIO. This is obtained by dividing the total credit sales by the account receivables. The ratio shows how many times the receivables have been collected.

ACCRUAL BASIS. Accounting method in which income and expenditure are entered as and when earned or incurred, although they may not have been received or paid.

ACCRUAL BASIS. A matching process whereby revenue is recognized as services are rendered and expenses are recognized as efforts are expended or services utilized to obtain the revenue, regardless of when cash is received or disbursed.

ACCRUAL METHOD. An accounting method that describes a method of keeping accounts whereby expenses incurred and income earned for a given financial year are shown in the books even though they may not have actually been paid or received during that period.

ACCRUE. Accumulation of a receivable or payable during a given period been though no explicit transaction occurs.

ACCRUED INCOME. The amount of dividend or interest deemed to have accrued during the period since the last distribution of income.

ACCRUED INTEREST. Interest accumulated on debentures since the last interest-payment date.

ACCUMULATED DEPRECIATION. Depreciation up-to-date not just one particular year's.

ACCUMULATED DEPRECIATION. The cumulative sum of all depreciation recognized since the date of acquisition of the particular assets described.

ACCUMULATED DIVIDEND. Dividend due to preference shareholders, not paid and carried forward on the balance sheet as a liability till it is paid. Skipped or passed dividends do not accrue to equity shareholders.

ACCUMULATION. When the price of a share rises as a result of increased buying pressure it is said to be under 'accumulation'.

ACCUMULATION AREA. A term used by technical analysts when the price of a share moves within a narrow range of ups and downs over a period. In the graph it will show as a side-ways movement. Technical analysts interpret this as accumulation or buying activity.

ACHIEVEMENT TEST. A test which measures skill proficiency.

ACID RAIN. Naturally occurring rain that contains dilute solutions to nitric acid and sulfuric acid that are formed when nitrogen oxides and sulfur oxide combine with atmospheric water vapour.

ACID TEST RATIO. The total cash accounts receivable and marketable securities divided by current liabilities.

ACQUIRED ADVANTAGE. A form of trade advantage due to technology rather than the availability of natural resources, climate etc.

ACQUIRED GROUP MEMBERSHIPS. Affiliations not determined by birth, such as religions, political affiliations, and professional and other associations.

ACQUIRER. The acquirer includes any individual company any other legal entity who intends to acquire or acquires substantial quantity of shares or voting rights of target company or acquires or agrees to acquire control over the target company along with persons acting in concert (PAC) with him.

ACQUISITION. (*See* Merger.)

ACQUISITION COST. The original historical cost of an asset acquired. Usually includes directly associated costs such as freight and installation.

ACQUISITION. The purchase of one company by another company.

ACROSS THE BOARD. Any movement in share prices which affects all the shares in the same direction up or down. An 'across the board settlement' with the employees of a company affects all of them from the highest paid to the lowest paid.

ACRS. *See* Accelerated cost recovery system.

ACTING IN CONCERT. When two or more investors act together with the same goal, *e.g.*, buying or selling shares of a particular company to push the price up or down, or accumulating stocks with the eventual purpose of securing a controlling interest in a company. They are acting in concert.

ACTIVE BOND MANAGEMENT. It means that increased volatility brings both greater opportunities as well as risks in managing fixed income securities.

ACTIVE INCOME. Income of a CFC that is derived from the active conduct of a trade or business. As specified by the U.S. internal revenue code.

ACTIVE MARKET. Characterized by frequent and large volume of trading of a particular share or shares in general. In such a market the gap between buying and selling prices is narrow. Also in such a market the buying or selling activities of financial institutions tend to have a lower impact than in a dull market.

ACTIVE MONETARY POLICY. When the fed increase the money supply in an attempt to bring down interest rates, thus pruning investment and aggregate demand.

ACTIVE RULE. A monetary policy rule that prescribes changes in the money supply in response to changes in the economy.

ACTIVE SHARES. Shares in which transactions take place everyday, can be called 'active shares'. The other shares can be relegated to the 'partially active and inactive categories'.

ACTIVITY ACCOUNTING. *See* Responsibility accounting.

ACTUAL COSTING. The method of allocating costs to products using actual direct materials, direct labour, and overhead.

ACTUARIAL. Calculation of premiums and matters connected with pension funds.

ACTUARIAL RATE OF RETURN. Accelerated Cost Recovery which could be withdrawn from the lease. It is calculated as a constant rate of return on the net cash investment in the lease over the period in which there is a positive net cash investment in the lease.

ACTUARIAL TABLES. Tables that give the probability of death for particular age groups. These tables are based on past experience with separate tables for men and women, different racial groups and for certain hazardous occupations. Such a table might indicate that at age 25, a white male would have 1 chance in 350 of dying within the next year and could on the average expect to live 36 more years (to age 72) for a 65 year old white male it might list his chance of dying in the next year as 1 in 10 and his future life expecting as ten years (to age 75).

A-D INDEX OR ADVANCE-DECLINE INDEX. A useful tool for detecting bullish or bearish trend in the stock market in which one divides the number of traded shares which have risen in prices by those which have fallen.

For example, if 200 shares have advanced and 100 declined on a particular day the A-D Index is 2. Index more than 1 indicates a bullish trend and less than 1 a bearish trend.

AD REFERENDUM. When referring to a contract, ad referendum indicates that while the contract has been agreed and signed, there are some matters to be discussed.

ADAPTIVE EXPECTATIONS HYPOTHESIS. Views expectations as evolving relatively slowly over time and being revised in light of past experience.

ADB. Asian Development Bank.

ADD BACK METHOD. The practice of beginning a statement of changes in financial position with net income and then adding or deducting income statement items not affecting working capital.

AD HOC COALITION. Any informal and temporary group organized to lobby for or against a law of government regulation.

AD HOC MARGIN. When a member of a stock exchange has an usually large outstanding position, the exchange collects this margin from him.

ADJUSTABLE PEG. An exchange rate which varies from time to time when it is pegged or tied to another or other currencies. India's Currency has an Adjustable peg.

ADJUSTING ENTRIES. The records made of and accounting transaction giving effect to the correction of an error, an accrual, a write-off, a repayment, a provision for bad debts or depreciation, or the like.

ADJUSTMENT CREDIT. Loans made to depository institutions to allow them to more gradually adjust their reserves and loan portfolios in response to changes in deposits.

ADJUSTMENTS. The key final process (before the computation of ending account balances) that assures the accountant that the financial effects of transactions are assigned to the appropriate time periods.

ADMINISTERED PRICE SYSTEM. A system in which the price is set without close regard to the costs. Obviously, it must be above the break-even price. It generally occurs in the oligopoly models and it tends to remain steady across variations input prices.

ADMINISTRATIVE COSTS. The direct costs incurred in running government regulatory agencies, including salaries of employees, equipment, supplies, and other such items.

ADMINISTRATIVE LEARNING. A stage in the development of social responsiveness within a company during which managers and supervisors learn the new practices necessary for coping with social problems and pressures.

ADMINISTRATIVELY GUIDED MARKET ECONOMY. An economic system in which there is a great deal of cooperation among government, management, and workers to achieve growth and full employment with low job turnover on a non-mandated basis.

ADMINISTRATORS. *See* Managers.

ADMISSION TO DEALING. When a particular share of a company is allowed to be entered in the official list of a stock exchange, it is said to be admitted to dealing.

ADR. American Depository Receipt, United States. Traded securities representing stock in foreign corporations.

AD VALOREM DUTY. A duty (tariff)

assessed as a percentage of the value of the item.

AD VALOREM. Ad velorem means 'according to the name' used to describe the rates of transfer stamp duty payable on a transaction as stamp duty.

ADVANCE CORPORATION TAX. Sum paid by a company to the inland revenue equivalent to the tax credits/issued to shareholders with their dividends as an advance payment of corporation tax for the relative trading period.

ADVANCE DECLINE LINE. It is one of the most important technical indicators of the condition of the stock market. It is the most common measure of market breadth. It is derived by taking the difference between the number of advancing issues and the number of declining issues each day. This daily figure is then added or subtracted each day to a cumulative number in order to determine the advance decline line. It is a measure which will often signal a major change in the direction of the market. Its purpose is to tell whether the market as a whole is gaining strength or losing strength.

ADVERSE IMPACT. Occurs when there is a substantially different rate in hiring, promotion, or other employment decisions which works to the disadvantage of members of protected groups.

ADVERSE SELECTION. In the loan market the situation that occurs as the interest rate rises and honest borrowers decide not to borrow. The bank is left with an adverse pool of borrowers — those who know they are more likely to default.

ADVERTISING AGENCY. An independent business which specializes in planning and carrying out the ventures or campaigns for other business firms.

ADVERTISING. Any type of sales presentation which is of a nonpersonal nature and is paid for by a sponsor.

ADVISORY SENTIMENT. It is often best used as an indicator of contrary option. It is common knowledge that stock market investment advisors tend to be trend followers. They tend to be bullish quite quickly after the market prices start rising. Conversely, when the market has been declining, advisors tend to get over pessimistic. The degree of advisors' pessimism can best be determined by the 'Sentiment index'.

AESTHETIC POLLUTION. Any thing that detracts from the beauty of nature.

AFFILIATED COMPANY. Very often certain operating units of a parent company are not owned 100 per cent.

AFFIRMATIVE ACTION. Refers to efforts by employers to identify problem areas in the employment of protected group members, and goals and steps to overcome those problems.

AFFIRMATIVE ACTION. A positive and sustained effort by an organization to identify hire, train if necessary and promote minorities women, and members of other groups who are underrepresented in the organization's workforce.

AFTA. *See* ASEAN Free Trade Receipt.

AFTER TAX. When a tax-payer is investing in loan investments like debentures or bonds or fixed deposits, it is the after tax return which is the real return not the rate(s) of interest. The relevant rate(s) of interest on the investor's slab of income should be decided from the earnings, and the actual return compared with returns from tax sheltered instruments, such as tax free bonds, or debentures which enjoy an interest exemption, under section (80) of the Income Tax Act.

AFTER TAX INTEREST RATE. The interest rate minus the amount of the interest payment that is due in income taxes. Calculated as the interest rate minus the interest rate times the tax rate.

AGE DISCRIMINATION in employment act.

AGENCY COSTS. The agency problems arising from the conflicts between share-holders, debenture-holders and managers are handled through monitoring and restrictive covenants, which involves cost. These costs are agency costs.

AGENCY FACTORING. This type of factoring basically used as a method of financing book debts under this the client continues to administer credit and operate sales ledger and the factor finances the book debts.

AGENCY SHOP. A shop agreement in which both union and nonunion employees pay union dues but a worker does not have to join the union in order to be or remain employed.

AGENDA. Details of business to be transacted at a meeting. An agenda has to be sent to every equity shareholder before a company holds the AGM.

AGENT. Any person performing an act on behalf of another person is called agent.

AGGREGATE DEMAND CURVE. A relation between the price

level and aggregate quantity of goods and services demanded holding other things such as an interest rates and the money supply constant.

AGING SCHEDULE. The aging schedule breaks down defers according to the length of time for which they have been outstanding.

AGM OR ANNUAL GENERAL MEETING. Meeting held once a year where the Directors of the company report to the shareholders' on the year's performance and any vacancies in the Board of Directors are filled by taking shareholders consent. The chief of the company comments on the future outlook of the company and answers questions from shareholders. Notice of the meeting along with a copy of the annual report has to be compulsorily sent to every shareholder, who may send a PROXY to attend on his behalf. Shareholders can insist that all resolutions on company policy be voted upon by the equity shareholders of the company. This meeting also receives the auditors' report.

AGRARIAN SOCIETY. A society in which agricultural activities dominate work and employ the largest proportion of the labour force.

AGREED VALUE POLICY. It is the sum to be paid out in the event of claim in insurance policy. It is often used for antiquities, jewellery and classic cars.

AIR POCKET STOCKS. Due to sudden and unfavourable news affecting a company or an industry (such as price control or liberalization of imports) there is a steep fall in the price of a share, creating a large gap between a day's closing price and the considerably lower opening price on the following day, an air pocket appears and the stocks are said to be air pocket stocks. Shares which are particularly prone to such falls are usually over priced in the first instance.

AIR POLLUTION. Gaseous elements or particles in the air.

AIR POLLUTION RIGHTS. A legal right to exceed established emission limits such right may be bought, sold or held for future use with approval of government regulators.

ALADI. *See* Latin America Integration Association.

ALL OR NONE. Instruction to the broker, fill the entire order : no partial execution; if you can't, let go.

ALLOCATION. Assigning one or more items of cost or revenue

to one or more segments of an organization according to cause, benefits received, responsibilities, or other logical measure of use.

ALLOTMENT. The number of shares or amount of stock forming part of a new issue and due to an applicant or existing holder.

ALLOTMENT ADVICE. Letter sent to a successful applicant for shares and debentures of a company informing him that he has been allotted.

ALLOTMENT LETTER. The document evidencing an allotment. It is a provisional letter in the case of a rights issue.

ALLOTMENT OF SHARES. Allotment can be made after the minimum sub-subscription stated in the prospectus has been fulfilled. In the event of over subscription the basis on which the shares are to be allotted is decided by the principal stock exchange in consultation with the company. Approval of the other stock exchanges where the shares are proposed to be listed is also required.

ALPHA FACTOR. The concept which measures the inherent volatility of a share. A share with an alpha factor of (say) 1.5 is slated to rise in price by 50% in a year on its inherent strength, such as growth in earnings per share regardless of the behaviour of the market (*See* BETA FACTOR).

ALPHA SHARES. The most frequently traded shares, also called specified shares also called, A group securities (*See* BLUE CHIPS).

ALTERNATIVE DELIVERY PROCEDURE. A delivery mechanism in which the long and the short agree to carry out physical delivery under terms or conditions that are different from the standardized contract rules prescribed by the exchange. The ADP is available only after the end of trading in a futures contract and after the longs and shorts have been matched by the clearing house.

AMBULANCE STOCKS. Securities recommended to an investor whose portfolio has done badly. Insurance Ombudsman : Official in charge of a service set up by insurance companies in 1981, to arbitrate in disputes between insurance companies and policyholders.

AMERICAN DEPOSITORY RECEIPT (ADR). A negotiable certificate issued by a U.S. bank in the United States to represent the underlying shares of a foreign corporation's stock held in trust at a custodian bank in the foreign country.

AMERICAN DREAM. An ideal goal or vision of life in the United States usually including material abundance and maximum freedom.

AMERICAN OPTION. An option that can be exercised at any time prior to the contracts expiration date.

AMERICAN STOCK EXCHANGE. At 86 Trinity Place, New York, the second largest stock exchange in America. Till 1921 it was known as the Kurb Exchange. Stocks and bonds listed at anex are usually those of medium to small-sized companies as also of a large number of oil and gas companies. It is dealing in foreign shares, more than in any other exchange.

AMERICAN SYSTEM. *See* U.S. terms.

AMEX. The American Stock Exchange.

AMORTIZATION. The systematic reduction of a lump-sum amount.

ANALOGUE COMPUTERS. Computers which are primarily measuring devices, measuring quantities on a continuous scale.

ANALYST. An investment professional, who makes buy or sell recommendations. Successful analysts not only influence the fortunes of their employees, but of the shares listed on the stock market as well.

ANALYTIC PROCESS. A production process in which raw materials are reduced to form products.

ANARCHY. A society with little or no government or social controls in which each person pursues individual interests without regard for others.

ANDEAN GROUP (ANCOM). A South American form of economic integration involving Bolivia, Colombia, Ecuador, Peru and Venezuela.

ANNUAL EQUIVALENT VALUE. The value is calculated by dividing NPV by the annuity factor.

ANNUAL MEETING. A yearly meeting called by a corporation's board of directors for purposes of reporting to the company's stockholders on the current status and future prospects of the firm.

ANNUAL REPORT. Formal financial statements, the Auditors' Report, together with the Directors' Report issued by a company. These financial statements are usually prepared at the end of the company's financial year.

ANNUALIZED BASIS. Statistical computation, whereby company figures covering periods of less than a year are extended to cover a full year. The computation takes into account seasonal variations, if any.

ANNUITY. A series of fixed payments starting at the beginning of each period for a specific number of periods is called an annuity.

ANOMALY. The situation where the price of a stock or share is out of line with other similar stocks or shares indicating an opportunity for a purchase or sale.

ANTICIPATED INFLATION. The amount of inflation that is expected.

ANTI-TRUST LAWS. *See* MRTP Commission.

AOL-TIME WARNER. AOL–Time Warner received approval for their $ 106 bn merger in December 2000. For the first time after receiving approval they reported combined earnings. The media and Internet Company has a net loss of $ 1.09 bn. While the total revenues of the combine were around $ 10.2 bn. However, AOL's Internet and cable services reported good growth.

APB OPINIONS. A series of thirty-one opinions to the accounting principles boar issued during 1962-73, many of which are still the accounting law of the land.

APB. *See* Accounting principles board.

APPLICATION FORM. A written summary of the applicants background — education, age, marital status work experience.

APPLICATION MONEY. The amount an investor is asked to pay along with the application for new issues usually less than the full value of the shares the remainder being either fully or partly collected on actual allotment. In the latter case, there will be a final call for the unpaid portion (*See* CALL MONEY).

APPLICATION OF FUNDS. A term featuring on the balance sheet of a company showing how the total funds of the company *i.e.*, share capital, reserves and surplus and loans are deployed. A part of it constitutes NET FIXED ASSETS; another part goes into investments; another towards CURRENT ASSETS, Loans and advances and the remainder is miscellaneous expenditure like technical know-how or royalty on the use of patents and processes.

APPRECIATION. When the dollar appreciates a dollar buys more units of foreign currency than before.

APPRENTICESHIP TRAINING. Training which involves learning a skilled trade, and includes both principles and practices of the specific skilled trade.

APPROACH TO MANAGEMENT. McKinsey' 7-s FRAME-

WORK. An analysis of management which organizes managerial knowledge around the following categories : strategy, structure, systems, style, staff, shared values, and skills.

APPROACH TO MANAGEMENT SYSTEM APPROACH. An analysis of management which emphasizes looking at managerial knowledge from the point of view of system.

APPROACH TO MANAGEMENT, CONTINGENCY OR SITUATIONAL APPROACH. An analysis of management that emphasizes the fact that what managers do in practice depends upon a given set of circumstances or the "situation" and that there is no single "best way" to manage.

APPROACH TO MANAGEMENT, EMPIRICAL OR CASE. An analysis of management as a study of experience from instances of managing.

APPROACH TO MANAGEMENT, GROUP BEHAVIOUR APPROACH. An analysis of management as a study in group behaviour patterns.

APPROACH TO MANAGEMENT, MANAGERIAL ROLES. A means of analyzing management by observing what managers actually do and from such observations come to conclusions as to what managerial activities (or roles) are.

APPROACH TO MANAGEMENT, MATHEMATICAL, OR "MANAGEMENT SCIENCE". An analysis of management primarily as a matter of developing mathematical models of managerial decision areas.

APPROACH TO MANAGEMENT, OPERATIONAL. An analysis of management which draws together knowledge that is unique to managing and knowledge from other fields pertinent to managing, and relates it to the task of managing in way most useful to the managerial practitioner, it is thus in part eclectic and part a summary of the central core of knowledge which exists in management situations.

APPROACH TO MANAGEMENT, SOCIO-TECHNICAL SYSTEMS. An analysis of management viewing managerial situations as involving a combination of interacting social and technical systems.

APPROPRIABILITY THEORY. The theory that companies will favour foreign direct investment over such non-equity operating forms as licensing arrangements so that potential competitors will be less likely to gain access to proprietary information.

APPROPRIATION. An authorization to spend up to a specified dollar ceiling.

APPROPRIATION. A term featuring on the balance sheet of a company showing how the net profits are deployed in distribution of dividends on preference shares and equity shares, transfer to general reserves, and balance carried forward.

APPROVED LIST. A list of various investments in which a mutual fund, the LIC, the Unit Trust of India, Pension funds etc. are allowed to make investments. The list also specifies in what proportion investments are to be made from the instruments so approved.

APTITUDE TEST. A test to measure the potential ability a person possesses to learn a new job.

ARBITRAGE. The simultaneous purchase and sale of the same security on different stock exchanges at different prices which yield a profit.

ARBITRAGERS. Buyers and sellers who try to take advantage of temporary profit opportunities caused by discrepancies between prices in various markets.

ARBITRAGEUR. Arbitrageur would buy the relatively cheap and sell the relatively expensive one.

ARBITRAGEURS. They buy and sell securities in more than one stock exchange to take advantage of the price differences in such exchanges.

ARBITRATION. Process where by an impartial entity determines the relative merit of different view-points and makes a decision called an "award". Settlement of claims differences or disputes between one member and another between a member and his clients, authorized clerks, sub-brokers etc., trough appointed arbitrators. It is a quasi judicial process that is faster and is an inexpensive way of resolving dispute. The exchange facilitates the process of arbitration between the members and their clients. The disputes between the parties are resolved through an arbitration in accordance with the bye laws of the exchange.

ARBITRATION. A process of settling a dispute by having a third party decide the terms of an agreement between the disputants, who must accept the arbitrator's decision.

AREA DIVISION. *See* Geographic division.

ARIEL. (Automated Real time Investments Exchange). Computerised dealing system for large scale investors by passing the stock exchange.

ARITHMETIC MEAN. The sum of all items divided by the number of items.

ARM'S-LENGTH PRICE. A price between two companies that do not have an ownership interest in each other.

ARM'S-LENGTH TRANSACTION. Assumes that the parties to it are unrelated, such parties may be the main company and its group of companies or subsidiaries, or members of the same family. This is done so that neither normal advantage to either party is surrendered, nor extra advantage gained.

ARMS INDEX. It measures the relative strength of volume entering advancing stocks against the strength of volume entering declining stocks, and is calculated as follows : Divide the number of advancing stocks by the number of declining stocks. Then divide the upside volume by the down side volume. Finally divide the first answer by the second result. Readings below 100 are bullish and above are bearish. Extreme readings of 1.50 or higher are very bearish and of 0.50 or lower very bullish. Climax readings would be at 2.00 and 0.30.

ARRANGEMENT REGARDING INTERNATIONAL TRADE IN TEXTILES. An agreement among government establishing rules on textile trade; also known as the multi-fibre arrangement (MFA).

ARREAR AGE. If interest on bonds or dividends on cumulative preference shares are not paid the company is said to be in arrear age. Dividends on ordinary shares can't be paid until cumulative dividends on preference shares are paid.

ARREARS. Interest or dividends payable on a fixed interest bearing security that were not paid when due.

ART. Practice; skill acquired by experience.

ARTICLES OF ASSOCIATION. Drafted along with the MEMORANDUM of association by the promoters of a company. The articles lay down the detailed rules and regulations for managing the companies affairs. This has to be submitted to the Registrar of Companies for his approval for the incorporation of the company. The articles are effectively the contractual terms between shareholders and directors.

ARTICLES OF CO-PARTNERSHIP. A written agreement between partners which sets the relationship between the partners as to contribution profit share authority etc.

ARTIFICIAL PERSON. Though the shareholders own the company, the company has an independent legal existence of its own, distinct from that of its shareholders. It is regarded by law as an independent entity. It is considered to be an 'artificial person' and is attributed by law with most of the legal rights and obligations which normally devolve on an individual person.

ARUBIENT AIR QUALITY STANDARD. (*See* Environmental Quality Standard.)

ASCENDING RIGHT ANGLE TRAINING. It is characterised by a top-line boundary that is horizontal and bottom line that is sloping upward. This formation occurs when demand is growing yet continues to meet supply at a fixed price. If demand continues the supply being distributed at that price will eventually be entirely absorbed by new buyers, and prices will then advance rapidly.

ASCRIBED GROUP MEMBERSHIP. Affiliation determined by birth, such as those based on gender, family, age, caste, and ethnic, racial or national origin.

ASEAN FREE TRADE AREA (ASEAN). A free trade area formed by the ASEAN countries on January 1, 1993, with the goal of cutting tariffs on all intra-zonal trade to a maximum of 5 per cent by January 1, 2005.

ASEAN. *See* Association of South East Asian Nations.

ASK PRICE. *See* Average option.

ASKED PRICE. The price at which a share is offered for sale on the floor of the stock exchange. It is the price at which the JOBBE or TARAVANIWALLAH will sell. This is countered by the BID price.

ASPIRIN COUNT THEORY. A light-hearted approach to the market behaviour which states that if aspirin consumption rises in the country about a year later the market will fall and *vice versa.* For another example of stock market scholarship. *See* HEMLINE THEORY.

ASSENTED. Description of stocks or shares where an offer to acquire them or to modify their rights has been accepted.

ASSESSMENT CENTRE. A technique to aid in the selection and evaluation of potential managers whereby candidates are subjected to various tests and exercises and their performance is observed and evaluated by assessors.

ASSESSMENT YEAR. An income tax year, known as the assessment year, is the period of twelve months beginning April of each year and ending on March 31 the next year.

ASSET COVERAGE. The concept becomes important when a company goes into liquidation. From the total book value of the assets are deducted and then the claims of creditors. And the ratio of what remains to the total value of preference shares represents the asset coverage for such shares. The asset coverage for equity shares is the ratio obtained after deducting all creditor's dues and the value of the preference shares, divided by the number of equity shares. The result is also called the net book value of equity shares.

ASSET FINANCING. This converts assets of a company into liquid cash in exchange for a security interest to be paid to a bank or a financing company, distinct from borrowing from banks. Usually it takes in the form of loans against accounts receivables (which is an asset) but inventories and fixed assets are being mortgaged to raise loans.

ASSET MANAGEMENT. *See* PORTFOLIO MANAGEMENT.

ASSET STRIPPING. Selling off the assets of a company for quick profit, rather than running the company for steady gain. The asset stripper is usually left with a shell company which he keeps alive. Not for regular business, but for other, usually dishonest purposes. Such as tax evasion.

ASSET TURNOVER. The ratio of sales to total assets available.

ASSET VALUE PER SHARE. The value of the assets of a company on balance sheet after allowing for the repayment of prior charges and creditors, divided by the number of equity shares in issue.

ASSETS. Items of value owned by a person or business such as cash plant goodwill etc.

ASSETS. Economic resources that are expected to benefit future activities.

ASSOCIATED COMPANY. An associated company is a company owned jointly by two other companies.

ASSOCIATING CAUSE AND EFFECT. According to this principle certain costs expire in a particular accounting period because they can be directly associated with specific revenue recognized during that period. Raw material consumed power and fuel or wages are examples of such costs.

ASSOCIATION OF SOUTH-EAST ASIAN NATIONS. A free-trade area involving the Asia countries of Brunei, Indonesia, Malaysia, the Philippines, Singapore, and Thailand.

ASYMMETRIC INFORMATION. A

situation where parties engaged in a transaction have different information for example in the loan market. When borrowers have better information about their ability to repay a loan than does the bank.

AT PAR. When the offer for sale of 'rights' is made at the face value of the shares, they are said to be issued 'at par'.

AT A PREMIUM. At a price higher than that printed on the share certificate *i.e.*, above par. When a well established company issues new shares, either as rights or to the public, it may ask for a higher price.

AT THE OPENING. An order to buy or sell at the opening of trading. This has a much better chance of being executed.

AT-THE-MONEY. A term referring to an option when the market value of the asset on which the option is written is equal to the strike price of the option.

ATTENTION DIRECTING. That function of the accountant's information supplying task which focuses on problems in the operation of the firm or which points out imperfections or inefficiencies in certain areas of the firm's operation.

AUCTION. An auction is a mechanism utilized by the exchange to fulfil its obligation to a counter party member when a member fails to deliver good securities or make the payment. Through auction the exchange arranges to buy good securities and deliver them to the buying broker or arrange to realize the cash and pay it to the selling broker.

AUCTION COMPANIES. Do not take title to goods which they offer for sale at public auction to highest bidder.

AUDIT. An examination that is made in accordance with generally accepted auditing standards. Its aim is to give credibility to financial statements.

AUDITOR'S REPORT. The written description of an auditor's finding together with the auditor's professional opinion regarding the credibility of management's financial statements.

AUDITOR'S REPORT. Auditor's report informs the shareholders whether the accounts of the company give a true and fair view of the state of the company's finances at the close of the company's accounting year, and of the profits made by the company for the said year.

AUTHORITY, ORGANIZATIONAL. *See* organizational authority.

AUTHORITY, PARITY WITH RESPONSIBILITY. The principle that responsibility for action should not be greater than authority delegated, nor should it be less. Authority is the discretionary power to carry out assignments and responsibility is the obligation owed a delegate to accomplish these activities.

AUTHORITY. It is the right to use resources to accomplish goals and the right to make decisions and to take action acquired to complete an assignment.

AUTHORIZED SHARE CAPITAL. The maximum number of shares that a company may issue, stated in the memorandum and articles of association of the company. A company may initially issue fewer shares. The authorized capital can be increased with the consent both of the shareholders and SEBI.

AUTHORIZED UNIT TRUST. A Unit Trust authorized by the development of trade under the provisions of the Preventions of Fraud (Investments) Act 1958.

AUTOCRATIC LEADER. One man rule.

AUTOMATIC DEBIT TRANSFER. Service provided in the UK by Giro Bank that, for a small charge, allows a business to collect regular sums of money from a large number of customer.

AVERAGE. Properly weighted and adjusted arithmetic mean of certain shares to represent general market behaviour or a particular class of shares.

AVERAGE OPTION. An option in which the final payoff is determined by the average price of the asset during a specified period. In a fixed strike average option, the payoff at maturity depends on the difference of the average and a fixed strike price. In a floating strike average option, the payoff at maturity depends on the difference of the spot price and the average.

AVERAGING DOWN. The purchase of a further holding of shares at a lower price (averaging down) or at a higher price (averaging up).

AVOIDABLE COST. Those costs that will not continue if an ongoing operation is changed or deleted.

B

B GROUP. The list of group B shares contains a few active shares but the vast bulk consists of partially active and inactive ones.

BABY BONDS. Bonds offered by registered friendly societies to minors. The funds are tax exempt.

BACK TO BACK LEASE. Equipment which is leased to a leasing company and then sub-leased to the actual user.

BACK-END LOAD. A kind of redemption charge, that an investor has to pay for withdrawing his money before the date of maturity, applies to time deposits, to discourage investors from withdrawing funds pre-maturely.

BACK-ENDED-LEASE. (*See* Front ended-lease.)

BACK-TO-BACK LOAN. One method of borrowing foreign currency. A deposit in one country is used to obtain a loan in another financed by a reciprocal transaction.

BACK UP. When the stock market has backed up it shows a sudden reversal of trend *i.e.*, a sudden fall in a rising market, or a sudden rise in a falling market.

BACKWARD INDUCTION. A technique used in pricing derivative securities. The value of the option is first determined at maturity, and then, by working backwards, the current value of the derivative is calculated.

BACKWARD INTEGRATION. Taking over of a company which produces raw materials or ancillaries by another company, which uses these products to manufacture finished goods. Backward integration guarantees, to a certain extent, quality control, an uninterrupted supply of raw materials and components at a fair price, and timely deliveries.

BACKWARDATION. The carry over charges in the case of the seller is called 'backwardation'.

BAD ACCOUNT. That is financially, very weak and high risky customer.

BAD DEBTS. Accounts receivable that cannot be collected.

BADLA. Badla in Hindi means

"something in return". This is a process where the buyer who has bought shares in the settlement does not wish to take the delivery of shares but wishes to carry over his purchase to next settlement. The consideration, which he pays (in case of Sidha Badla) or receives (in case of backwardation or Undha Badla) for such a carry over, is called as badla.

BAGGING THE STREET. It is concealment of information about the sale of stock from dealers and specialists by institutional investors or broker. Such an information may include reasons why the stock is being sold off, and the number and price of the shares in question.

BAIL BOND. Bail bond is an extension of motor insurance, taken out in the UK, that can bc used to pay the bail of a UK motorist taken into custody in Spain.

BALANCE. The difference between the total debits and the total credits in an account at any particular time.

BALANCE CERTIFICATE. Certificate representing balance of stocks or shares back to vendor after sale of part only of holding.

BALANCE CHARGE. The difference between the sale proceeds and the tax written down value of equipment for tax purposes.

BALANCE OF GOODS AND SERVICES. The value of a country's exports of merchandise trade minus imports.

BALANCE OF PAYMENTS. An accounting summary of the value of payments between households, firms, and government in one country and the rest of the world.

BALANCE OF PAYMENTS. Statement that summarizes all economic transactions between a country and the rest of the world during a given period of time.

BALANCE OF TRADE. Difference in value, over a period of time, between a country's imports and exports of merchandise. When exports exceed imports, the country has a favourable balance of trade, and when imports exceed exports the balance is unfavourable. Often shortened to BOT.

BALANCE ON SERVICES. That part of the balance of payments accounts that consists of exports and imports of services including such things as military expenditures tourism transportation services and investment income such as dividends, interest income and royalties.

BALANCE SHEET. A financial statement showing the nature and amount of the assets owned by the company, the liability it owes prepared on a given date.

BALANCED FUNDS. It is a mutual fund which invests in equity shares, debentures, government bonds, and Unit Trust certificates so as to balance gain with risk. A balanced fund usually offers a higher yield than a fund which consists only of equity shares (as the yield from good equity shares is usually lower than debenture or bond yields), but its share price rises slowly. In a bear market a balanced fund performs well, whereas in a bull market all-equity shows a faster capita appreciation.

BALANCED MUTUAL FUND. A mutual fund which invests in equity shares, debentures, government bonds, and unit trust certificates so as to balance the gain with risk. A balanced fund usually offers a higher yield than a fund which consists only of equity shares but its share price rises slowly. In a bear market a balanced fund performs well, whereas in a bull market an all equity fund shows a faster capital appreciation.

BALANCED SCHEMES. Mutual Fund schemes that aim to provide both growth and income by periodically distributing a part of the income and capital gains they earn. They invest in equities and fixed income securities in the proportion indicated in their offer documents. In a rising stock market, the NAV of these schemes may not normally keep pace. The scheme suits investors looking for a combination of income and moderate growth.

BALANCE-OF-PAYMENTS DEFICITS. An imbalance of some specific component within the balance of payments, such as merchandise trade or current, account, that implies that a country is importing more than it exports.

BALANCE-OF-PAYMENTS SURPLUS. An imbalance in the balance of payments that exists when a country exports more than it imports.

BALLOON MATURITY. Long term deposits or investments in which larger repayments are due in the later years.

BALLOON MORTGAGE. Mortgage in which a lumps has to be paid at the end of the mortgage period to pay off the outstanding principal and interest. It is also called non-amortizing mortgage.

BALLOON OPTIONS. A Balloon Options an option that "Balloons" in size once a certain trigger is reached. It is most commonly used in

FX markets but can also be used in interest rate, equity and commodity markets.

BALLOON PAYMENT. A final payment of debt instalment which is considerably larger than the previous payments.

BALLOON STOCKS. Loans, which are not repaid in fixed instalments. They are repaid as and when funds come in.

BALLOT. A random basis of allotment of shares when a new issue has been over subscribed. A typical announcement of allotment on the basis of a ballot works like

No. of shares applied of	Basis of allot-ment	No. of shares allotted	No. of allot-tees
100	1 : 37	100	27344
200	1 : 28	100	26532
300-500	2 : 49	100	15641
600-1000	1 : 20	100	10897
and so on.			

The above chart shows the allotment in a highly over-subscribed issue.

BAND KE BAAD. The prices offered by unauthorised dealers in stocks outside the official hours of the stock exchange.

BAND PASS FILTER. *See* LOW PASS FILTER.

BANK BORROWINGS. Banks provide funds for financing a firm's fixed assets. Such loans will be grouped under long-term liabilities. In India, it is a common practice to include both short and long term borrowings under loan funds.

BANK CHARTER. Approval from a regulatory agency to form a bank granted by the comptroller of the currency or state banking commission.

BANK CREDIT. Bank credit includes loans, cash, credits and overdrafts and inland bills and foreign bills purchased and discounted. Bills exclude those re-discounted with RBI and IDBI.

BANK DEPOSITS. A firm can deposit its temporary cash in a bank for a fixed period of time. The interest rate depends on the maturity period. For ex. the current interest rate for a 30 to 45 days deposit is about 5% and for 180 days to one year is about 8%. The default risk of the bank deposits is quite low since most banks in India are owned by the government.

BANK FOR INTERNATIONAL SETTLEMENTS (BIS). A bank in Basel, Switzerland that facilities transactions among central banks, effectively the central banks.

BANK NOTE. A written document issued by a bank and promising to pay the bearer on demand. A note issued by a bank which is payable to the bearer on demand and is intended to circulate as money.

BANK PANIC. A period during which banks throughout the banking system face an increased desire for currency by depositors which manifests itself as a widespread withdrawal of deposits from the banking system.

BANK RATE. The rate of interest at which the Reserve Bank of India will lend to the other banks in the country's banking system. It is also known as the minimum lending rate or the base rate.

BANK REFERENCES. Another source of collecting credit information in the bank where the customer maintain his accounts.

BANKER'S ACCEPTANCE. A written demand, which has been accepted by a bank, to pay a specified amount at a future date.

BANKING HOLDING COMPANIES. Corporations that hold one or more banks.

BAR CHART. A chart, using either vertical or horizontal bars, for data presentation.

BAR TRUSTEE. One who holds an asset to the order of the owner. Usually used where a trust has ended permitting a new owner to take control of the asset (*See* nominee).

BARGAIN PURCHASE OPTION. A provision allowing the lessee, at his option, to purchase the leased asset for a price which is sufficiently lower than the expected fair market value (at the date such option becomes exercisable), the exercise of the option appears, at the inception of the lease, to be reasonably assured.

BARGAIN RENEWAL OPTION. A provision allowing the lessee, at his option, to renew the leased for a rental sufficiently lower than the expected fair rental for the property (at the date the option becomes exercisable), the exercise of the option appears, at the inception of the lease, to be reasonably assured.

BARGAIN. Any transaction carried out by a stock broker with a jobber.

BARGAINING SCHOOL THEORY. A theory holding that the negotiated terms for foreign investors depend on how much investors and host countries need each other's assets.

BAROMETER. Economic and market data which represent larger trends, used in economic forecasting. The more significant data are consumer spending start in housing, and interest rates.

BAROMETER STOCK. A share, usually a blue chip, which is

taken to show the state of the stock market. It is widely held, frequently traded share with a stable price record.

BARRIER OPTION. A path dependant option the payoff of which depends on the payoff to an ordinary option and whether a pre-specified barrier has been crossed. Common examples include down-and-in options, down-and-out options, up-and-in options, and up-and-out options.

BARRIERS OF TRADE. Practices of nations which restrict the international exchange of goods — quotas, embargoes and tariffs.

BARTER. The exchange of goods and services directly for other goods and services without the use of money.

BASE CAPITAL ACCORD. The Basel Committee on Banking Supervision is a Committee of banking supervisory authorities, which was established by the central bank Governors of the Group of Ten countries in 1975. In the Basel Capital Accord of July 1988 explicit reference is made to off-balance-sheet netting *vis-à-vis* the same counter party, but not to the offsetting of on-balance-sheet assets and liabilities. Over recent years, certain methods of on-balance-sheet netting have developed and the Basel Committee has decided that the time has come to establish certain principles for the guidance of its members and of other countries.

BASE CURRENCY. The currency whose value is implicitly 1 when a quote is made between two currencies; for example if the cruzeiro is trading at 29692.5 cruzeiros per dollar is the base currency and the cruzeiro is the quoted currency.

BASE MARKET VALUE. Average market price of a group of shares at a given time, used for plotting changes in market indexing.

BASE PORTFOLIO. Specimen portfolio against which the performance of a managed fund can be compared.

BASIC BALANCE. The net current account plus long-term capital within a country's balance of payment.

BASIS. The purchase price of an asset for tax purpose. The taxable gain is the difference between the sale price and the basis (usually purchase price plus other expenses less depreciation).

BASIS POINT. A basis point equals 0.01 per cent or one-hundredth of a percentage point.

BASIS PRICE. The price on which an investor calculates his capital gains when he sells his shares or bonds.

BASLE ACCORD. An international agreement to establish capital adequacy standards for banks.

BATHTUB ANALOGY. The advance-decline line can best be understood by the 'bathtub analogy'. Imagine the market as a bathtub and the water level as represented by the advance decline line. Advancing stocks raise the water level and declining stocks lower the water level.

BEAR. A bear is a speculator who takes a pessimistic view of the future. He expects the price of a particular share to fall in the immediate future. He sells the shares which he does not possess at their current market price.

BEAR CYCLE. An extended period, usually shorter than a bull cycle, when share prices generally keep falling and the stock market INDICES keep going down. *See* BEAR.

BEAR HUG. Term used in takeover situation, meaning an indication to the board of a target company that an offer of takeover is under consideration. A strong bear hug is a formal notice to the target company of an intended takeover. A steady bear hug is an indication from a target company that it will favourably consider a takeover, but at a higher price than offered.

BEAR MARKET. A market in which stock prices are moving downward.

BEAR RAID. Manipulation by a group of investors or bears selling a large number of shares 'short' in an attempt to bring down their prices. They then keep the difference between their selling price and the new lower price.

BEAR SLIDE. General downward movement of share prices towards conditions characterised by BEAR MARKET.

BEAR SPECULATOR. A bear speculator is one who sells the shares in expectation of a fall in price.

BEAR TRAP. An erratic movement of share price downwards, encouraging investors to SELL SHORT. When the market corrects itself and prices go up, unwary investors get caught in the bear trap. *See* BULL TRAP.

BEARER BOND. A bond on which the owners name is not registered but is the property of whoever holds them at a specific time.

BEARER SECURITY. A security does not require the registration of the owner's name in the company's book. The owner's name is not shown on the security certificate also. The transfer of such a security takes place by mere delivery.

BEARISH. When the market is dominated by a lot of bear activity and there is a falling trend in prices, the market is said to be 'bearish'.

BEATING THE MARKET. Getting a higher return on investments higher than the market average is possible, but difficult, as the market beats, more often than not.

BED AND BREAKFAST. The selling of a security one day and buying it back on the following day in order to establish a capital gain or loss for tax purposes.

BEHAVIOURALLY ANCHORED RATING SCALES (BARS).

BELL WHETHER STOCK. Bell whether literally means a sheep that leads the herd, often bearing a bell, hence a share which assumes a position of market leadership. If it moves up the market is buoyant and if it declines, the market falls. It is not, as some people suppose a share that is supposed to hold firm in stormy conditions.

BELLS AND WHISTLES. They are the extras, like options added to a financial product to make it more attractive.

BELLY UP. A company in its last stage of existence, likely to go bankrupt soon looks like a dead fish which floats with the belly up.

BELOW PAR. A price lower than the face value of a share.

BENEFITS are rewards available to an employee or group of employees as a part of organizational membership.

BERMUDA OPTION. An option that can only be exercised at a fixed number of intervals over its life. It is a cross between a European and an American option.

BEST FIT LINE. The line drawn through the points on the scanegram that is chosen by a statistical procedure to fit the best straight-line to the scatter of points.

BEST TERMS. Broker's commission at rates which do not include sharing with an agent.

BEST. An instruction to a broker to deal 'at best' means to deal at the best price obtainable, *i.e.*, without imposition of a limit.

BETA. Beta is a measure of the percentage change in the price of a stock relative to the percentage change of a market index.

BETA COEFFICIENT OR BETA FACTOR. A measure of performance of a particular share or class of shares in relation to the general movement of the market. If a share has beta of 1 its rise and fall corresponds exactly with the market; with a beta of 2 its rise or fall is double, *i.e.*, when the market falls by 10 per cent it falls by 20 per cent with a beta of 0.5, the particular share will rise by only 5 per cent if the market rises by 10 per cent and falls by 5 per cent if the market falls by 10 per cent. Shares with negative beta coefficients are CONTRARIAN SHARES.

BETA RATIO. Relates stock performance to market performance. For a Z per cent change in the market, a stock will tend to change by BZ per cent where b is the stock's beta ratio.

BETA SHARES. Listed but infrequently traded, Shares of companies with a generally low equity capital.

BID. The offer by a jobber to buy a stock or share. Hence, 'bid price' is the price at which stocks, shares or units in a unit trust can be sold by a holder (*See* Offer).

BID AND ASKED. A 'bid' is the price a prospective buyer is willing to pay whereas 'asked' is the price a seller is willing to accept.

BID AND OFFER. Bid is the price of a share prospective buyer is prepared to pay for a particular scrip. Offer is the price at which a share is offered for sale.

BID PRICE. It is the price a prospective buyer of a share is prepared to pay on the floor of the stock exchange at a particular auction. This is in response to the jobber's ASKED PRICE.

BID SPREAD. The difference between BID PRICE and ASKED PRICE.

BID-ASK SPREAD. The difference between the ask price and the bid price.

BID-UP. When demand exceeds supply the trend will be up as buyers 'bid up' the price.

BIFR. Board of Industrial Finance and Reconstruction.

BIG BOARD. The name for the New York Exchange.

BIG EIGHT. The eight largest American Accounting Firms. Arthur Anderson and Co., Coopers and Ly Brand, Ernst and Whinny, Delistle Haskings & Sells, Peat Marwick Mitchell and Co., Price Water House and Co., Touch Ross and Co. and Arthur Young and Co.

BIG TICKET LEASE. A lease in which the asset's capital cost is very high.

BILL OF EXCHANGE. A written order by one party to another party (usually a bank) to pay a third party a specified sum of money.

BILL OF EXCHANGE. *See* Commercial bill of exchange.

BILL OF LADING. A document

that is issued to a shipper by a carrier, listing the goods received for shipment. Information on a document issued by a carrier to cover a shipment of merchandise.

BILL OF LEADING. A document which represents ownership of goods in transit.

BILL OF MATERIALS. A specification of the utilities of direct material allowed for manufacturing a given quantity of output.

BILLS DISCOUNTING. Bills discounting consists of the client drawing bills of exchange for goods and services on buyers, and then discounting it with bank for a charge. Thus, like factoring, bill discounting is a method of financing.

BILLS PAYABLE. They are the promises made in writing by the firm to make payment of a specified sum to creditors at some specific date.

BINARY OPTION. *See* digital option.

BINARY SYSTEM. A two-digits number system, 0 to 1 used in the digital computer to represent various quantities.

BINOMIAL MODAL. A model that describes the random evolution of the price of an asset over time. The model assumes that at the end of each interval the asset price can have one of two possible values.

BIODEGRADE. A process of natural decomposition in which a substance is slowly absorbed back into the natural environment.

BIOMASS. Any plant or animal material or waste by-products such as wood chips or municipal solid wastes that can be used to generate energy.

BIOSPHERE. The land, air, water and natural conditions on which life on earth depends.

BIRPI. *See* International Bureau for the protection of Industrial Property Rights.

BIS. *See* Bank for International Settlements.

BIT. A binary notation, one (1) represents the presence of a value and is called a bit while a zero (0) represents the absence of a value and is defined as a no bit.

BLACK BOOK. It refers to the company's preplanned strategy to be put into action in the event of a hostile takeover bid.

BLACK KNIGHT. An unwelcome takeover bidder.

BLACK MARKET. The foreign-exchange market that lies outside the official market.

BLACK TRADING. Stock market disaster, so named as the first such took place on Friday 24 September 1869.

BLACK'S MODEL. A model for pricing a futures option using

a lognormal distribution for the underlying futures price.

BLACK-SCHOLES MODEL. A model for pricing stock options using a lognormal distribution for the underlying stock price.

BLANK SALES. Sale of securities by BEARS who do not possess the securities at the movement of selling, but hope to buy them at a lower price when the market has fallen.

BLANK TRANSFER. A blank transfer is made when the seller fills in only his name and signature in the transfer form and does not fill-in the buyer's particulars or the date of sale. The buyer can then sell these shares without registering them in his name. This process may be repeated many times without the shares being sent to the company for making changes regarding their ownership. A record of such transactions can be found on the reverse of the transfer deed where the delivering broker writes his name and the date. It must, therefore, be checked that valid transfer forms have been delivered as the transfer deeds have a limited life of one year or till the date of closure of the register of members, whichever is later.

BLIND ADVERTISEMENT.

BLOCK. Fixed assets are referred to as block.

BLOCK TRADE. A trade involving 10,000 shares or more often handled by a block trader.

BLOCK TRADER. One who assembles orders on the passive side of block trade and manages the transaction.

BLOCK TRADES. Trades in a common stock over 10,000 shares.

BLOWING THE WHISTLE. (*See* Whistle blowing.)

BLOW-OUT. A new issue which is subscribed on the opening day. It is also called out of the window issue.

BLUE CHIP STOCK. Stock of the largest and best known companies in the United States.

BLUE CHIPS. The ordinary shares of leading companies.

BM & F. Bolsa Mercandily De Futures.

BOARD OF DIRECTORS. A plural executive that is a committee, with power to exercise authority and make decisions which normally stands at the top of a corporation and is charged by law with the responsibility of "managing" the corporation.

BOARD OF DIRECTORS. A group of persons elected by shareholders votes to be responsible for directing the affairs of a corporation establishing company objectives and policies selecting top level managers and reviewing company performances.

BOARD OF GOVERNORS. Consists of screen members appointed by the U.S. presidents and conformed by the U.S. senate responsible for monetary policy and regulation of the banking industry by the federal reserve system.

BODY LANGUAGE. The way people move their bodies, gesture, position themselves etc., to convey meaning to others.

BOILER ROOM. 'High pressure' investments selling from small office rooms by a number of smooth-talking salesmen luring suckers on the telephone. The cacophony of their talk in a congested room creates boiler-room conditions.

BOLTON INDEX. It is by the square root of the difference between the ratio of advances to unchanged and the ratio of declining to unchanged a/u-d/u. The analyst calculates this using the unchanged issues as a basic component. The reason for calculating the square root was that it eliminates a strong down word bias.

BONA FIDE OCCUPATIONAL QUALIFICATION (BFOQ).

BOND. Long-term debt instruments of corporations.

BOND DISCOUNT. Bonds which are purchased for less than their face value.

BOND MARKET. In the context of the US, that is a market in which association broker/dealers and banks in a government and federal agency securities, deal in municipal securities, mortgage backed securities, and money market securities.

BOND PREMIUM. A bond foi which the buyers pays more than its face value.

BOND TRUST. A public mutual fund investing only in government or corporate fixed interest securities. Although the returns are relatively low, the risk to the investor is minimal.

BOND WASHING. It is the practice of buying bonds dividends and selling ex-dividend to reduce the rate of tax payable on the transaction. The dividends on the bond becomes a capital gain on which a lower rate of tax is payable than if the tax were paid on the proceeds as dividend income.

BONDED WAREHOUSE. A building or part of a building used for the storage of imported merchandise under supervision of the U.S. Customs Service and for the purpose of deferring payment of customs duties.

BONFIRE OCCUPATIONAL QUALIFICATION (BFOQ) is a legitimate reason why an employer can exclude persons on otherwise illegal bases of consideration.

BONUS ISSUE. Issue of shares to existing holders and with no payment to be made, representing an increase in issued capital by converting reserves into shares and thus only arising from an accounting change (*See* SCRIP ISSUE).

BONUS PLAN. A payment system to provide an incentive for employees to produce more and thus earn more.

BONUS SHARES. Sometimes companies capitalize a part of their reserves by the issue of "bonus" shares. Bonus shares are issued free of cost to the existing shareholders in proportion to their existing shareholding. This results in an increase in the paid-up capital of the company. Since bonus shares are issued free of cost, they do not bring-in any additional funds to the company. The issue of bonus shares is essentially a book transfer, thereby a certain sum of money, representing the amount capitalised, is transferred from a company's reserves to the accounting head, share capital. Bonus shares have the effect of increasing the shareholding of each shareholder without any change in the proportionate ownership of the company.

BOOK. The day to day records of a jobber of shares bought and sold.

BOOK CLOSURE AND RECORD DATE. When a company declares a dividend or announces a bonus share or right issue or wants to convey a meeting of the shareholders, it becomes necessary to freeze the list at a point of time to take stock of the shareholders entitled to the benefit. This is known as closure of register of members or just book closure. During the period of book closure, no transfer of share is undertaken by the company.

BOOK CLOSURE. Before a company declares a dividend or issues bonus or rights shares, it closes its register of members for a certain period from one week to a month, during which no transfer of shares is registered. Only those shareholders whose names appear on the register after the book closer are eligible to receive dividends and bonus shares and entitled to rights shares. After the book closure shares are quoted ex-dividend, ex-bonus (if bonus has been announced) or ex-rights (if announced) prices, which carry xd, xb, and xr after the figures. Dates of book closure are announced in financial newspapers and journals. While buying shares it is prudent to ask the broker what the book closure dates are. Delay in lodging share transfer forms with the company many sometimes result in the loss of dividends, rights, or bonuses.

BOOK DEBT. Debt recorded in an account book.

BOOK KEEPING. Systematic keeping of books of accounts.

BOOK LOSS. Loss not actually sustained as the investor hasn't sold when the price has fallen. Book loss induces some depression of mind, but does not actually pinch the investor's pocket unless, of course, the book loss keeps mounting and the investor is forced to sell at a considerable loss, if he can sell at all.

BOOK LOSS OR PROFIT. A loss or profit on paper, not realized.

BOOK PROFIT. As a noun, unrealised profit when shares which an investor holds have appreciated in price, but the shareholder has not sold any, it induces a sense of well-being without bringing in any tangible profit. It is only in the verbal use of the term, *i.e.*, to sell shares when they have appreciated in price. That real profit come. Hence, the stock market adage; unbooked profit is only book profit.

BOOK VALUE. The carrying amount in the accounts, net of any contra accounts. For example, the book value of equipment is its acquisition cost minus its accumulated depreciation.

BOOK VALUE. Book value per share indicates the portion of shareholders' funds, that accrue to each equity share. It is an evaluation of shareholders' funds on a per share basis.

$$\frac{\text{EQUITY SHARE CAPITAL} + \text{SHAREHOLDERS' RESERVES}}{\text{Total no. of equity shares subscribed}}$$

BOOK VALUE. The value of an asset shown in accounts, generally representing cost price plus additions, net of depreciation.

BOOK VALUE METHOD. *See* Accounting rate of return.

BOOK VALUE OF EQUITY SHARES.

$$^{*}F = \frac{\text{Total value of equity share capital} + \text{reserves and surplus}}{\text{Total number of equity shares}}$$

This value indicates the asset coverage that each equity share represents in the company. It represents the net-worth of assets that each share commands.

*F = Female.

BOOK VALUE PER SHARE. It is net-worth divided by the number of shares.

BOOKING CENTRE. An offshore financial centre whose main function is to act as an accounting centre in order to minimize the payment of taxes.

BOOKING PROFIT. Making profit by selling a share which has gone above its purchase price. When shares, which an investor holds, go up in price the investor has made only a notional profit, which is meaningless, except in a DRY RUN PORTFOLIO. Only when he actually sells them he makes some tangible profit.

BOOK-STRAP. It is a cash offer for controlling stake in a company which if accepted, is followed by another (usually at a lower price) for the reminder of the shares.

BOOM. The top of a favourable trade cycle, when the prosperous outlook is reflected in the upward movement of share prices. The opposite of SLUMP. BOOM often tends to end suddenly.

BOOM. In boom condition the frequency and volume of share market transactions reach a very high level. As a result almost every share listed on the stock exchange becomes an active share.

BOOTS TRAP ACQUISITION. Term used in connection with a friendly takeover. Threatened with a hostile takeover the target company exchanges some of its assets for shares held by dissident share-holders. Then the target company sells the rest of the company to a friendly acquirer. The friendly acquirer thus gets 100 per cent of the target company for less than he would have paid otherwise. The target company has virtually helped finance part of the takeover.

BOOTSTRAP. It is a cash offer for a controlling stake in a company which if accepted, is followed by another (usually at a lower price) for the remainder of the shares.

BORROWED CAPITAL. The money raised from outsiders is called 'borrowed capital'.

BORROWED RESERVES. Reserves that banks borrow from the fed and other depository institutions without collateral.

BOTTOM LINE. The net profit or loss figures in an analysis of a company's performance.

BOTTOM LINE. Business profits or losses usually reported in figures on the late or bottom line of a company's income statement.

BOTTOM OUT. When shares have hit their lowest and are

slowly vising they are said to be on their path of recovery where they are bottomed out.

BOTTOM-UP APPROACH TO INVESTING. Looking for individual shares with outstanding performances or potential without considering economic trends, on the assumption that individual companies can still do well, even though the industry to which they belong may not be doing well. The companies are often chosen with the help of fundamental analysis, research reports or personal knowledge of their products. Its opposite is TOP-DOWN investing.

BOTTOM-UP INVESTING. An investment strategy that considers the fundamental factors driving individual stock performance before considering the economic prospects affecting the industry wish in which that company operates.

BOUNDARIES. *See* systems, boundaries.

BOUNDARY AGENT ROLE. A work role that links an organization with its environment.

BOUNDARY CONDITION. The payoff to derivative security at expiration or at an exercise date.

BOUNDED RATIONALITY. Rational action limited because of lack of information, lack of time, or ability to analyze alternatives in the light of a goal sought, unclear goals, or the human tendency not to take risks in making a decision, to play it safe. See also satisfying.

BOUTIQUE. Relatively new form of financial services company, operating in much the same way as a high street shop into which customers walk to seek investment advice and service. It is also known as a financial supermarket.

BRAINSTORMING. An approach to improve problem discovery and solving by encouraging unfettered suggestions and ideas, usually from a group of individuals.

BRANCH (FOREIGN). A foreign operation of a company that is not a separate entity from the partner that owns it.

BRANCH STORE. An extension of a retailing outlet, usually a downtown store opening a new store to compete with other stores in shopping centre and operating under the same policies as the parent store.

BRAND. A particular good identified with a company by means of name, logo, or other method, usually protected with a trademark registration.

BREAD AND BREAKFAST DEAL. Transaction formerly used to

minimize the impact of capital gains tax. A shareholder sold his or her holding at a loss after the trading closed for the day, and registered the loss for tax purposes. Next morning, the shareholder bought his or her holding back. The tax advantages of the same were withdrawn from the UK in 1998; The US term for bed-and-breakfast deal is swap.

BREADTH OF THE MARKET. Indicated by the percentage of shares involved in an upward or downward movement of the stock market. If two-thirds of the shares listed in a stock exchange participate during a trading session, the market is said to have a good breadth *i.e.*, the trend it shows is representative, and is not influenced by the price of a few heavily traded shares. *See* also A-D INDEX.

BREAK-EVEN ANALYSIS. Break-even analysis is a specific way of presenting and studying the interrelationships between costs, volume and profits. It provides information to management in a most lucid and precise manner. The bieak-even point is the point of sales and volume at which total revenue is equal to total cost. It is a no-profit-no-loss point.

BREAK-EVEN POINT ANALYSIS. Charting and analyzing relationships usually between sales and expenses to determine at what size or volume point an operation breaks even between a loss and a profit it can be used in any problems area where marginal effects can be pinpointed.

BREAK FORWARD. A foreign exchange forward contract where one party has the right, but not the obligation to terminate the contract at one or more predetermined times during the life of the transaction. It is also known as a Cancelable Forward. The interest rate version of the Break Forward is known as a cancelable swap.

BREAK OUT. When the price breaks out of the range of resistance levels, it moves either up or down beyond the resistance levels. Such level *i.e.*, price level is called break out.

BREAK UP VALUE OF SHARES. The net asset or net-worth of the company, divided by the number of shares issued.

BREAK WAY GAP. They occur as prices break away from an area of congestion. Typically prices will break away from an ascending or descending Triangle with a gap. The gap implies that the change in sentiment has been strong and that the ensuing move will be powerful.

BRETTON WOODS. Under this fixed exchange rate system the United States agreed to peg the U.S. dollar to a given amount of gold and other nations pegged their currency to the U.S. dollar.

BRETTON WOODS AGREEMENT. An agreement among IMF countries to promote exchange rate stability and to facilitate the international flow of currencies.

BRIBE. Something of value given to someone in power to influence materially that person's decision in favour of you compared with others.

BROAD MONEY. Money held for spending.

BROADENING FORMATIONS. They usually have bearish implications. They appear frequently at tops. The theory is that five minor reversals are followed by a substantial decline. Reversal 3 and 5 occur at successively higher points than first top and reversal 4 occurs at a lower point than reversal 2. Broadening Top formation usually suggests a market that is lacking support from the 'smart money' and is beyond control. During the early stages of the formation, well informed selling is completed and in the latter pages less informed will participate. The price and wings are unpredictable and volume is irregular as to which direction the breakout goes.

BROKER (IN FOREIGN EXCHANGE). Specialists who facilitate transactions in the interbank market.

BROKER. *See* Member of stock exchange.

BROKER. A person (Agency) who arranges the purchase and sale of an asset by acting as an intermediary between the purchaser and the seller.

BROKERAGE FIRMS. Firms which link buyers and sellers of financial assets.

BROWNIAN MOTION. A stochastic process the increments of which are normally distributed with zero mean and variance proportional to time.

BSE. Bombay Stock Exchange.

BUBBLE. When stock prices are pushed up to an abnormally high level unsupported by any fundamentals, it is said to have developed a bubble. The market crash on 11th and 12th May, which in two days trading burst the bubble of 4,546 points reached on 2nd April 1992 observed on 2nd May 1992 that the Indian stock markets had the shun of a bubble about to burst.

BUBBLE CONCEPT. A pollution control plan that determines compliance by measuring combined total emissions from an industrial installation, rather than from each of the plants individual pollution sources.

BUCKET SHOP. A brokerage firm which is not a member of the recognised stock exchange. The term formerly used to describe of low ginmill where beverages were dispensed in small amounts in buckets.

BUDGET. A plan expressed usually in financial terms.

BUDGET. A statement of plans and expected results expressed in numerical terms : a "numberized" programme.

BUDGET SUMMARY. A master summary of operating and capital budgets, usually with a forecast income statement and balance sheet.

BUDGET VARIANCE. The difference between an actual and a budget amount. Also see control budget variance.

BUDGET ZERO-BASE. *See* Zero-Base budgeting.

BUDGET, PROGRAMME. *See* Programme budgeting.

BUDGETS, VARIABLE OR FLEXIBLE. *See* Variable budgets.

BUDLIWALLA. The member who finances those carry-over transactions is called a 'budliwalla'.

BUFFER-STOCK SYSTEM. A partially managed system that utilizes stocks of commodities to regulate their prices.

BUILD-OPERATE-TRANSFER (BOT). This an arrangement in which private entity is responsible for the financing, construction and operation of an infrastructure facility for a specific period after which the facility is transferred to the government.

BULGE BULGE. Sudden, short-lived price rise that may apply to the entire stock market or an individual share.

BULL. A bull is a speculator who takes an optimistic view of the future. He expects the price of a particular share to rise in the immediate future. Therefore, he buys these shares at their current prices with the hope of selling them subsequently at higher prices.

BULL CYCLE. An extended period during which share prices are generally rising and the stock market indices show an upward trend. *See* BULL & BEAR CYCLE.

BULL CHARGE. Bull pushing up share prices vigorously.

BULL MARKET. The primary trend usually consists of three phases. In first phase known as 'accumulation' business conditions are poor and the public is generally discouraged with the stock market. The business conditions and corporate earnings begin to improve in second phase. The third phase is characterised by highly publicized 'good news'. Price gains are often spectacular and the public becomes heavily involved.

BULL MARKET TERMS. Shoot up, show an uptrend, rise, soar, gain, gain smartly, rally, move up, firm up, flare up, lump, turn, bullish, lookup, upswing, improved sentiments, bears covering short sales, escalate go up, shoot up, boom.

BULL SPECULATOR. A speculator who purchases shares in expectation of a rise in price is called a bull speculator.

BULL TRAP. An erratic movement of share prices upwards, encouraging investors to buy in anticipation of further rise in prices when the market corrects itself. The prices come down, trapping unwary investors. *See* BEAR TRAP.

BULLISH. The bull is said to "buy long" as opposed to the bear who sells "short" when the stock market is dominated by a lot of bull activity and there is a rising trend in prices, the market is said to be "bullish". And the market is referred to as a "bull market".

BUNDESBANK. The German central bank.

BUREAU EXERCISE PRICES OR DIFFERENT EXPIRY DATES.

BUREAU for the protection of industrial property right for the protection of industrial property rights.

BURN OUT TURNAROUND. Rebuilding the fortunes of a company which would otherwise go in for liquidation.

BURN RATE. The rate at which a new enterprise uses up its VENTURE CAPITAL.

BURYING THE BODY. Concealing unpleasant financial facts in a mass of figures and misleading headings on a balance sheet. "Miscellaneous," "other" or "sundries" are such headings which may conceal the fact of bad investments or product failures.

BUSINESS. The activity of organizing resources in order to produce and distribute goods and services for society.

BUSINESS AND SOCIETY. The study of the relationship of business with its entire social environment.

BUSINESS CYCLE INDEX. An index that indicates the position of the economy on a business cycle.

BUSINESS ETHICS. The application of general ethical principles to business behaviour.

BUSINESS INFRASTRUCTURE. The basic underlying structure of facilities and services essential to the operation of a market based business system, including a monetary system, standard weights and measures transportation networks, a legal system to make and enforce laws and similar components.

BUSINESS UNITS. *See* strategic business units.

BUSTED BONDS. Certificates of securities issued by famous companies which have gone into liquidation or countries which have repudiated their debts (*e.g.* Russian or Chinese bonds). Bought in hope of eventual repayment, or more commonly, as collectors' items.

BUTTERFLY. A term used in options trading. The strategy comprises simultaneous buying and selling call options.

BUTTERFLY SPREAD. A combination of a vertical bull spread and vertical bear spread with the same expiration date on all options and the same strike price on all short options.

BUY AND HOLD STRATEGY. Accumulating shares of a company over the years for long term growth benefits and foremost capital gains tax on profits. This requires far less of the investor's time, than the buy and sell strategy, which means trading frequently in shares.

BUY AND SELL STRATEGY. Active share trading strategy in which shares are bought at dips and sold at peaks. Since the lowest dip and highest peak are seldom identified, it amounts to buying low and selling high, not holding on to a share or shares for long. As such a strategy results in short term gains, the government claims nearly half the profits in income tax.

BUY BACK. Repurchase of convertible or nonconvertible debentures or the non-convertible part partly convertible debentures before the stipulated period, at par or at a discount, by companies or banks. Buy back promises, however, should be lightly taken, as companies devise methods to keep the sellers at bay.

BUY CHEAP AND SELL DEAR. It is one of the most frequently quoted maxims in the share market buying a share at a cheap or low price and selling at high price seems to be the most obvious way of making money. Share prices are high or low because there is a reason for it.

BUY LOCAL LEGISLATION. Laws that are intended to favour the purchase of domestically sourced goods or services over imported ones, even though the imports may be a better buy.

BUY ORDER. The buy order executed by the buyer to the broker (stock broker). It contains the name of the company, the number of equity shares intended to be bought and instructions regarding the price at which they are to be bought.

BUY OUT. Buying the controlling shareholding of a company to takeover its assets and business. A buy out can be made through negotiations or through accumulation of shares from the stock market or purchase of shares of a major shareholder. When money is borrowed from financial institutions to finance the purchase it is called a leveraged buy out in which case the loan is repaid from cash generated by the company's business or from the sale of its assets.

BUY ZONE. A parallel line equidistant between the basic trend line and return line forming upper channel and lower channel. The lower channel is called 'buy zone'. A return line can also be used to forewarn an impending change in trend. When prices move up to the area of the return line. One can consider the market is weakening.

BUYING CLIMAX. If the situation characterises with criteria which are similar to those of the selling climax *i.e.*, Advancing issues account for 70 per cent or more of total issues and declining issues 15 per cent or less. Buying climax takes place generally near intermediate bottoms and is often followed by new high, its significance is not as great as a selling climax.

BUYING THE BOOK. Buying up all the shares on a JOBBER'S account book at the current ASKED PRICE, usually under instruction from a financial institution or a stock broker acting on behalf of someone trying to accumulate a particular share.

BUY-SELL DECISION RULES. The rules are very simple, but it requires careful FUNDAMENTAL ANALYSIS to arrive at the real value of a share.

Rule 1. If the price of a share is lower than its value, *buy*.

Rule 2. If the price of a share is higher than its value, *sell*.

Rule 3. If the price of a share equals its value, *hold*.

C

C.L. LOT. Carload lot. The rate charges for shipping a full rail car of freight.

C.V. = C.R. × share price.

CACM. *See* Central American Common Market.

CALCULATED INTANGIBLE VALUE. It is the ability to use its tangible assets to outperform other companies in the industry that have similar assets.

CALL. An option to purchase an asset at a set price at some particular time in the future.

CALL FEATURE OF BOND OR PREFERRED STOCK. Option available to company to repurchase securities at set price over pre-specified period.

CALL MONEY. Instalment in paying for new issues when requested by the company. When all the calls have been paid the share is endorsed as fully paid up. Shareholders then have to send the certificates to the company for endorsement, with proof of payment of call money.

CALL MONEY MARKET. The inter bank call money market is the cone of the formed money market banks borrow from the call money market in order to meet sudden demand for funds for payments and 1-0 obtain funds to meet any likely short talk in their cash reserve to meet the CRR application or in liquid assets required to be hold to meet the SLR stipulation.

CALL OPTION. Gives a buyer the right to buy a financial asset at a specified price up to a specified expiration date. An option giving the buyer the right to purchase the underlying asset at a fixed strike price. A call gives the investor the right to purchase a particular stock at affixed price until a specific date.

CALL PREMIUM. The additional yield purchasers of callable bonds must receive in order to be willing to be exposed to call risk.

CALL PROVISION. A stipulation in a bond or preferred stock contact enabling the issuing firm to call back (repurchase) the outstanding bond or preferred stock at a predetermined price.

CALL RISK. The risk that a bond will be called.

CALLABLE BONDS. Bonds that the issuer may call or redeem after a specified period.

CALLABLE SWAP. An interest rate swap where one party has the right to cancel the swap at a certain time without any additional costs.

CALLED-UP-CAPITAL. Of the issued share capital, the entire amount may not be called-up. If some Rs. 5/- (say) is called-up for payment out of Rs. 10/- (face value), that portion is known as called-up capital. And the balance which is not yet called for payment is uncalled-up capital.

CALLS-IN-ADVANCE. (*See* Calls-in-arrear.)

CALLS-IN-ARREAR. Out of the called up capital, on the date of balance sheet, some amount may be outstanding. Such amount not yet paid by the shareholder is called-in-arrear amount. The amount that has been received by the company is called the paid-up amount. Some shareholders instead of only paying the called up capital they may pay the full amount. This supplies amount which has not yet been called for by the company, but has been paid in advance is known as the calls-in-advance amount.

CAMBRIDGE CONSTANT. The reciprocal of velocity.

CAMBRIDGE THEORY OF MONEY DEMAND. Asserts that people have two motives for holding money (a) to make transaction (b) to store wealth.

CANADA-U.S. FREE TRADE AGREEMENT. An agreement enacted in 1989, establishing a free-trade area involving the United States and Canada.

CAP. A series of European interest rate call options often used by a party that has issued a floating rate note. The cap ensures that the effective interest rate paid on the debt is capped at a fixed rate.

CAP AND COLLAR MORTGAGE. Mortgage with fixed upper and lower limits of the variable interest rates.

CAP FINANCING. It is the financing provided by a second lender to borrower when the financing provided by the first lender is insufficient.

CAPACITY UTILIZATION. When plant and machinery are installed they have a rated capacity *i.e.*, under optimum utilization they can produce a certain quantity of goods working a single shift. The rate of utilization of that plant capacity is expressed in percentage. The nature of demand for the company's product often regulates capacity utilization sometimes, owing to a glut of commodity in the market, *e.g.*, fertilizer industry, the government regulates capacity utilization when there are no such controls, a low capacity utilization is generally bad news for the company under conditions of a seller's market, a company may achieve more than 100 per cent capacity utilization by working more than one shift.

CAPITAL. In accounting, this word is too general by itself. In most cases, capital implies owners' equity. Money generated by long-term debt is also often called capital.

CAPITAL. In common business usage, it funds in the business. In economic terminology, it exists as a labour-saving device, equipment, Machinery, etc.

CAPITAL ACCOUNT. That portion of the balance of payments that keeps track of investment by U.S firms households, and government overseas and investments by foreigners in the U.S. A measure of transactions involving previously existing readier than currently produced assets.

CAPITAL ACCUMULATION. The amount of funds a firm can accumulate to provide for the operation of the business.

CAPITAL ADEQUACY RATIO. This is a measure of the amount of bank's capital expressed as a percentage of its risk weighted credit exposures. Two types of capital are measured — tier one capital which can absorb losses without a bank being required to cease trading *e.g.*, ordinary share capital, and tier two capital which can absorb losses in the event of a winding up and so provides a lesser degree of protection to depositors, *e.g.*, subordinated debt. The higher the capital adequacy ratio the bank has, the greater the level of unexpected losses it can absorb before becoming insolvent.

CAPITAL ALLOWANCE. The amount of depreciation allowed by the income tax to be offset against taxable profits.

CAPITAL ASSET PRICING MODEL. A theory which shows the relationship between risk and return for efficient and inefficient portfolios.

CAPITAL BUDGET. A statement showing the forecast of cash receipts, cash disbursements, and net cash balanced over a period of time.

CAPITAL BUDGETING. Long-term planning for proposed capital outlays and their financing.

CAPITAL COSTS. An alternate term for fixed costs, emphasizing the fact that fixed costs are needed in order to provide operating facilities and an organization ready to produce and sell at a planned volume of activity.

CAPITAL DISTRIBUTION. A distribution by a company out of capital profits, or by way of reduction in the nominal value of the capital.

CAPITAL EMPLOYED. Net assets used in a business to make profits.

CAPITAL FLIGHT. Movement of large sums of money from one country to another, or within a country from one state to another, to find a more congenial investment climate. The flight may take place because of political uncertainties, high inflation, labour unrest, military *dictatorship* or violence in general.

CAPITAL GAIN. The increase in the value of an asset over and above the cost of obtaining that asset. Gains made from capital transactions, *e.g.*, buying and selling of financial securities and real estate.

CAPITAL GEARING OR CAPITAL LEVERAGE. *See* Leverage.

CAPITAL ISSUE. The issue of shares by a company, whether new issue or premium issue or rights issue.

CAPITAL LEASE. A lease in the US is classified and accounted for by a lessee as a capital lease if it meets any of the following criteria. (a) The lease transfers ownership to the lessee at the end of the lease term; (b) The lease contains an option to purchase property at a bargain price; (c) The lease term is equal to 75 per cent or more of the estimated economic life of the property (exceptions for used property leased toward the end of its useful life).

CAPITAL LOSS. Loss incurred when investments are sold at a price lower than the purchase price. If the sale is within a year of the purchase, it is a short-term capital loss. If it is after an year, long term capital loss is sustained. In income tax returns long term capital losses can only be set off against long term capital gains. Whereas short term capital losses can be set off against short term capital gains, or against current income from other sources.

CAPITAL MARKET INSTRUMENT. A money market instrument with a maturity of more than one year.

CAPITAL MARKET. Sources from which long-term capital is raised for the selling up and sustained growth of companies. The stock exchange is a part of the capital market, not only because it readily provides money for new or existing ventures, but also because it helps investors to trade in their shares and maintain the liquidity of investments. Investment in public and rights issues, convertible and non-convertible debentures, therefore, becomes an attractive propositions and companies are also to raise the resources they need. The capital market is distinct from money market (blanks and leading institutions) which provides short term finance.

CAPITAL RATIONING. Refers to a situation where the firm is constrained for external or self-imposed reasons to obtain necessary funds to invest in all investment projects with positive NPV. Under capital rationing the management has not simply to determine the profitable investment opportunities but if has to decide to obtain that combination of the profitable projects which yields highest NPV within the available funds.

CAPITAL REDEMPTION RESERVE FUND. When a company redeems its preference shares, the nominal value of the shares is put in this fund, which becomes part of the paid up capital of the company, with no obligation to pay dividend although the fund can be used towards issuing bonus shares.

CAPITAL STRUCTURE OF COMPANIES. The capital of a new company consists of issued and subscribed equality shares. Redeemable preference shares and secured and unsecured loans. When the company is making profits, that part of profits remaining undistributed among the shareholders is transferred to reserves and becomes part of the capital structure. *See* FINANCIAL STRUCTURE.

CAPITAL SURPLUS. The excess received over the part or state or legal value of the shares issued.

CAPITAL SURPLUS. The difference between the nominal or face value of shares sold by a company to the public and the sum realized by selling them as a PREMIUM ISSUE.

CAPITAL TRANSFER TAX. A cumulative tax applied to gifts made during a lifetime and assets left at death.

CAPITAL TURNOVER. Revenue divided by invested capital.

CAPITAL TURNOVER. Annual sales divided by paid up equity, studied over a period shows the extent to which a company can grow without additional capital investment.

CAPITAL-INTENSIVE. A project that requires large investments in capital assets especially machinery and equipment is called capital intensive. Automobiles, oil refineries, and steel production are capital intensive and may keep the investor waiting for rewards, unless these make a high profit within a short time or keep the cost of borrowing low. Capital intensive may also mean high proportion of fixed assets to labour or raw materials.

CAPITALISM. An economic system characterized by private ownership, pricing, production and distribution of goods.

CAPITALIZATION. Conversion of FREE RESERVES of a limited company into capital by issuing bonus shares.

CAPLET. One of the component interest rate call options in a cap.

CAPPED MORTGAGE. It is a mortgage with a fixed upper limit to its variable interest rate.

CAPTIVE FINANCE COMPANY. Usually a wholly owned subsidiary of a consumer product company to finance purchases from the parent company. Some automobile finance companies belong to this category.

CAPTIVE FUND. Fund wholly owned by a larger body than individual entrepreneurs.

CAPTIVE MARKET. A market waiting for a particular product, its demand, considerably outstripping the supply. Also a product for which there is an assured buyer.

CAREER is the sequence of work-related positions occupied throughout a person's life.

CAREFUL PERSONALITY TYPE.

CARIBBEAN COMMUNITY AND COMMON MARKET (CARICOM). A customs union in the Caribbean region.

CARICOM. *See* Caribbean Community and Common Market.

CARRY FORWARD. A speculator may carry forward the transaction if he feels that the share price will further make bigger profit by holding. In such case he may ask his broker to carry forward his transaction to the next account if he is not willing to pay for the transaction.

CARRY OVER MARGIN. The amount which operators must deposit in order to carry over their transaction from one SETTLEMENT period to another. Stock exchange authorities periodically impose such margins in order to curb excessive speculation. The margin varies in amount based on the level of speculative activity and may be imposed either on bulls or bears or both.

CARTEL. A restrictive trade association of a number of companies bonding a market by carrying it up among themselves, reaching an agreement to peg prices at certain levels, controlling supplies etc. so as to check unfair profits. OPEC is an example of an oil cartel.

CASCADE TAX. Tax imposed at each stage of production. For instance, a company may pass on from one country to another as each stage of production is carried out and attracts taxation at each stage of production.

CASH BASIS. A process of accounting whereby revenue and expense recognition depend solely on the timing of various cash receipts and disbursements.

CASH BASIS. Method of accounting in which income and expenditure are entered only when cash is received or paid out. Opposite of accrual basis.

CASH BREAK-EVEN POINT. When eliminated the non-cash item from revenues and costs the breakeven point on cash basis can easily be computed. In most cases depreciation would be the non-cash expense included in fixed costs.

CASH BUDGET. A schedule of expected cash receipts and disbursements.

CASH BUDGET. Cash budget is the most important component of financial budgets. The major objective of the cash budget is to plan cash in such a way that the company always maintain sufficient cash balance to meet its needs and uses the idle cash in the most profitable manner.

CASH COW. A share which yields consistently high rate of dividends. Also a currently profitable business but one which does not have very bright growth prospects and is, therefore, used to fund other enterprises.

CASH CREDIT. An arrangement whereby the bank allows the borrower to borrow upto a certain limit, the cash credit limit.

CASH DELIVERY. A relatively new procedure for settling future obligations is cash delivery. This procedure is a substitute for physical delivery. The mechanism of cash delivery is that the price of the relevant contract at the close of trading.

CASH FLOW. A general term that must be interpreted carefully. Most strictly, cash flow mans inflows or outflows of cash. Frequently, the term is used loosely to represent funds provided by operations.

CASH FLOW. Usually equivalent to retained profits plus depreciation.

CASH INVESTMENT. An investment which can be converted back into the money (originally invested) on demand or after a short period of notice.

CASH LIST. Group B securities, unspecified shares or non cleared securities.

CASH MARKET. It is referred to as the actual or spot market, where the commodities themselves are bought and sold on a negotiated basis. Most of the time, the contract calls for the actual delivery of a commodity.

CASH OFFER. A cash offer is a straightforward means of financing a merger. It does not cause any dilution in the E.P.S. and the ownership of the existing shareholders of the acquiring company. It is also unlikely to course wide fluctuations in the share prices of merging companies. The shareholders of the target company get cash for selling their shares to the acquiring company.

CASH PROFIT. Profit before depreciation and tax are deducted.

CASH RATIO. The ratio of cash and marketable securities to a company's current liabilities. The ratio indicates how soon a company can pay back its creditors. *See* QUICK RATIO.

CASH SETTLEMENT. Settlement for the purchase or sale of an investment which is due the day after the transaction.

CASH SHARES. *See* Non-cleared securities.

CASH SURRENDER VALUE. The accumulated savings element of a life insurance policy that can be recovered on cashing in the policy or borrowed against at a specified interest rate.

CASH-AND–CARRY. An investment strategy that duplicates the payoff to a forward contract.

CASH-AND-NEW. When shares bought during the account are sold free of commission at the end of the account and are immediately repurchased for the new-account.

CASINO SOCIETY. Investors who put their money into undervalued corporate assets volatile futures contracts or other speculative ventures in an effort to make fast money.

CASTE. A social class separated from others by heredity.

CATS AND DOGS. Shares of small, new, poorly financed or loss making companies infrequently traded are called cats and dogs. These may show appreciation in a bull phase but in a bear phase become practically untradeable.

CAVEAT EMPTOR. Beware of a 'maxim' in Indian market which is still not adequately protected either against unscrupulous brokers or against defaulting companies. Once the Securities and Exchange Board of India gets sufficiently, it is hoped that investor interest will be adequately protected, but not till then. Beware of brokers who pay very late, show suspiciously low price and delay to execute orders till the opportunity is lost.

CBOE. Chicago Board of Options Exchange. An exchange that has promoted the organized trading of call options.

CBOT. Chicago Board of Trade US based largest futures exchange.

CBT. Chicago Board of Trade.

CD (CUM-DIVIDEND RATE). An investor who buys a share at the cum-dividend (cd) rate is entitled to the dividend for which the books are being closed. Stock exchange authorities normally fix the dates on which shares are to be quoted at "cd" or "xd" rates.

CEFTA. *See* Central European Free Trade Association.

CENTRAL AMERICAN COMMON MARKET (CACM). A customs union in Central America.

CENTRAL BANK. A country's Central bank (In India, the Reserve Bank) issues currency, administers monetary policy, regulates the working of its subsidiaries, holds reserves of other banks, regulates foreign exchange policies and is supposed to protect public interest in general.

CENTRAL EUROPEAN FREE TRADE ASSOCIATION (CEFTA). An association which went into effect on July 1, 1992 with an initial membership of the Czech Republic, Slovakia, Hungary, and Poland, and whose goal is to establish a free trade area that includes the basic trade structure of the EU by the year 2000.

CENTRAL STATE CONTROL. A socio-economic system in which political social and economic power is concentrated in a Central government that makes all fundamental decisions for the society.

CENTRALIZATION OF AUTHORITY. The tendency to restrict delegation of decision making in an organization structure, usually by holding authority at or near the top of the organization structure.

CENTRALIZATION. Decision-making is reserved at central points in the organization. It is the extent to which decision making authority/ responsibility is concentrated.

CENTRALIZED AUTHORITY. Exists in government ownership economic systems where almost all business decisions are made by a central government level.

CENTRALLY PLANNED ECONOMY (CPE). *See* Command economy.

CERTAINTY EQUIVALENT. A certain cashflow which is equal in desirability to an uncertain cashflow.

CERTIFICATE OF ACCEPTANCE. A document whereby the lessee acknowledges that the equipment to be leased has been delivered to him, is acceptable to him, and has been manufactured or constructed in accordance with the specifications.

CERTIFICATE OF INCORPORATION. A certificate usually issued by a State government authorizing a group of individuals to establish a business in the legal form of a corporation (*See* Federal chartering).

CERTIFICATE OF ORIGIN. A shipping document that determines the origin of products and usually validated by an external source, such as a chamber of commerce it helps countries determine the specific tariff schedule for imports.

CERTIFICATE. The document of a title to registered stock or shares.

CERTIFICATES OF DEPOSIT. Called CDs special redeemable debt obligation issued by banks whose terms usually run from 90 days to 4 years.

CERTIFIED CHEQUE. The cheque that is guaranteed not to bounce as it is issued by a bank with a guarantee of payment. The bank is legally obligated to honour it. The funds to cover it are immediately withdrawn from the depositor's account.

CERTIFIED MANAGEMENT ACCOUNTANT. A designation given by the institute of management accounting of the national association of Accountants to those who pass a set of examinations and met specified experience and continuing education requirements.

CERTIFIED PULIC ACCOUNTANT. In the US an accountant earns this designation by a combination of education, qualifying experience, and the passing of a three and one-half day written national examination.

CERTIFIED TRANSFER. A transfer form or deed certified to the effect that the certificate in respect of the stock or shares transferred is held at the offices of the registrar for the company awaiting the completed document.

CFC. *See* Controlled foreign corporation.

CHAEBOLS. Family run conglomerates in South Korea.

CHAIN STORE. A store under the control of central ownership which stocks and distributes similar lines of goods.

CHAIRMAN OF THE BOARD. The highest ranking authority in a company. The chairman of the board of directors may be an eminent person or a representative of the controlling group. If he is also the chief executive or managing director of the company, he holds considerable executive authority, otherwise he may be treated simply as a venerable figure head. The chairman presides over the annual general meeting and summarized version (unless it is short) of whose speech is often published in the newspaper along with his photograph.

CHANGE AGENT ROLE. A work role that promotes different behaviour in others and/or different conditions in the environment.

CHANGE IN DEMAND. A shift in the entire demand curve caused by a change in income, tastes, expectations, or other determinants of demand.

CHANGE IN QUALITY DEMANDED. A movement along a given demand curve.

CHANGE IN QUANTITY SUPPLIED. A movement along a given supply curve.

CHANGE IN SUPPLY. A shift in the entire supply curve.

CHANGE OF NAME OF COMPANIES. A company may change its name by passing a special resolution at a meeting of shareholders. A recent example is the change of name of IEL to ICI. A change of name, however, does not absolve a company of any of its legal obligations. A change of name may also be occasional by a simple spelling mistake.

CHANGES STATEMENT. A statement of changes in financial position.

CHANNEL OF DISTRIBUTION. The route a product follows to reach the final consumer.

CHARACTERISTIC LINE. A regression line representing the relationship between the return on an individual security and the return on the market portfolio. The slope of the characteristic line is the beta of the security.

CHART ANALYSIS. The use of graphs and charts to analysis prices and trading behaviour and to anticipate future price movements.

CHART OF APPROVAL AUTHORIZATIONS. A technique by which the various authority delegations of an enterprise are charted in a matrix from showing the mature of the subjects over which authority exists and the organizational positions where decision making authority rests.

CHART. Visual display of the movement of prices or indices. (*See* also BAR CHART, LINE CHART POINT — AND FIGURE CHART.)

CHASTITY BONDS. They are the bonds that become redeemable at par value in the event of a takeover.

CHATTELS. Movable property; Opposite of fixtures.

CHEAP MONEY. Easily borrowable money supplied at low rates of interest. Cheap money promotes industrial development and improves the investment climate. When lending is restricted and interest rates are high it is bad for the industry as well as investment.

CHEAPEST TO DELIVER. The bond in a futures contract this is least expensive to deliver on the contract.

CHECK OFF. The practice of deducting union dues by the employer.

CHECKS. Negotiable instruments ordering a bank to pay someone a certain sum of money on demand.

CHERRY PICKING. When a credit rating agency carefully shifts a pool of assets in order to give a very high credit worthiness rating to the one it chooses it is doing 'cherry picking'.

CHICAGO MERCANTILE EXCHANGE (CME). The largest commodity exchange in he world, dealing primarily in agriculture products, U.S. treasury bill, coins and some metals.

CHINESE WALL. Watertight compartments in a business house which keeps the information of each department confidential so that those inside the company may not take advantage of such inside information.

CHOICE CRITERION. Often used as a synonym for objective function.

CHOOSER OPTION. An option for which during the life of the option, the option owner can pick either a call option or a put option.

CHRONOLOGY is a structured review of activities during a period of time.

CHURNING. Overactive trading of customer accounts in order to generate commission or income is called churning.

CIA. The Central Intelligence Agency a U.S. governmental agency charged with gathering intelligence information abroad.

CIRCUIT BRAKERS. It is a mechanism by which exchanges temporarily suspend the trading in a security when its prices are volatile and tend to breach the price band.

CIS. Collective investment schemes.

CIVIL AERONAUTICS BOARD. A federal agency which regulates air transportation.

CIVIL LAW SYSTEM. A legal system based on a very detailed set of laws that are organized into a code, countries with a civil law system, also called a codified legal system, include Germany, France and Japan.

CIVIL LAW. Law that deals with difference between individuals.

CIVIL LIBERTIES. The freedom to develop one's own views and attitudes.

CIVIL RIGHTS ACT. A federal act passed in 1964 that prohibits discrimination in employment as to race, colour, religion, sex, or national origin.

CLASS RATE. Rates charges for shipping products grouped into the same class.

CLASSICAL VIEW OF MONEY DEMAND. Considers income to be the primary determinant of money demand.

CLASSIFICATION OF DEPOSITS. Classification of deposits by maturity refers to outstanding amount of term deposits as on the date of the term return. Maturity refers to original period of deposits.

CLASSIFICATION. A grouping of objects with the same data structure and behaviour.

CLAW BACK. The statutory reduction in life assurance tax relief when a qualifying policy is surrendered within four years.

CLEAN BALANCE SHEET. A balance sheet with no debt items, showing that the company hasn't any outstanding.

CLEAN DESCRIBES. The price of a stock after allowing for any accrued interest reflected in the market price.

CLEAN FLOAT. Controller of Capital Issues may determine the price of a new issue or a rights issue. When there is no such intervention, free market forces determine the price of an issue, it is a clean float.

CLEARING HOUSE. Transaction in group A shares can be settled between members by using the facilities of the "Clearing house" attached to the stock exchange.

CLEARING MEMBER. A member of the clearing-house. Each clearing member must be a member of an exchange but not all members of an exchange are members of a clearing-house. All trades made by a non-clearing member must be registered with and eventually settled through a clearing member.

CLEARING PROGRAMME. The transactions entered during this period of a week are to be settled either by payment for purchase or by delivery of share certificates sold on notified days which are made known to the members of the exchange through a clearing programme.

CLOSED ECONOMY MODEL. A model that does not consider the impact of international trade on the economy.

CLOSED SHOP. Requires individuals to join a union before they can be hired.

CLOSED-END-MUTUAL FUND. It is an investment company which has a fixed number of shares traded on the stock market after their initial public issue.

CLOSED-END-FUND. In this type of fund, investors have to commit their money to the fund for a particular period of time as specified by the terms of the offer. The main drawback here is that since an exit is not available from the fund itself; units of such funds are normally traded on stock exchanges at a discount to their existing net asset values (NAVs). However, this discount reduces as funds approach their redemption dates.

CMA. *See* Certified management accountant.

COAL GASIFICATION. A process of making a gaseous fuel from solid coal.

COAL LIQUEFACTION. A process of making a liquid fuel from solid coal.

COBOL. Common Business Oriented Language, a computer language.

COCOM. *See* Coordinating committee on Multilateral sports.

CODE OF CONDUCT. A set of principles guiding the actions of their contacts with societies.

CODETERMINATION. A process by which both labour and management participate in the management of a company. Codetermination is a practice whereby union or worker representatives are given positions on a company's board of directors.

CODETERMINATION. A system of corporate governance providing for labour representation on a company's board of directors.

CODIFIED LEGAL SYSTEM. *See* Civil law system.

COEFFICIENT OF VARIATION. A measure of depression

defined as standard deviation divided by expected value.

CO-GENERATION. An energy conservation process that used steam twice once for generating electric power or for producing heat and a second time for a supplemental use.

COLLABORATIVE ARRANGEMENT. A formal, long term contractual agreement among companies.

COLLAR. An interest rate contract that establishes a cap and a floor on a specified rate of interest that is to be paid can also be used in commodity foreign currency, and equity market.

COLLATERAL. Property or assets pledged as a security against default on a loan.

COLLATERAL. Collateral under a lease is the equipment which is leased : Property or assets pledged as a security against default on a loan.

COLLATERAL TRUST BONDS. Bonds backed by securities of the company (such as stocks).

COLLECTIVE BARGAINING. It is the process whereby representatives of management and workers negotiate over wages, hours, and conditions of employment. Workers through a spokesman, bargain collectively rather than individually for wages and other issues.

COLLECTIVE BARGAINING. The legally protected right of employees to organize for purposes of bargaining with an employer concerning wages, working conditions, and benefits.

COLLUSION. The act of two or more firms conspiring to act in concert in their pricing or output decisions in order to make both firms better off.

COMECON. *See* Council for Mutual Economic Assistance.

COMEX. Commodity exchange, NEW YORK.

COMMAND AND CONTROL SYSTEM. A pollution control system based on government regulations environmental and emission standards and legal penalties for noncompliance.

COMMAND ECONOMY. An economic system in which resources are allocated and controlled by government decision.

COMMERCIAL BANKS. A depository institution which is relatively unrestricted in its ability to make loans and which is legally able to accept demand deposits.

COMMERCIAL BILL OF EXCHANGE. An instrument of payment in international business that instructs the importer to forward payment to the exporter.

COMMERCIAL INVOICE. A bill for

goods from the buyer to the sells.

COMMERCIAL PAPER. An unsecured promise to pay back a specified amount at a designated time in the future. The maturity at issue is no more than 270 days. Commercial paper is usually sold at a discount from the face amount. Any type of security that promises payment of debt.

COMMISSION AGENT. A type of intermediary that sells a manufacturer's agency that deals with multinational enterprises.

COMMISSION MERCHANTS. Do not take title to goods but have physical possession of merchandise and are paid on a commission basis.

COMMITMENT PRINCIPLE. A group of persons to whom, as a group, some matter is committed for purposes of information, advice, interchange of ideas, or decision.

COMMITTED COSTS. Those field costs arising from the possession of plant and equipment and a basic organization and thus are affected primarily by long-run decisions as to the desired level of capacity.

COMMITTEE. A group of persons to whom, as a group, some matter is committed for purposes of information, advice, interchange of ideas, or decision.

COMMODITIES. Basic raw materials or agricultural products.

COMMODITY AGREEMENT. A form of economic cooperation designed to stabilize and raise the price of a commodity.

COMMODITY DERIVATIVE. A derivative written on a commodity.

COMMODITY EXCHANGES. A commodity exchange is merely a meeting place where buyers and sellers meet to transact business for their own behalf or on their client's behalf.

COMMODITY FUND. An entity in which funds contributed by a number of people are pooled together to trade futures and option contracts under professional management.

COMMODITY FUTURES. A futures contract written on a commodity.

COMMODITY FUTURES TRADING COMMISSION (CFTC). The commodity futures trading commission (CFTC) act of 1974 of the USA established the commission. CFTC has specific powers under the Act. One important area of jurisdiction is the approval of new contracts. CFTC regulates future market trading rules including the daily permitted maximum price fluctuations certain features of the delivery process and minimum price fluctuation limits.

COMMODITY FUTURES TRADING COMMISSION. The federal agency responsible for regulating futures markets in the United States.

COMMODITY MONEY. A physical commodity that is used as money even though it has alternative non-monetary uses.

COMMODITY RATE. Rates charged for shipping bulky items, such as coal or sand.

COMMODITY SWAP. A swap in which counter parties exchange cash flows based on at least one commodity price.

COMMON MARKET. A form of regional economic integration in which countries abolish internal tariffs use a common external tariff, and abolish restrictions on factor mobility.

COMMON AGRICULTURAL POLICY (CAP). An EU policy aimed to form trade, price supports and modernization programmes in agriculture.

COMMON CARRIER. A carrier offering its services to the general public, regulated by various state and federal agencies. The same rates must be charged to all customers.

COMMON COST. A cost that is common to all the segments in question and is not clearly or practically allocable except by some questionable allocation base.

COMMON LAW SYSTEM. A legal system based on tradition precedent and custom and usage, in which the courts interpret the law based on those conventions; found in the United Kingdom and former British colonies.

COMMON LAW. Unwritten law that is established by judges interpreting all written law.

COMMON STOCK. Stock representing the class off owners having a "residual" ownership of a corporation.

COMMON STOCK. A certificate of ownership of the corporation form of business ownership. It generally has full voting rights and shares the excess profits after other forms of debt and ownership have been paid.

COMMUNICATIONS SKILL. Ability of manager to effectively send information to all other individuals in the firm.

COMMUNISM. A form of totalitarianism initially theorized by Karl Marx in which the political and economic system are virtually inseparable.

COMMUNITY.

COMMUNITY EMPLOYEE OWNED FIRM (CEF). A company owned wholly or in part by a combination of its employees and other persons and groups in the firms local community.

COMMUNITY RELATIONS. The involvement of business with the communities in which it conducts operations.

COMPANIES ACT. A comprehensive price of legislation regulating the functioning of Joint Stock Companies in India.

COMPANY OBJECTION. An investor sends the certificate along with the transfer deed to the company for transfer. In certain cases the registration is rejected because of signature difference or if the share are fake, forged or stolen, etc. in such cases the company returns the shares along with the letter which is termed as a company objection.

COMPARABLE ACCESS. A protectionist argument that companies and industries should have the same access to foreign markets as foreign industries and companies have to their markets.

COMPARABLE WORTH. It is the concept that jobs requiring comparable knowledge skills and abilities should be paid similarly.

COMPARATIVE ADVANTAGE. The theory that there may still be global efficiency gains from trade if a country specializes in those products that it can produce more efficiently than other products.

COMPARATIVE MANAGEMENT. The study and analysis of management in different environments and in various countries.

COMPENSATION COMMITTEE. Usually is a subgroup of the board of directors composed of outside directors.

COMPETENT PARTIES. A requirement of valid contracts which does not include drunkards, insane persons, convicts or individuals under 21 years of age (in some states 18).

COMPETITION. A struggle to survive and excel. In business different firms compete with one another for the customers dollars.

COMPETITIVE MARKETS. A market where all traders act as price takers.

COMPLEMENTS. Goods or services that tend to be used jointly and thus have the property that when the price of one increases the demand for the other decreases.

COMPLETE CROWDING OUT. Describes a situation in which crowding out is complete. So that the increase in government spending cause a reduction in the sum of investment and consumption spending of an equal of an equal but opposite magnitude.

COMPLETE CURRENCY MULTIPLIER. Indicates how much currency holdings will change due to a change in the monetary base.

COMPLETE MONEY MULTIPLIER. Determines the factor by which the money stock (currency plus deposits) change due to a change in the monetary base.

COMPLETED STAFF WORK. Implies presentation of a clear recommendation to a superior based upon full consideration of a problem clearance with persons importantly affected, suggestions about avoiding any difficulties involved, and, often, the preparation of necessary paperwork for implementing recommendations so that the receiving person can accept or reject the proposal without further study, long conferences, or unnecessary work.

COMPLIANCE COSTS. The costs incurred by business and other organizations in complying with government regulations such as the cost of pollution control machinery or disposing of toxic chemical wastes.

COMPONENT PERCENTAGES. Analysis and presentation of financial statement in percentage form to aid comparability.

COMPOSITE STRATEGIES. A group of srategies in various related areas that a company or other enterprises may have.

COMPOUND DUTY. A tax placed on goods traded internationally based on value plus units.

COMPOUND GROWTH (ECONOMIC POPULATION). Growth in production or population that incorporates periodic increase into the (production or population) base thereby compounding or multiplying the amount of growth experienced.

COMPOUND OPTION. An option written on one or more options.

COMPTROLLER. *See* Controller.

COMPTROLLER OF THE CURRENCY. An office of the treasury which regulates the formation of national banks from time to time to verify their financial health.

COMPUTER AIDED DESIGN. The application of computer technology to design products much more quickly than with the traditional paper and pencil approach.

COMPUTER AIDED MANUFACTURING. The application of computer technology to the manufacturing process. The ultimate goal for some companies is "computer-integrated manufacturing" which computerizes the total manufacturing process.

COMPUTER LANGUAGE. The instructions which contain the operations the computer is to perform written in a specific language which the computer can interrupt.

CONCENTRATION STRATEGY. A strategy by which an international company builds up operations quickly in one or a few countries before going to another.

CONCENTRATION (CORPORATE ECONOMIC INDUSTRIAL MARKET). When relatively few companies are responsible for a large proportion of overall economic activity, production, or sales.

CONCEPTUAL SCHEMA (IN A RELATIONAL DATA BASE). A design form the perspective of an entire enterprise.

CONCEPTUAL SKILL. The ability of a manager to see the overall picture.

CONCILIATION. It is a process in which an outside entity attempts to help two deadlock parties continue negotiation and arrive at a solution. A third party, the conciliator, attempts to get labour and management together to discuss issues involved in their disagreement.

CONDITIONAL SALE/LEASE. A term for a lease which in substance is a conditional lease.

CONDITIONAL SALE. A transaction for purchase of an asset in which the user for income tax purpose is treated as the owner of the equipment at the outset of the transaction.

CONDITIONAL VALUE. The value that will ensue if a particular event occurs.

CONFIRMED LETTER OF CREDIT. A letter of credit to which a bank in the exporter's country adds its guarantee of payment.

CONFORMITY. A person's dependence on the norms of others without independent thinking.

CONSERVATISM. A characteristic of accounting systems that implies that companies are hesitant to disclose high profits or profits that are consistent with their actual operating results; more common in Germanic countries.

CONSERVATISM. Selecting that method of measurement which yields the gloomiest immediate results.

CONSIDERATION. A requirement of valid contracts which means all parties must contribute some thing of value. It refers to behaviour indicating trust warmth friendship and mutual respect between the leader and the group members.

CONSOLIDATED STATEMENTS. Statements that combine legally separate companies as though they were a single fused entity.

CONSOLIDATION. An accounting process in which financial statements related entities, such as a parent and its subsidiaries are combined to yield a unified set of financial statements; in the process transactions among the related enterprises are eliminated so that the statements reflect transactions with outside parties.

CONSORTIUM LEASE. A lease in which a number of lessors participate. The usual reason for this is that the cost or the potential risk is too high to be bone by one lessor.

CONSORTIUM. A temporary combination of two or more companies for the purposes of bidding for a large project. These are formed to obtain a competitive edge over other bidders, as the pooling of financial and technical resources enable them to offer an attractive package.

CONSTANT DOLLARS. Those monetary units restated so as to represent the same general purchasing power.

CONSTANT YIELD SWAP. An interest rate swap in which both parts are floating.

CONSTRAINT INDEX. A quantitative score that reflects the level of a nation's environ-ment for effective business operations.

CONSULAR INVOICE. A document that covers all the usual details of the commercial invoice and packing list, prepared in the language of the foreign country for which the goods are destined, on special forms obtainable from the consulate or authorized commercial printers.

CONSUMER ADVOCATES. Persons who act to protect the interests of the consumer.

CONSUMER BEHAVIOUR. Actions of individuals involved in deciding which goods and services to purchase.

CONSUMER GOODS. Goods purchased and used by the final consumer for his personal or household use.

CONSUMER LOANS. Loans obtained by individuals for intermediate-term purchased such as automobile purchases as well as merchandise purchased with credit card.

CONSUMER MOVEMENT. The actions of consumer advocates to improve products and business practices.

CONSUMER MOVEMENT. (*See* Consumerism).

CONSUMER PRICE INDEX. A measure of the cost of typical wage-earner purchases of goods and services expressed as a percentage of the cost of these same goods and services in some base period.

CONSUMER PRICE INDEX. The consumer price index measures the percentage change in the expenditure of family for buying a fixed "basket" of commodities and services. Since January 1999, the prices of the basket representing the consumption of the urban families in 1997 are measured according to Household expenditure Survey, 1997-First Findings, and the official index is presented on the base of the period : average 1998 = 100.0 there are in fact several Consumer Price Indices. Each tracks the retail prices of goods and services for a different group of people, because the consumption patterns of different groups differ.

CONSUMER RESPONSIBILITIES. The obligations of consumers to act fairly, intelligently, honestly and helpfully towards sellers.

CONSUMER RIGHTS. The legitimate claims of consumers to safe products and services adequate information free choice, a fair hearing and competitive prices.

CONSUMER SOVEREIGNTY. The freedom of consumers to influence production through the choice they make.

CONSUMER SOVEREIGNTY. The idea that consumers, through their purchases decide what will be produced by business firms.

CONSUMER-DIRECTED MARKET ECONOMY. An economy in which there is minimal government participation while growth is promoted through the mobility of production factors, including high labour turnover.

CONSUMERISM. A social movement that seeks to augment the rights and powers of buyers in relation to sellers.

CONSUMPTION GOODS. Goods and services demanded by households.

CONTINENTAL TERMS. *See* European terms.

CONTINGENCY APPROACH TO LEADERSHIP. A theory that leadership depends upon the group task situation and the degree to which the leader's style, personality, and approach fit the group.

CONTINGENCY MANAGEMENT. Managing which recognizes differences or contingencies in people, at various times as in actual situations, also referred to as "situational management", an approach that emphasizes that there can be no "one best way" in all situations.

CONTINGENCY MODEL OF LEADERSHIP EFFECTIVENESS. A leadership model developed by Fred Fiedler that postulates that a leader's effectiveness dependents on three variables. (1) how well a leader accepted by subordinates, (2) the degree to which subordinate's positions are routine and clearly spelled out in contrast to being vague and undefined, and (3) the formal authority in the position occupied by a leader.

CONTINGENCY PLANNING. Planning for possible future environments which are not expected to occur but which may occur; if this possible future is widely different from that premised, alternative premises and plans are required.

CONTINGENCY STRATEGIES. Strategies developed to be used when unforeseen events or circumstances may make a selected strategy obsolete or unsuitable.

CONTINGENT PREMIUM OPTION. *See* Paylater option.

CONTINGENT RENTALS. Rentals in which the amounts are dependent upon some factors other than passage of time.

CONTINUITY CONVENTION. *See* going concern convention.

CONTINUOUS BUDGET. A budget that perpetually adds a month in the future as the month just ended is dropped.

CONTINUOUS BUDGETING. Continuous budgeting provides for a system of revising the budget for the changing conditions continuously.

CONTINUOUS PRODUCTION. A production process that produces a standardized product. Raw materials are continually fed into the production process.

CONTINUOUS TRADING. A market where trading can take place continuously in time.

CONTINUOUSLY COMPOUNDED INTEREST RATES. Interest rates in which interest is compounded continuously.

CONTRA ACCOUNTANT. A separate offsetting account. Examples are allowance for uncollectible accounts and accumulated depreciation.

CONTRACT. Agreement between two or more persons to perform certain acts.

CONTRACT CARRIER. A carrier which offer its services to an individual person or firm. This carrier may charge different rates to customers served.

CONTRACT CONCESSIONS. An agreement reached between a labour union and an employer to reduce monetary benefits, change work rules, and/or modify fringe benefits in an existing labour contracts in order to improve the competitive standing of the employer firm.

CONTRACT HIRE. Expression for an operating lease, usually

for vehicles or handling equipment. Lessor carries the residual value risk, and the fixed rentals may include a maintenance charge.

CONTRACT MANUFACTURING. The company in concern (in this case UB), enters into a contract with an individual/organization, termed as a 'contractor'. The contractor selected will be responsible for manufacturing a product with the company's (UB's) name on its. The bottom line in contract manufacturing is to assemble a working product and deliver it, on time, and in the specified budget.

CONTRACT MARKET. A commodity futures market or an exchange that qualifies under the commodity futures Trading Commission Act.

CONTRACTUAL. A obligation include those financial obligations like interest lease rentals and financial payments that are matters of contract and should not be defaulted.

CONTRIBUTED CAPITAL. The total amounts invested by owners at the inception of a business or subsequently, usually distinguished from capital arising from retained income.

CONTRIBUTION APPROACH. A method of preparing income statements that separates variable costs from fixed costs in order to emphasize the importance of cost behaviour patterns for purposes of planning and control.

CONTRIBUTION MARGIN. Excess of sales price over variable expenses. Also called marginal income. May be expressed as a total, as a ratio, or on a per unit basis.

CONTROL. The planning, implementation, evaluation and correction of performance to ensure that organization objectives are achieved.

CONTROL FACTOR UNIT. A measure of workload. Examples are lines per hour and pieces mailed per hour.

CONTROL OF OVERALL PERFORMANCE. Control designed to measure the total performance of an enterprise, an integrated division of it, or a major programme or project.

CONTROL PROCESS. In managing, the basic process involves (1) establishing standards, (2) measuring performance against standards, and (3) correcting for undesirable deviations.

CONTROL UNIT. The computer component which directs and controls the internal flow of information according to instructions contained in the computer programme.

CONTROL-BUDGET VARIANCE. *See* Flexible-budget variance.

CONTROLLABLE COST. A cost that may be directly regulated at a given level of managerial authority, either in the short run or in the long run.

CONTROLLED FOREIGN CORPORATION (CFC). A foreign corporation of which more than 50 per cent of the voting stock is owned by U.S. shareholders (taxable entities that own at least 10 per cent of the voting stock of the corporation).

CONTROLLED SAMPLE. A non-probability sample, and includes convenience and judgment samples.

CONTROLLER. The chief management accounting executive also spelled comptroller.

CONTROLLING. The management function of checking that plans are carried out successfully in accordance with stated company objectives.

CONVENIENCE BUILD. The implied or non-pecuniary return from holding a commodity. It is also a measure of the degree backwardation in a market.

CONVENIENCE GOOD. A good sold through many retail outlets sold at a low unit price it is nationally advertised as well as being purchased frequently with little or no thought given to making the purchase. Also, the quality is standardized.

CONVENIENCE STORE. This store is usually located away from major shopping centres, open long hours and sells national brand name merchandise at higher prices.

CONVENIENCE VALUE. The value to storing a commodity for its use in production.

CONVENIENCE YIELD. The convenience value expressed as a per cent.

CONVENTIONAL INVESTMENT. Conventional Investment can be defined as one whose cash flows take the pattern an initial cash outlay followed by cash inflows.

CONVERGENCE. Refers to the tendency of cash and futures prices to come together (*i.e.*, the basis shrinks) as a futures contract approaches expiration.

CONVERGENCE THEORY. A theory that as nations industrialize they are inevitably pulled toward similarity (also known as convergence hypothesis).

CONVERSION COSTS. Direct labour plus factory overhead.

CONVERSION FACTOR. A pricing factor used to determine the prices of T-bonds or T-notes eligible for delivery on futures contracts. These factors are provided by exchanges.

CONVERSION RATIO AND CONVERSION PRICE. The conversion ratio is the number of ordinary shares that on investor-cum-receive when he exchanges his convertible debenture. The conversion price is the price paid for the ordinary share at the time of conversion.

CONVERSION VALUE. The conversion value of a convertible debenture is equal to the conversion ratio multiplied by the ordinary shares market price.

CONVERTIBILITY. The ability to exchange one currency for another currency without restrictions.

CONVERTIBLE BONDS. Bonds convertible into shares of common stock.

CONVEXITY. A measure of the bonds sensitivity to large changes in the bond's yield.

COOLING PERIOD. Banks, under collateralized lending could borrow after 4 weeks. An additional period of 2 weeks are allowed.

COOPERATIVE CHAIN. Retailers who form their own wholesaling organization in order to compare with cooperative chains.

COOPERATIVE SYSTEM. A system, as perceived by Chester Barnard, as one whose purpose is cooperation and which comprises physical, biological, social, and psychological elements.

COORDINATING COMMITTEE ON MULTILATERAL EXPORTS (COCOM). An agreement among western industrial nations to limit militarily useful exports to communist countries disbanded in 1991 after the former Soviet Union broke up.

COORDINATION. Achieving harmony of individual and group efforts toward the accomplishment of group purposes and objectives.

COPYRIGHT. The right to reproduce, publish, and sell literary, musical, or artistic works.

COPYRIGHT. Exclusive right conveyed by federal statue to reproduce and sell a book, design, pamphlet, drawing, or other creations, and to forbid the publication of excerpts or other limitations.

COR-DOR. An option portfolio a call option and a put option, both equally out of the money write a call option and a put option. Each further out-of-the-money than the call and put options that were purchased. All options have the same time to expiration.

CORNER. A market situation where a trader or group of traders acting in unison own the available supply of an asset.

CORPORATE BOND. A debt instrument issued by a corporation that states it will make specified interest payments (typically twice each year) and a principal amount or "face value" (usually $1000) at maturity (say 30 years from the date of issue).

CORPORATE CULTURE. The common values shared by employees in a corporation, which form a control mechanism that is implicit and helps enforce other explicit control mechanisms.

CORPORATE GOVERNANCE. The Cadbury Report, the financial aspects of corporate governance, which was published on December 1992, focused the corporate governance debate in four main areas. (1) The responsibilities of executive and non-executive directors for reviewing and reporting on performance to shareholders. (2) The case of establishing audit committees. (3) The principal responsibilities of auditors. (4) The links between shareholders, board of directors and auditors. The report contained a Code of Best Practice, most elements of which were adopted as part of the London Stock Exchange's Listing Rules for all quoted companies. Beyond the detail, the Cadbury Report states that, "Corporate governance is the system by which companies are directed and controlled".

CORPORATE GOVERNANCE. Any structured system for allocating power in a corporation that determines how the company to be governed.

CORPORATE LEGITIMACY. Public acceptance of the corporation as an institution that contributes to society's well-being.

CORPORATE SOCIAL INVOLVEMENT. The interaction of business corporations with society.

CORPORATE SOCIAL RESPONSIBILITY. There is no complete agreement about the definition of this term. In a broad context it means that corporation consider seriously the impact of the enterprise's actions on society.

CORPORATE SOCIAL RESPONSIBILITY. A business obligations to seek socially beneficial results along with economically beneficial results in its actions.

CORPORATE SOCIAL RESPONSIVENESS. The ability of a corporation to relate its operations and policies to the social environment in ways that are mutually beneficial to the company and to society.

CORPORATE STAKEHOLDER. A person or group affected by a corporations' policies and actions.

CORPORATE STOCK. An equity instrument that represents ownership of a share of the assets and earnings of a corporation.

CORPORATE TAKE OVER. The acquisition or merger of one corporations by another.

CORPORATION. Organizations that are 'artificial beings' created by individual state laws.

CORPUS. The total inevitable funds available with a mutual fund scheme. If already invested the then corpus is worth the current market values of the instrument into which it is invested.

CORRECTION. A correction means prices had gone too high and had to come down to realistic levels.

CORRECTIVE ADVERTISING. Advertising sometimes required by government that is intended to correct misleading claims made by the advertiser in earlier ads.

CORRELATION. A measure of the cause-and-effect relationship between variable.

CORRESPONDENT (BANK). A bank in which funds are kept by another usually foreign, bank to facilitate check clearing and other business relationships.

COST ACCUMULATION. Gathering of costs in some organized way via an accounting system.

COST ALLOCATION. Assignment of an re-assignment of a cost or group of costs to one or more cost objectives.

COST APPLICATION ALSO CALLED COST ABSORPTION. The allocation to products rather than to departments.

COST APPROXIMATION. *See* Cost estimation.

COST BEHAVIOUR PATTERN. *See* Cost function.

COST BENEFIT ANALYSIS. A systematic method of calculating the costs and benefits of a project or activity that is intended to produce benefits.

COST BENEFIT CRITERION. As a system is changed, its expected additional benefits usually must exceed it expected additional costs.

COST EFFECTIVE. Carrying out an activity by prudent and efficient use of resources.

COST EFFECTIVENESS ANALYSIS. Seeking the best ratio of benefits and costs; this means, for example, finding the least costly way of reaching an objective, or getting the greatest value for given expenditures.

COST ESTIMATION. An attempt to specify some underlying relationship between x and y over a stimulated relevant range of x that may be of interest. An approximation of how a cost truly behaves. The approximation is in linear rather than nonlinear form.

COST FUNCTION. A relationship between a cost and one or more variables such as the total cost of repairs in relation to miles driven.

COST METHOD FOR INVESTMENTS. The method whereby the initial investment is recorded at cost and dividends are recorded as income.

COST OBJECTIVE. Any activity for which a separate measurement of costs is desired. Examples include departments, products, territories, etc.

COST OF CAPITAL. As used in third book, and in many finance books, a synonym for required rate of return.

COST-OF-CARRY. The costs associated with holding (or carrying) a commodity or an asset. These include financing costs, storage costs and insurance costs.

COST OF EQUITY. Shareholders' required rate of return which equates the present value of expected dividends with the market value of the share is the cost of equity.

COST OF GOODS SOLD. Cost of merchandise that is acquired and resold.

COST OF RETAINED EARNINGS. The rate of return on dividends foregone by the equity shareholders.

COST OF SALES. *See* Cost of goods sold.

COST POOL. A group of individual costs that is allocated as a group to cost objectives in some plausible way.

COST-ALLOCATION BASE. A common denominator used to trace the cost or costs in question to the cost objectives. Examples are direct-labour-hours and machine-hours.

COST/BENEFIT ANALYSIS. It is comparing what efforts will cost with the benefits received to see which is greater.

COST-SACRIFICE made for goods or services.

COST-OF-LIVING ADJUSTMENT. An increase in compensation given to an expatriate employee when foreign living costs are more expensive than those in the home country.

COUNCIL FOR MUTUAL ECONOMIC ASSISTANCE (CMEA or COMECON). A regional form of economic integration that involved essentially those communist countries considered to be within the Soviet bloc; terminated in 1991.

COUNCIL OF MINISTERS. One of the five major institutions of the FU; composed of one member from each country in the EU and entrusted with making major policy decisions.

COUNTER CYCLICAL POLICY. Policy actions aimed at counteracting business cycle influences on the economy.

COUNTER PARTY. The opposite party to a financial contract.

COUNTER PARTY RISK. The risk that a counter party to a contract might default.

COUNTER TRADE. A reciprocal flow of goods or services valued and settled in monetary terms.

COUNTERVAILING DUTY. An import duty imposed to protect a home industry against what is regarded as unfair foreign competition.

COUNTRY ANALYSIS. A process of examining the economic strategy of a nation state, taking a holistic approach to understanding how a country and in particular its government has behaved, is behaving and may behave.

COUNTRY RISK ANALYSIS COUNTRY. Risk is a broad concept that refers to the risks emanating from an underlying combination of economics, finance, geo-politics, sociology, and history issues. As the new global economy raises the level of uncertainty and complexity for the international firm's cross-border strategy, country risk analysis has become today an essential component of strategy decisions regarding export, investment, partnership, mergers, as well as takeovers.

COUNTRY SIMILARITY THEORY. The theory that a producer having developed a new product in response to observed market conditions in the home market, will turn to markets that are most similar to home.

COUNTRY SIZE THEORY. The theory that larger countries are generally more self-sufficient than smaller countries.

COUPON. The interest payment made on a bond.

COUPON BOND. A bond that makes coupon payments.

COUPON RATE. The percentage of the face value of a bond that will be paid each year as an interest payment.

COUPON RATE. The coupon on a bond divided by the face value of the bond.

COURT OF JUSTICE. One of the five major institutions of the EU composed of one member from each country in the EU and serves as a supreme appeals court for EU law.

COVERED CALL. A position in a call option with an opposite position in the underlying asset.

COVERED INTEREST ARBITRAGE. An arbitrage possibility that occurs when two countries have interest rates, a spot exchange rate, and a forward exchange rate that allow an arbitrager to profit.

COVERED OPTION. A written option that is covered by an offsetting cash or futures position in the underlying asset or by an offsetting option position with specific characteristics. As such, it has little or no risk.

CPE (CENTRALLY PLANNED ECONOMY). *See* Command economy.

CRAFT UNION. Unions comprised mainly of skilled craft worker, such as carpenters.

CRAFT UNION. A union whose members poses a particular skill or craft, such as carpentry or plumbing.

CRAM-DOWN DEAL. It is a situation in which the shareholders are forced to accept undesirable terms because of lack of attractive alternatives in the event of a merger or a leveraged buyout.

CREATIVITY. The ability to develop new concepts, ideas, and problem solutions.

CREDIT. In accounting, means one thing and one thing only — "right," as distinguished from 'left'. It typically refers to an entry in an account or the balance of an account.

CREDIT CRUNCH. Situation in which loan that must be repaid over a short time-scale (short credit) becomes scarce and thus more expensive than loans that must be repaid over a long period of time (long credit).

CREDIT DERIVATIVES. Credit derivatives are used generally to describe financial instruments that are specifically designed to allow for the separate trading in, and management of, credit risk. Credit derivatives are designed to transfer credit risk from a party to another. Credit risk is not like other market risks in that it is an event risk and not a price risk. Simply put, credit derivatives are designed to transfer credit risk from a party to another. It is done so that one can offload risk that he already has. The person undertaking to accept the risk is paid for it and hopes that the event (default) does not crystallize.

CREDIT FILE. A firm maintains a credit file for each customer. The firm's trade experiences, with the customer and his performance report based on financial statements submitted by him will be recorded in his credit file. A regular examination of the customers credit file will reveal to the firm the credit standing of the customers.

CREDIT INVESTIGATION. It is a difficult task a firm use numerical credit scoring to appraise credit applications when it is dealing with a large number of small customers. The firms based on its past experience or empirical study may identify both financial and non financial attributes the measure the credit standing of a customer.

CREDIT RISK. The risk that an issuer of debt securities or a borrower may default on its obligations.

CREDIT STANDARDS. They are criteria to decide the types of customers to whom goods could be sold on credit.

CREDIT TERMS. It refers to the conditions under when the supplier sells on credit to the buyer, and the buyer is required to repay credit.

CREDIT UNIONS. A depository institution that operates as a cooperative, accepting deposits from and lending to only a closed group such as employees of a specific company, members of a specific labour union, or even members of a specific church, unlike savings and loans credit unions typically do not make mortgage loans.

CREEPING ACQUISITION. Gradual increase in the shareholding through open purchase on the stock exchange with the aim of increasing ones holding in the desired company.

CREOLIZATION. The process by which elements of an outside cultural are introduced.

CRISI. Credit Rating Information Service of India.

CRISIS STOCK. Its performance will in lack ("some-things check it") times but not all that well in a rising market.

CROSS BORDER LEASE. In case of cross border lease the lessor and the lessee are situated in two different countries. Because the lease transaction takes place between parties of two or more countries. It is called cross-border lease. It involves relationships and tax implications more complex than the domestic lease when the lease transaction takes place between the parties manufacturer/lender, lessor and lessee in three different countries, it is called foreign-to-foreign lease.

CROSS HEDGING. Hedging a commodity by using a futures contract on a different but related commodity. A cross hedge I based on the premise that the price movements of the two com-modities are related.

CROSS RATE OPTION. A foreign currency option for which the numerate is not dollars but a foreign currency.

CROSS RATE. An exchange rate between two currencies used in the spot market and computed from the exchange rate of each currency in relation to the U.S. dollar.

CROSS SECTIONAL ANALYSIS. Another way of comparison is to compare the ratios of one firm with some selected firms in the same industry at the same point of time. This kind of comparison is known as cross-section analysis. In most cases it is more useful to compare the firm's ratios with ratios of a few selected competitors who have similar operations. This kind of comparison indicates the relative financial position and performance of the firm.

CROSS-BORDER LEASING. Where the lessor and lessee are in different countries under different legal systems.

CROSS-LICENSING. The exchange of technology by different companies.

CROSS-SELLING AGREEMENTS. Cross-selling means offering related items when a customer places an order. For example when a customer is served a burger, the waiter can inquire whether the customer would like fries with it.

CROWDING OUT. Describe the effect of increases in government purchases on other private spending government borrowing raises interest rates and hence reduces investment and consumption spending.

CROWDING OUT IN THE OPEN ECONOMY. In the open economy an increase government spending financed by borrowing causes an increase in the interest rate which not only reduces consumption and investment, but also net exports counteracting the increase in government spending. It is most severe when exchange rates are flexible.

CROWN JEWELS. They are the most desirable entities within a diversified corporation as measured by asset value, earning power and business prospects. The crown jewels usually figure prominently in takeover attempts; they are the main objectives of the acquirer and may be sold by the takeover target to make the rest of the company less attractive.

CRUSH SPEED. The purchase (or sale of soybean futures and the simultaneous sale or purchase) of soybean oil and soy-meal futures.

CSCE. Coffee, Sugar and Cocoa Exchange, New York.

CTN. Cotton Exchange, New York.

CULTURAL DISTANCE. The amount of difference between two social systems.

CULTURAL RELATIVISM. The belief that behaviour has meaning and can be judged only in its specific cultural context.

CULTURE SHOCK. A generalized trauma one experience in a new and different culture because of having to learn and cope with a vast array on new cues and expectations.

CULTURAL SHOCK. A person's disorientation and insecurity caused by the strangeness of a different culture. (Also known as culture shock.)

CULTURE. The specific learned norms of a society, based on attitudes, values and beliefs.

CUM-DIVIDEND. A stock trading before a dividend is paid.

CURRENCY. Coins and paper money.

CURRENCY LIABILITY OF CENTRAL GOVERNMENT.

CURRENCY BOARD. A currency board is an arrangement under which a country fixes its exchange rate and maintains 100 per cent backing of its money supply with foreign exchange. As reserves, it holds high-quality, interest-bearing securities denominated in the reserve asset. The currency board makes profits from the difference between the interest on the securities that it holds and the expense of maintaining its note and coin circulation. It remits to the government all profits beyond what it needs to pay expenses and maintain its reserve ratio.

CURRENT ACCOUNT. That portion of the balance of payments that consists of the merchandise account, the services account, and the balance of unilateral transfers. Part of balance of payments which refers to national income and expenditure, including visible and invisible trade.

CURRENT ASSETS. Cash plus hose assets that are reasonably expected to be converted to cash or sold or consumed during the normal operating cycle.

CURRENT COST. Cost stated in terms of current market prices instead of historical cost.

CURRENT LIABILITIES. Liabilities that fall due within the coming year or within the normal operating cycle if longer than a year.

CURRENT LIABILITIES. Current liabilities are debt payable within are accounting period.

CURRENT RATIO. The ratio of current assets to current liabilities.

CURRENT YIELD. The ratio of the annual coupon payment to the price paid for the bond.

CURRENT-ACCOUNT BALANCE. Exports minus imports of goods services and unilateral transfers.

CURRENT-COST METHOD. *See* Current cost.

CURRENTLY ATTAINABLE STANDARDS. Standards expressing a level of economic efficiency that can be reached with skilled, diligent, superior effort.

CURRENTLY ATTAINABLE STANDARDS. Standards expressing a level of economic efficiency that can be reached with skilled, diligent, superior effort.

CURRENT-RATE METHOD. A method of translating foreign currency financial statements that is used when the functional currency is that of the local operating environment.

CUSTODIANS. Custodians are connected to exchange. At the end of each day, they receive a report of all trades done on behalf of their clients. The custodians are required to confirm such trades. The last date for confirmation of trades is one day after close of trading period *i.e.*, Wednesday. Any trades, which are not confirmed by the custodians, are reverted back to the trading member. Custodians had to develop software and modify their procedures to meet the exchange schedules.

CUSTOMS DUTIES. Taxes imposed on imported goods.

CUSTOMS UNION. A form of regional economic integration that eliminates tariffs among member nations and establishes common external tariffs.

CUSTOMS VALUATION. The value of goods on which customs authorities charge tariffs.

CUTOFF RATE. Minimum desired rate of return.

CUTOFF RATE. The ratio of current assets to current liabilities.

CYCLICAL VARIATION. A measure of the business cycle.

D

D/A TERMS. Documents against Acceptance where the documents to title of the goods are given to the purchaser only after the purchaser accepts gives his acceptance to the draft Bill of Exchange/Hundi.

DAILY COMPOUNDING. Sometimes compounding may be done continuously. For example, banks may pay or charge interest continuously they call it daily compounding.

DAILY MARGINS. Normally payable in respect of every contract outstanding at the end of the day, generally at the rate of 5 to 10 per cent of the contract value which can be hiked to higher levels depending upon the volatility of the market. The higher rates being made applicable to bulls in a rising market and to bears in a falling market.

DAILY PRICE LIMITS. The maximum and minimum daily price movement allowed on a futures contract.

DAY-ORDER. A day order as the name suggests, is an order which is valid for the day on which it is entered. If the order is not matched during the day, at the end of the training day, the order gets cancelled automatically.

DDB. *See* Double-declining-balance depreciation.

DEALER IN NON-CLEARED SECURITIES. The dealer in non-cleared securities specialises in buying selling on his own account shares which are not on the active list. He is generally prepared to buy what is on offer & sell what is required but the price at which he deals varies with the activity of the particular stock.

DEBENTURE. A bond that is not backed by any specific collateral, but is instead backed by "the full faith and credit" of the selling firm or institution.

DEBENTURE. A security with a general claim against all unencumbered assets rather than a specific claim against particular assets.

DEBENTURE BONDS. Bonds backed by financial reputation of a company.

DEBIT. An entry on the left side of an account.

DEBT FUND. A fund that invents in debt securities it attempts generates a study income while preserving the investors principal the returns from such funds are generally better than those from money market mutual funds and gift funds. These funds are generally presented by investors not willing to take on a higher risk.

DEBT INSTRUMENT. A written promise by a borrower to pay the owner of the instrument a specified amount in the future. Asset requiring payments of fixed amounts, such as a government or corporate bond.

DEBT MARKET. A market where lenders provide funds to borrowers for some specified period of time. The market for trading debt instruments.

DEBT-EQUITY RATIO. Indicator of financial leverage. Compares assets provided by creditors to assets provided by shareholders. Determined by dividing long-term debt by common stockholder equity.

DEBTORS TURNOVER. Debtors turnover is found out by dividing credit sales by average debtors. Debtors turnover indicates the no. of Times the debtors turnover each year. Generally the higher the value of debtors turnover the more efficiency is the management of credit.

DEBT-SERVICE RATIO. The ratio of interest payments plus principal amortization to exports.

DEBT-TRAP. During the periods of low profits a highly debt finance company suffers great strain it cannot even pay the interest charges of creditors. As a result their pressure and control are further tightened to meet their working capital needs the firm finds difficulty in getting credit. It may have borrow on highly unfavourable terms. Thus it get entangled in a debt-trap.

DECENTRALIZATION. It is the extent to which decision making authority/responsibility is dispersed downward.

DECENTRALIZATION OF AUTHORITY. The tendency to disperse decision-making authority in an organization structure.

DECENTRALIZATION OF PERFORMANCE. The geographic dispersal of operations in an enterprise.

DECERTIFICATION. It is a process whereby a union is removed as the representative of a group of employees.

DECIMALIZATION. In preparation for the industry-mandated conversion from fractional pricing to decimal pricing in the US equities and options markets, instinct is continually planning to ensure that all products and services are decimal complaint by the industry imposed targets. The conversion will result in a new display format and potentially decrease the Minimum Price Variation (MPV) at which securities will be traded. These are pricing increments will result in volume and frequency impacts on the securities industry. Clients can also e-mail their decimalization inquiries directly to Instinet at decimal@instinet.com.

DECISION MAKING. The selection from among alternatives of a course of action; a rational selection of a course of action.

DECISION MODEL. A formal method for making a choice that often involves quantitative analysis.

DECISION SUPPORT SYSTEMS (DSS). The application of computers to facilitate the decision-making process of semi-structured tasks.

DECISION TABLE. A convenient technique for showing the total expected value of each of a number of contemplated acts in the light of varying probabilities of the events that may take place on the varying values of each act under each of the events.

DECISION TREES. An approach toward seeing risks and probabilities in a problem situation involving uncertainty, or chance events, by sketching in the form of a "tree" decision points, chance events, and the probabilities involved in various courses that might be undertaken.

DECLINING FIRMS. Firms that would earn on investment the rate of return less than the minimum required by investors. Investors of such firm would like earnings to be distributed to them so that they may either spend it or invest elsewhere to get a rate higher than earned by the declining firms.

DEEP POCKET VIEW. It refers to the theory that some subsidiary companies might have access to more funds than an independent firm of a similar size. It further argues that the subsidiary may call upon greater resources of its present to engage in competition with independents in the sector.

DEEP-DISCOUNT BOND (DDB). It is zero interest bond.

DEFAULT RISK. The risk that a borrower will not fully repay the principle and interest on a loan.

DEFAULT RISK PREMIUM. The difference between the interest rate charged on safe loans, loans considered default-free, and the interest rate charged on loans that have a higher default risk.

DEFAULT-FREE. A payoff to a security that has no possibility of default.

DEFERRAL. The postponing of taxation of foreign source income until it is remitted to the parent company.

DEFERRED CHARGE. An expenditure not recognized as a cost of operations of the period in which incurred but carried forward to be written off in one or more future periods.

DEFERRED CREDIT. Often used as a synonym for deferred revenue or as a description for deferred income tax. In its book-keeping application, the term refers to an amount that is classified as a liability that will eventually be transferred as a credit to revenue or a credit to expense.

DEFERRED EQUITY FINANCING. By issuing convertible debentures, the firm is in turn selling ordinary shares in future. A company would do so when it considers the current market price of its share to below, but wants to issue shares at a higher price.

DEFERRED INCOME. *See* Deferred revenue.

DEFERRED INCOME. It represents fund required by the firm for goods and services, which it has agreed to supply in future.

DEFERRED INCOME TAX (LIABILITY). A liability in the balance sheet that represents the additional federal income taxes that would have been due if a company had not been allowed to deduct greater amounts for expenses for income-tax-reporting purposes than are recorded for financial-reporting purposes. Also see interpreted tax allocation.

DEFERRED REVENUE. Income received or recorded before it is earned.

DEFERRED SWAP. A forward swap.

DEFINED BENEFIT PLAN. It is one in which the retirement benefits to be paid to the employees and the method of determining those benefits is set so that the employer's contribution can be statistically determined.

DEFINED CONTRIBUTION PLAN. It is one in which the employer's contribution rate is set and the employees' retirement benefits depend upon the contributions and emplyees' earning levels.

DEFLATIONARY GAP. The difference between the actual level of investment and the level necessary to restore full employment.

DE-GEARING. Reduction of risk or leverage, examples include

cutting borrowing and reducing exposures to forces which a company or dealer cannot control.

DELEGATION OF AUTHORITY, PROCESS OF. The determination of results expected from a subordinate, the assignment of tasks, the delegation of authority for accomplishing these tasks, and the holding of people responsible for the accomplishment of such tasks.

DELIVERY DATE. The date on which the underlying asset is exchanged for a cash payment on a forward contract or a futures contract.

DELIVERY MONTH. The calendar month during which delivery as a futures contract must be made.

DELIVERY PERIOD. Whenever a book closure or record date is announced by a company, the exchange sets a no delivery period for that security. During this period, trading is permitted in that security. However, these trades are settled only after the no delivery period is over. This is done to ensure that investor's entitlement for corporate benefits.

DELIVERY PRICE. The price used in determining the value of a contract held to maturity.

DELIVERY STOCK. The quality of a commodity that meets exchange specified quality standards and is available for delivery at exchange specified locations (such as approved warehouse).

DELPHI TECHNIQUE. A technique normally used for forecasting such future events and conditions as technological developments by obtaining estimates of experts in a field and feeding back summaries of these estimates for additional estimates by those experts, until a reasonable degree of convergence in estimates is obtained.

DELTA. A measure of how much an option's premium changes for a given unit change in the underlying asset price must be made.

DELTA NEUTRAL. A portfolio position that has a delta of zero.

DEMAND CURVE. The relationship between the price of a good or service and its quality demanded.

DEMAND DEPOSITS. Checking accounts in commercial banks. Deposits in depository institutions which can be withdrawn by depositors upon demand *i.e.* whenever they choose. Demand deposits are transferable by cheque.

DEMAND FOR NET EXPORTS. The demand for exports minus the demand for imports.

DEMATERIALIZATION. Dematerialization is the process by which shares in the physical/ paper form are cancelled and credit in the form of electronic. Balance is maintained in highly secure system at the depository.

DEMOCRACY. A political system that relies on citizens participation in the decision making process.

DEMOCRATIC SOCIALISM. The belief that economics and politics are so closely connected that the voters should rely on their elected governments to control the economic system.

DEMOTION. Downward movement to a job of lesser responsibility and pay.

DENOMINATOR VARIANCE. Same as production volume variance.

DEPARTMENT. A distinct area, division, or branch of an enterprise over which a manager has authority for the performance of specified activities and results.

DEPARTMENT STORE. A store which is described as a collection of speciality stores under one roof.

DEPARTMENTATION BY CUSTOMER. The grouping of activities around customers.

DEPARTMENTATION BY FUNCTION. The grouping of activities in departments in accordance with the characteristic functions an enterprise undertakes; for example, in a manufacturing company marketing, production, engineering, and finance.

DEPARTMENTATION BY PROCESS OR EQUIPMENT. The grouping of activities around a process or type of equipment used, such as electronic data-processing or painting departments.

DEPARTMENTATION BY PRODUCT. The grouping of activities around a product or product line.

DEPARTMENTATION BY TERRITORY. The grouping of activities by territory segments; geographic departmentation.

DEPENDENCIA THEORY. The theory holding that LDCs have practically no power when dealing with MNEs as host countries.

DEPENDENCY. A state in which a country is too dependent on the sale of one primary commodity and/or too dependent on one country as a customer and supplier.

DEPOSIT FLOAT. The amount of cheque sent by a customer which is not yet collected is called collection of deposit float.

DEPOSITORY INSTITUTION DEREGULATION AND MONETARY CONTROL ACT OF 1980 (DIDMCA). Legislation designed to solve problems created in part by disintermediation.

DEPOSITORY INSTITUTIONS. Institutions which accept deposits from individuals and use the funds to participate in the debt market (*i.e.* to make loans).

DEPOSITORY TRUST COMPANY. It is the principal depository company owned jointly by the New York Stock Exchange (NYSE) and American Stock Exchange (AMEX).

DEPRECIATION. Depreciation of the U.S. dollar means the dollar buys fewer units of foreign currency than before.

DEPRECIATION. The amount of life of an asset used over a period of time.

DEPRECIATION. The allocation of the acquisition cost of plant, property, and equipment to the particular periods or products that benefit from the utilization of the assets.

DEPRECIATION TAX SHIELD. Depreciation is a deductible expense and saves taxes. It is equal to the amount of depreciation multiplied by the tax rate.

DEREGULATION. The removal or scaling down of regulatory authority and regulatory activities of government.

DERIVATIVE. A foreign-exchange instrument such as an option or futures contract that derives its value from some underlying financial instrument.

DERIVATIVE SECURITY. A financial contract the value of which is derived from some underlying asset.

DERIVATIVES MARKET. Market in which forward contracts futures, options, and swaps are traded in order to hedge or protect foreign exchange transactions.

DERIVED ASSOCIATION. An association that is defined in terms of other association.

DERIVED DEMAND. An individual bank's demand for deposits is called a derived demand because it is derived from the demand for loans that bank try to satisfy.

DESCRIPTIVE STATISTICS. Quantitative data used to describe a particular characteristic such as the number of births.

DESIRED CURRENCY TO DEPOSIT RATIO. The amount of excess reserves bank's wish to hold as a fraction of demand deposits.

DETACHABILITY. A warrant can be either detachable or non-detachable. If a warrant can be sold separately from the debenture to which it was originally attached, it is called a detachable warrant. A debenture holder may sell his warrant when its price increased continues holding the debenture. VARIATION OF WARRANTS: A warrant is an option to buy a stated number of a company is ordinary sharer at a given exercise price on or before a specified maturity date.

DETERMINANTS OF DEMAND. Variable that determine the position of demand curve changes in them shift the curve.

DETERMINANTS OF SUPPLY. Variable that determine the position of the supply curve : changes in them shift the curve.

DETERMINISTIC INTEREST RATES. Future interest rates that are known with certainty.

DETINUE. It is a legal term which means action to recover same thing that has been detained.

DEVALUATION. A formal reductions in the value of a currency in relation to another currency the foreign currency equivalent of the devalued currency falls.

DEVELOPING COUNTRY. A poor country also known as a third world country or a less developed country.

DIA TERMS. Documents against acceptance where the documents to title of the goods are given to the purchaser only after the purchaser accepts given his acceptance to the draft bill of exchange/hundi.

DICTIONARY OF OCCUPATIONAL TITLES. A book listing 25,000 titles and descriptions and published by the department of labour.

DIFFERENTIAL COST. *See* Incremental cost.

DIFFERENTIATION. A characteristic of an open system, and a social in particular, by which it tends to become more specialized in its structure and behaviour patterns.

DIGITAL COMPUTER. Computers, which work directly with numbers and alphabetic and special characters.

DIGITAL OPTION. An option that at maturity pays one dollar if in-the-money, zero otherwise.

DIRECT CONTROL. Control techniques designed to identify and correct for deviations in plans.

DIRECT COSTING. That type of product costing which charges fixed manufacturing overhead immediately against the revenue of the period in which it was incurred, without assigning it to specific units produced. Also called variable costing or marginal costing.

DIRECT FINANCE. Finance that occurs when savers lend funds directly to borrowers.

DIRECT FINANCING LEASE. Under accounting rules, a non-leveraged lease by a lessor (not a manufacturer or dealer) where the lessee meets criteria definitions of a capital lease (see above) plus the extra requirement that the collection-ability surround the amount of reimbursable costs to be incurred by the lessor under the lease.

DIRECT FOREIGN INVESTMENT. *See* Foreign direct investment.

DIRECT IDENTIFICATION DRAWBACK. A provision that allows U.S. firms to use imported components in the manufacturing process without having to include the duty paid on the imported goods in costs and sales prices.

DIRECT INVESTMENT. *See* Foreign direct investment.

DIRECT LABOUR. All labour that is obviously related to and specifically and conveniently traceable to specific products.

DIRECT LEASE. Same as a direct financing lease.

DIRECT MATERIAL. All raw material that is an integral part of the finished good and can be conveniently assigned to specific physical units.

DIRECT METHOD. A method that ignores other service departments when any given service department's costs are allocated to revenue-producing or production departments.

DIRECT QUOTE. A quote expressed in terms of the number of units of the domestic currency given for one unit of a foreign currency.

DIRECT SELLING. A sale of goods by an exporter directly to distributors of final consumers rather than to trading companies or other intermediaries in order to achieve greater control over the marketing functions and to earn higher profits.

DIRECTING. The management function dealing with the face-to-face supervision of employees.

DIRECTIVE. A proposed form of legislation in the EU.

DIRECTIVE COUNSELLING. An approach in which the counsellor asks specific questions.

DIRTY FLOAT. Situation where the exchange rate is determined by supply and demand, but the government influences supply and demand by buying and selling currency.

DISCHARGE. The action of one party not having to meet his obligation to a contract because other parties to the contract have not fulfilled their obligation.

DISCOUNT (IN FOREIGN EXCHANGE). A situation in which the forward rate for a foreign currency is less than the spot rate, assuming that the domestic currency is quoted on a direct basis.

DISCOUNT BOND. A zero coupon bond.

DISCOUNT PAYBACK. The number of years required in recovering the costs outlay on the present value basis is the discounted payback period.

DISCOUNT RATE. The interest rate charged by the fed on its loans to depository institutions.

DISCOUNT RATE. As used in capital budgeting, the minimum desired rate of return.

DISCOUNT STORE. This store features a wide variety of goods at low prices.

DISCOUNT WINDOW. Banks and other depository institutions can "go to the window" to borrow from the fed. Presentation of assets as collateral is not required, banks merely promise to repay the loan in the future.

DISCOUNT YIELD. Measure of yield frequently used in the case of treasury bills, but which understates the actual yield to maturity.

DISCOUNTED CASH FLOW. Technique for assessing the present value of future income and payments which takes into account of the time value of money.

DISCOUNTING. A financial institution lending money to a business with a customer's debt obligation to the business as security of the loan.

DISCOVERY PREMIUM TO NAV. The difference between the unit price and the NAV in percentage terms if the price is higher than the NAV, the units are trading at a premium if the price is lower the units are trading at a discount.

DISCRETELY COMPOUNDED INTEREST RATES. Interest rates that include compounding over discrete time periods.

DISCRETIONARY COSTS.

DISCRETIONARY COSTS. Fixed costs arising from periodic, usually yearly, appropriation decisions that directly reflect top-management policies. Also called programmed costs or managed costs.

DISCRETIONARY MONETARY POLICY. A situation where the fed has the flexibility to respond however it sees fit. Without any constraint to follow some pre-existing rule.

DISCRETIONARY ORDER. This order gives a specific among at discretion to a broker.

DISCRIMINATION (EEOC DEFINITION). It is the use of any test that adversely affects hiring, promotion, transfer or any other employment or membership opportunity of classes unless the test has been validated and is job related; and/or an employer can demonstrate that alternative hiring, transfer, or promotion procedures are unavailable.

DISCRIMINATION (IN JOBS OR EMPLOYMENT). Unequal treatment of employees based on non-job-related factors such as race, sex, age, national origin, religion, colour, and physical or mental handicap.

DIS-INTERMEDIATION. Describes the phenomenon of depositors withdrawing funds from financial intermediaries in favour of direct finance.

DISPLACED LOG NORMAL DISTRIBUTION. A log normal distribution the mean of which is translated along the horizontal axis.

DISTRIBUTION. The course-physical path or legal title — that goods take between production and consumption.

DISTRIBUTION LOGISTICS. An operations research optimizing model that treats the entire materials flow system of an enterprise — from sales forecasting through purchasing and processing of materials, inventorying them, to shipping of finished goods to sales warehouses — as a single system.

DISTRIBUTOR. A merchant in a foreign country that purchases products from the manufacturer and sells them at a profit.

DIVERSIFICATION. Spreading your investment dollars over two or more different assets often done to reduce risk.

DIVERSIFICATION STRATEGY. A strategy by which an international company produces or sells in many countries to avoid relying on one particular market.

DIVERSIFIED PORTFOLIO. A portfolio which invests among a variety of securities with different risk, reward, and correlation statistics so as to minimize unsystematic risk.

DIVERSION IN TRANSIT. A service offered by rail carriers which permits a shipper of goods to reroute his goods to a destination from the original destination while the goods are in transit.

DIVESTMENT. Reduction in the amount of investment.

DIVIDEND. A cash payment made to a common stock.

DIVIDEND. A return-on-investment payment made to the owners of shares of corporate stock at the discretion of the company's board of directors.

DIVIDEND CAPITALIZATION. The value of a share today is a function of cash inflows expected by investors and risk associated with those cash inflows. Cash inflows expected from an equity share consists of dividends expected to be received by the owner while holding the share and the price which he expects to obtain when the share is sold.

DIVIDEND DECISION. Dividend decision is the major financial decision. The financial manager must decide whether the firm should distribute all profits or retain them or distribute a portion of them and retain the balance. The pay-out ratio is equal to the per cent of dividends to the earning available to the shareholders.

DIVIDEND PAY-OUT RATIO. The dividend pay-out ratio is DPS divided by the EPS (earnings per share).

DIVIDEND PER SHARE. It is the earnings distributed to ordinary shareholders divided by the number of ordinary shares outstanding.

DIVIDEND YIELD. The ratio of the annual dividends per share to the price of the stock.

DIVIDENDS. Ordinarily distributions of assets that liquidate a portion of the ownership claim.

DIVIDENDS. Earnings paid to shareholders.

DOCUMENTS OF TITLE. Instruments that denote ownership or merchandise or goods which can be transferred by endorsement.

DOLLAR RETURN. One plus the per cent return.

DOLPHIN. Dolphin in an informed term referring to a person who buys shares in new issues and then sells for high profits as soon as train opens. Dolphin is an informal term referring to a person who buys shares in new issues and then sells for high profits as soon as trading opens.

DOMINANT STRATEGY. Situation in game theory where one player has an action or strategy that is best, regardless of what the other players do.

DOMINO EFFECT. An action being effected by a previous action is known as domino effect.

DORMANT PARTNER. A partner who assumes no active role in the business and who is not known as a partner to the public.

DOUBLE COINCIDENCE OF WANTS. A situation that occurs in a barter transition between two individuals the first individual wants, and the second individual has a good or service that the first individual wants.

DOUBLE-DECLINING-BALANCE DEPRECIATION (DDB). A form of accelerated depreciation that results in first-year depreciation being twice the amount of straight-line depreciation when zero terminal disposal value is assumed.

DOUBLE DIPPING. The structuring of leases to draw benefit from the benefits on capital investment in more than one country.

DOUBLE TAXATION. Under this system, shareowners' earnings are taxed twice. First, the corporate tax is levied on the profits at the level of the company, and then, the profits are distributed as dividends and such dividends are taxed as ordinary income in the hands of shareholders.

DOW JONES AVERAGE. Index of stock prices composed of four different averages of stock.

DOWN-AND-IN OPTION. For down-and-in options, a lower level (barrier) is specified for the asset price on which the option is written. For a down-and-in call (put) option the contract becomes a standard call (put) option if the price of the underlying asset falls below the barrier. If the price of the underlying asset never falls below the barrier during the life of the contract, the contract expires worthless.

DOWN-AND-OUT OPTION. For down-and-out options, a lower level (barrier) is specified for the asset price on which the option is written. For a down-and-out call (put) option the contract ceases to exist if the price of the underlying asset falls below the barrier. If the price of the underlying asset near falls below the barrier during the life of the contract, the contract expires as an ordinary call (put) option.

DRAW. It is an amount advanced to an employee and repaid from future commissions earned by the employee.

DRAWBACK. A provision allowing U.S. exporters to apply for refunds of 99 per cent of the duty paid on imported components provided they are used in the manufacture of goods that are exported.

DRIP FEED. Funding a new company in a number of stages rather an at once.

DRR. Debenture redemption reserve.

DTB. Deutsche Terminborse, Frankfurt, Germany.

DUAL BANKING. The system of banking in which banks can obtain either a state or a national charter.

DUAL RATE OF RETURN. An internal rate of return measure. An arbitrary reinvestment rate applied to periods in which cash surpluses arise under the lease.

The appropriate pre-tax borrowing rate as determined by interactive procedures.

DUAL TRADING. Floor brokers execute the order at the market place/floor at the exchange to trade future contracts that are accepted by FCMS. Floor traders are individual members at the exchange who act as agents for FCMS they made trading to their own accounts as well as for customer's account this practice is known as dual trading.

DUE DATE. It is the date by which the supplier expects payments.

DUMPING. Selling goods abroad at a lower price than charged for them in the home market. It is an example of discriminating monopoly. If the monopolist covers all his fixed expenses in the home market he can add to his total profit even if the price he fixes for foreign buyers is little more than sufficient to cover his marginal cost. Dumping gives rise to strong protests from producers of similar goods in the country in which the goods are dumped.

DUOPSONY. It is a market in which there are only purchases of type of goods and services but a number of competing suppliers.

DURABLE GOODS. Tangible goods which can be expected to last for a relatively long time even though used repeatedly.

DURATION. A measure of the average life of a bond.

DURESS. When threat or other action causes a person to perform an act against his will.

DUTY. A government tax (tariff) levied on goods shipped internationally.

DYNAMICALLY COMPLETE. A market where any derivative can be synthetically replicated using a dynamic trading strategy.

DYSFUNCTIONAL BEHAVIOUR. Actions taken in conflict with to-management goals.

E

EARNED SURPLUS. A virtually archaic term for retained income.

EARNINGS. The excess of revenues over expenses.

EARNINGS CAP. Limit of earnings introduced in the 1989 Financial Act for pension purposes. It represents the maximum earnings that can be pensioned. It does not apply to scheme members under approval basis before 1989 or to retirement annuities.

EARNINGS PER SHARE. Net income divided by the number of common shares outstanding.

EARNINGS YIELDS. Hypothetical figure that provides a reliable measurement of the worth of an investment. It is reached by relating a company's divisible net earnings to the market price of the investment. Sometimes, with reference to fixed interest securities, the term is used interchangeably with flat yield.

EBIT. The appropriate measure of profit is operating profit. Operating profit is equivalent to earnings before interest and taxes (EBIT). This measure of profit shows earnings arising directly from the commercial operations of business without the effect of financing. On an after tax basis profit to investors is equal to : EBIT (I-T) where T is corporate tax.

ECOLOGICAL BALANCE. A natural equilibrium maintained among any group of living things and environment they occupy.

ECOLOGY. The study of how living things plant and animals interact with one another and with their environment.

ECONOMIC COMMUNITY OF WEST AFRICAN STATES (ECOWAS). A form of economic integration among certain countries in West Africa.

ECONOMIC EXPOSURE. The foreign exchange risk that international business face in the pricing of products the source and cost of inputs, and the location of investment.

ECONOMIC GOODS AND SERVICES. Anything of value produced

by an economic system; includes all products and services.

ECONOMIC GROWTH. An increase in the economy's ability to produce real output of goods and services.

ECONOMIC INTEGRATION. The abolition of economic discrimination between national economies such as within the EU.

ECONOMIC LIFE OF LEASED PROPERTY. The estimated remaining period during which the property is expected to be economically usable by one or more users, with normal repairs and maintenance, for the purpose for which it was intended at the inception of the lease.

ECONOMIC LOT SIZE. Synonym for economic order quantity.

ECONOMIC SYSTEM. The system concerned with allocation of scarce resources.

ECONOMIC VALUE ADDED (EVA). It is the value-added to shareholders by generating operating profit in excess of the cost of capital employed in the business.

ECONOMICS. A social science concerned chiefly with the description and analysis of the production, distribution and consumption of goods and services.

ECONOMIES OF SCALE. The lowering of cost per unit as output increases because of allocation of fixed costs over more units produced.

ECOSYSTEM. All of the plants and animals, together with their natural environment living together in an interdependent system.

ECOWAS. *See* Economic Community of West African States.

ECU. *See* European Currency Unit.

EEC PATENT CONVENTION. An important cross national patent convention that involves the members of the EU objectives should be, and whether revised plans needed to meet these objectives.

EEC. *See* European Economic.

EFFECTIVE INTEREST RATE. If compounding is done more than once a year, the actual rate of interest paid (or received) is called the effective interest rate, and it would be higher than the nominal interest rate.

EFFECTIVE TARIFF. The real tariff on the manufactured portion of developing countries' exports which is higher than indicated by the published rates because the *ad valorem* tariff is based on the total value of the products which includes raw materials that would have had duty free entry.

EFFECTIVENESS LAGS INCREASE. The time between when a policy action is made and when they result in changes in the economy.

EFFICIENCY VARIANCE. The standard price for a given resource, multiplied by the difference between the actual quantity of inputs used and the total standard quantity of inputs allowed for the number of good outputs achieved.

EFFICIENT CAPITAL MARKET. One in which market prices 'fully reflect' all information available at a given time.

EFFICIENT MARKETS. A theory that states that asset prices accurately reflect relevant information.

EFFICIENT MARKETS HYPOTHESIS. It states that the current price of an asset such as a share of stock, reflects all available information about the value of the asset.

EFFICIENT PORTFOLIO. The portfolio which has the highest expected returns for a given level of risk is called an efficient portfolio.

EFTA. *See* European Free Trade Association.

ELABORATION. The tendency of an open system, and social system in particular, to enlarge its boundaries or create a new suprasystem with wider boundaries.

ELASTIC (PRODUCT DEMAND). A condition in which sales are likely to increase or decrease by a percentage that is more than the percentage change in income.

ELASTIC CURRENCY. A money supply which can be easily converted from demand deposits into currency.

ELASTICITY. A measure of how responsive one variable is to a change in another variable. For instance, the elasticity of supply of deposits is the percentage change in the quantity supplied of deposits divided by the percentage change in the interest rate paid on deposits.

ELECTORAL POLITICS. Activities undertaken by business and other interest groups to influence the outcome of elections to public office.

ELECTRONIC DATA INTERCHANGE (EDI). The electronic movement of money and information via computers and telecommunications equipment.

EMBARGOES. Keeps goods from entering a nation may be on a product or nation basis.

EMC. *See* Export Management Company.

EMISSION STANDARD. A legally defined specific amount of a pollutant permitted to be discharged from a polluting source in a given period of time (compare with Environmental-quality standard).

EMOTIONAL BUYING MOTIVE. A decision to buy which involves little or no thought.

EMPATHY. Viewing an issue as another person would view it.

EMPATHY EMPIRICAL PROBABILITY.

EMPIRICAL PROBABILITY. The likelihood of the occurrence of an event cannot be determined without experimentation.

EMPLOYEE SAFETY. A work environment that provides personal protective equipment control of exposure to air contaminants and clean orderly work areas.

EMPLOYEE STOCK OWNERSHIP PLAN (ESOP). It is a stock bonus plan whereby employees gain ownership in the firm for which they work.

EMPLOYEE STOCK OWNERSHIP PLAN (ESOP). A company plan that encourages employees to invest money in that company's stock.

EMPLOYEE-ASSISTANCE PROGRAMME. It provides counselling and other help to employees having emotional, physical, or other personal problems.

EMPLOYEES ASSOCIATION. A union whose membership is made up almost entirely of professional, state and local government workers.

EMPLOYER'S ASSOCIATION. Joining together of employers of different firms to present united efforts in dealing with labour unions demands.

ENCOUNTER GROUP TRAINING. A group training method in which intense personal discussion may threaten the privacy of one or more participants.

ENDOGENOUS MONEY SUPPLY. Upward sloping money supply curve that results when the determinants of the money supply — most notably the currency to deposit ratio and the desired excess reserve ratio — are endogenous and depend on economic variables like interest rates.

ENDOWMENT INSURANCE. A form of life insurance where premiums are paid for a specific period of item and the insured is covered during that time. If he is living at the end of the premium period, he collects the face value.

ENGINEERED COST. Any cost that has an explicit, specified physical relationship with a selected measure of activity.

ENLIGHTENED SELF-INTEREST MODEL OF SOCIAL INVOLVEMENT. The view that social responsiveness and long run economic return are compatible.

ENTER THE MARKET. In the case of an OS sell orders the order gets triggered if the last traded price is less than or equal to the OS sell order price.

ENTERPRISE OF THE AMERICA. A proposed series of bilateral trade relationships between the United States and Latin American countries, based on a "hub and spokes" concept and eventually resulting in one huge multilateral relationship involving the America.

ENTERPRISE SELF-AUDIT. The making by an enterprise of an audit, or appraisal, of its position, where it is heading under present programmes, what its ABC Agreement : In a US brokerage firm, an agreement with an employee detailing the rights of the company if it buys the membership of the New York Stock Exchange on his or her behalf.

ENTITY. A specific area of accountability that is the focus of the accounting process. It may be a single corporation, a tax district, a department, a papermaking machine, or a consolidated group of many interrelated corporations.

ENTREPRENEURS. People with the ability to see an opportunity, to obtain the necessary capital, labour, and other inputs, and to know how to put together an operation successfully, and with the willingness to take the personal risk of success or failure.

ENTRY AND EXIT LOADS. These are shares to investors to sell (exit) or buy (enter).

ENVIRONMENT — CLIMATE. The external conditions in host countries that could significantly affect the success of a foreign business enterprise.

ENVIRONMENT —ECONOMIC. That environment of managers which has to do with such elements as capital, materials, labour availability, quality, and price, price levels, productivity, availability of high-quality entrepreneurs and managers government fiscal and tax policy, customers, and demands for goods and services.

ENVIRONMENT — ETHICAL. That environment of managers which has to do with generally accepted sets of standards of personal conduct.

ENVIRONMENT — POLITICAL. That environment of managers which has to do with the complex of laws, regulations, and government agencies and their actions.

ENVIRONMENT — SOCIAL. That environment of managers which has to do with the attitudes, desires, expectations, degrees of intelligence, belies, and customers of people in any people in any given group or society; social forces.

ENVIRONMENT—TECHNOLOGICAL. That environment of managers which has to do with such laments as knowledge of ways of doing things; inventions; and techniques in the areas of processes, machines, and tools.

ENVIRONMENTAL FORECASTING. Forecasting the future environment — economic, technological, social, ethical, and political — as it may affect the enterprise.

ENVIRONMENTAL IMPACT STATEMENT. A report on the expected environmental effects of a planned development such reports are required when federal funding or federal jurisdiction is involved.

ENVIRONMENTAL QUALITY STANDARD. A legally defined specific amount of a pollutant permitted to be present in an areas, such as a plant where toxic substances are used in a region where auto traffic is heavy (compare with Emission standard).

ENVIRONMENTAL RESPONSIBILITY. The responsibility of business to help maintain a quality environment by helping to eliminate all forms of pollution.

ENVIRONMENTAL SCANNING. Examining an organizations environment to discover trends and forces that may have an impact on the organization.

EPC. *See* European Patent Conventions.

EQUAL EMPLOYMENT OPPORTUNITY. The principle that all persons otherwise qualified should be treated equally with respect to job opportunities workplace conditions, pay fringe benefits and retirements provisions.

EQUAL OPPORTUNITY. The chance for all persons and groups in society to compete on the same basis for personal and social goals. Equal opportunity does not guarantee personal or social or economic equality because some persons are more talented or luckier than others.

EQUAL RESULTS. A goal to insure that all people in a social system actually have equal benefits such as education and income.

EQUALIZATION RESERVE. Return on capital invested in a unit trust. All investors in a trust receive an equal sum per unit held, although some may only have invested in the period since the last distribution. The distribution paid on the latter's stock therefore comprises the dividend and an equalization that brings the return up to par.

EQUATION OF EXCHANGE. MV = PY; links aggregate spending in an economy and the stock of money.

EQUILIBRIUM. Situation where there is no tendency for the price to change any further.

EQUIPMENT TRUST BONDS. Bonds used to finance the purchase of new equipment (used chiefly by railroads).

EQUITIES. The claims against or interests in the assets. The creditors' claims are liabilities and the owners' claims are owners' equity or, in the case of corporations, stockholders' equity.

EQUITY. It is the perceived fairness of what the person does (inputs) compared with what the person receives (outcomes).

EQUITY ALLIANCE. A situation in which a cooperating company takes an equity position (almost always a minority) in the company with which it has a collaborative arrangement.

EQUITY CAPITAL. Capital of the company that belongs to the owners of the company in man cases holder of ordinary shares. Funds obtained for the business by selling ownership.

EQUITY FUND. A fund that invests primarily in stocks, the riskiest asset class available in Indian markets. Such funds show volatile performance with equity prices fluctuating daily and can show significant loses well. Baring this risk, these funds can show superior performance to others as equities can yield greater capital appreciation than other asset classes.

EQUITY INSTRUMENTS. Shares of common stock : represent the ownership of a share of a firm.

EQUITY KICKER. A loan guaranty that the lender will relieve.

EQUITY MARKET. A market where ownership shares of companies are bought and sold.

EQUITY METHOD. A basis for carrying long-term investments at cost plus a pro-rata share of accumulated retained income since acquisition. Equivalent units — the expression of output in terms of doses or amount of work applied thereto.

EQUITY METHOD OF ACCOUNTING. Where ownership of voting common stock is between 20 to 50 per cent, the accounting profession adopts the view that the holding company has effective control of dividend policy of the subsidiary. The initial cost of the investment in the subsidiary stock is shown separately as a long-term investment under assets on the holding company's balance sheet. As time passes, the investment account is adjusted upward for the holding company's share of subsidiary profits, and downward for its share in subsidiary losses and for dividend received. This is referred to as the equity method of accounting for subsidiaries.

EQUITY SWAP RATIO. When a company merges with another company, recommend Equity swap ratio on the basis of which merging company shares are equated with the shares of merged company.

EQUIVALENT MARTINGALE PROBABILITIES. The probabilities for computing the risk neutral value.

ERGONOMICS. It is a study of workers and choices that confront them in ordinary working situations. Ergonomics has as its goal an increase in the efficiency of the workforce and therefore the productivity.

ERRATIC FLUCTUATIONS. Changes of a short-term duration, difficult to measure and predict because of their un-expectedness.

ESCHEAT. The reversion of property to the state when a person having no legal heir dies without making a valid will.

ESCROW. Property or money held by a third party until the agreed upon obligations of a contract are met.

ESSENTIAL-INDUSTRY ARGUMENT. The argument holding that certain domestic industries need protection for national security purposes.

ESTOPPEL. In law, Estoppel holds a person liable for his previous actions. It is generally used to prevent a denial of responsibility.

ETC. *See* Export trading company.

ETHICS. The rules or principle that define right and wrong conduct.

ETHICS CODE. A written statement that describes the general value system and ethical rules of an organization.

ETHNOCENTRIC BUSINESS. A company whose business standards are based on its home nations customs markets and laws.

ETHNOCENTRISM. A belief that one's own group is superior to others also used to describe a company's belief that what worked at home should work abroad.

EURO. The legal currency of the eleven participating countries of the European union.

EURO-BONDS. Bonds that are denominated in a currency other than that of the country of origin.

EURO-CREDIT. A loan, line of credit, or other form of medium, or long-term credit on the Eurocurrency market that has a maturity of more than one year.

EUROCURRENCY MARKET. An international wholesale market that deals in Eurocurrencies.

EUROCURRENCY. Any currency that is banked outside of its country of origin.

EURODOLLAR CONTRACTS. Derivative securities written on Eurodollar deposits.

EURODOLLAR FUTURES CONTRACT. A futures contract written on a Eurodollar deposit.

EURODOLLARS. Dollars banked outside of the United States.

EURO-EQUITY MARKET. The market for shares sold outside the boundaries of the issuing company's home country.

EUROPE 1992. Legislation enacted by the EU and designed to eliminate most key barriers to trade of goods and services by December 31, 1992.

EUROPEAN COMMISSION. One of the five major institutions of the EU; composed of a president, six vice presidents and ten other members whose allegiance to the EU and serving as an executive branch for the EU.

EUROPEAN COMMUNITY (EC). The predecessor of the European Union.

EUROPEAN COUNCIL. One of the five major institutions of the European Union; made up of the heads of state of each of the EU members.

EUROPEAN CURRENCY UNIT (ECU). A unit of account based on a currency basket composed of the currencies of the members of the EU.

EUROPEAN ECONOMIC COMMUNITY (EEC). The predecessor of the European Community.

EUROPEAN FREE TRADE ASSOCIATION (EFTA). A Free-trade area among a group of European countries that are not members of the EU.

EUROPEAN MONETARY SYSTEM (EMS). A cooperative foreign exchange agreement involving most of the members of the EU and designed to promote exchange-rate stability within the EU.

EUROPEAN OPTION. An option that can be exercised only on the option expiration date.

EUROPEAN PARLIAMENT. One of the five major institutions of the EU; its representatives are elected directly in each member country.

EURO-SCLEROSIS. Popular term for a seizure (breakdown) in the Euro markets caused by illiquidity or some other financial panic.

EVENTS. Set of relevant occurrences that can happen synonym for states of nature.

EX ANTE REAL INTEREST RATE. *See* Real interest rate.

EX POST REAL INTEREST RATE. The nominal interest rate minus the actual inflation rate.

EXCESS MATERIAL REQUISITIONS. A form to be filled out by the production staff to secure any materials needed in excess of the standard amount allotted for output.

EXCESS RESERVES. Reserves in excess of required reserves.

EXCHANGE FOR PHYSICAL ORDER. This order permits the exchange of a futures position for a physical position.

EXCHANGE OF FUTURES FOR PHYSICAL (EEP). An alternative delivery procedure for futures contracts where there is an exchange of a specified quantity of the cash instrument for the equivalent quantity of futures contracts at mutually agreed-upon terms and at a mutually agreed-upon price. Partners to an EEP must notify the clearing-house of such transaction.

EXCHANGE RATE. The number of dollars you have to give up for each unit of the foreign currency.

EXCISE DUTY. Duty levied on home produced goods, either to control consumption and thus influence spending, or to raise revenue.

EX-DIVIDED DATE. The day on which a common stock makes a dividend payment.

EXEMPT EMPLOYEES. Those who are not required to be paid overtime under the Fair Standards Act.

EXERCISE. The action taken by the holder of an option contract either to acquire the underlying asset at the options strike price or to the underlying asset at the option's strike price.

EXERCISE DATE. It is the date on which the option is actually exercised. In the case of European Options, the exercise date is the same as the expiration date while in the case of American Options; the options contract may be exercised any day between the purchase of the contract and its expiration date (see European/American option).

EXERCISE PRICE. The price at which the underlying asset may be purchased or sold when an option is exercised.

EXERCISE RATIO. It states the number of ordinary shares they can be purchased at the E.P. per warrant. The same as the conversion ratio in the case of the convertible securities.

EXIT INTERVIEW. An interview conducted with personnel

leaving the firm to determine the cause of their leaving.

EXOGENOUS MONEY SUPPLY. Vertical money supply curve that results when changes in interest rates do not alter the currency to deposit ratio or the desired excess reserve ratios of banks.

EXOTIC OPTION. A non-standard option.

EX-PATRIATE. It is a person working in a country who is not a national citizen of that country.

EXPECTATIONS HYPOTHESIS. The hypothesis that longer-term interest rates are an average of the shorter term interest rates expected to prevail during the life of the longer-term asset.

EXPECTED VALUE. The some of the outcomes weighted by their probabilities.

EXPECTED VALUE. A weighted average of all the conditional values of an act. Each conditional value is weighted by its probability.

EXPEDITING PAYMENT. Gifts to lesser government and private employees primarily to assure that they carry out promptly cooperatively and efficiently the duties for the gift giver that their job normally requires them to do.

EXPENDITURE. Cash or other resources paid, or to be paid, for an asset purchased or service acquired.

EXPENSE. The cost of a earning revenue is called an expense.

EXPENSES. Generally a gross decrease in assets from delivering goods or services.

EXPIRATION DATE. The maturity date of a derivative security.

EXPIRATION OF RIGHTS DATE. It is the date before which existing shareholders should transfer the shares to be eligible for rights issue.

EXPIRED COSTS. Expenditures from which no further benefit is anticipated, an expense, a cost absorbed over the period during which benefits were enjoyed or a loss incurred.

EXPIRED COSTS. Expired costs are the ones that have helped to produce revenues. They are recognized as expenses in the income statement. They are also known as revenue expenditure.

EXPLICIT TRANSACTIONS. Events such as cash receipts and disbursements that trigger nearly all day-to-day routine entries.

EXPLODING WARRANT. Warrant introduced on order to dilute to the need for an additional capital.

EXPORT OF JOBS. A business beginning or expanding a branch in another nations which may cause a loss of jobs in the business home operations.

EXPORTS. Goods and services produced in the U.S. and sold to the rest of the world.

EXPROPRIATION. (*See* Nationalization).

EX-SPLIT DATE. The day on which the stock split occurs.

EXTENDED CREDIT. Represents long-term lending to troubled depository institutions.

EXTENDIBLE BONDS. A bond for which the bondholder has no option to extend the maturity of the bond.

EXTERNAL DATA. Data pertaining to activities outside an individual firm.

EXTERNALLY. A positive or negative side effect of production or consumption in a market system.

EXTINCTION. It is the absence of a response to a situation.

EXTREME LOOKBACK OPTIONS. For a call option, the payoff at maturity depends on the maximum value of the price of the underlying asset over the life of the option.

F

FABRICATION. One category of the synthetic process of production in which materials are combined to form a product. The materials are not altered.

FACE VALUE. The amount paid when a financial instrument, like a Treasury Bill, matures.

FACTORING. It is a method of converting a non-productive and inactive asset into a productive asset by selling receivables to a company that specializes in their collection and administration. Factoring commission is paid for credit evaluation and collection and other services and to cover bad-debt losses.

FACTORY BURDEN. *See* factory overhead.

FACULTATIVE-OBLIGATORY REINSURANCE. It is a type of treaty agreement whereby the insurer can choose whether or not to reinsure a risk, but once chosen, the re-insurer must accept.

FAIR LABOUR STANDARDS ACT.

FAIR RENTAL. The expected rental for equivalent property under similar terms and conditions of FASB (Financial Accounting Standard Board).

FAIR VALUE. The theoretical value of a option or futures contract derived from a mathematical evaluation model. It is also referred to as the no arbitrage value.

FAIRY GODFATHER. A prospective supporter or investor in a particular company.

FALLEN ANGEL. The company, or shares in a company, whose rating has recently fallen significantly.

FAS 13. Technical statement of Financial Accounting Standards Board, November 1976.

FASB. Financial Accounting Standards Board.

FASB STATEMENTS. Official rules and regulations regarding external financial reporting issued in a numbered series by the Financial Accounting Standard Board.

FDIC. Federal Deposit Insurance Corporation.

FEDERAL CHARTERING. A proposed plan for giving the federal government power to issue certificates of incorporation.

FEDERAL DEBT. The total amount the federal government owes its creditors.

FEDERAL DEPOSIT INSURANCE. Insurance issued by the FDIC that guarantees the full payment to owners of certain deposit accounts at member banks.

FEDERAL DEPOSIT INSURANCE CORPORATION. Established in 1934 to insure depositors against loss due to bank failure.

FEDERAL EMERGENCY RELIEF ACT.

FEDERAL FUNDS. Short-term loans of reserve deposits between banks.

FEDERAL FUNDS RATE. Rate at which banks can borrow funds from another bank to obtain funds on a short-term basis.

FEDERAL OPEN MARKET COMMITTEE. The policy-making arm of the federal Reserve System.

FEDERAL PERSONAL INCOME TAXES. Interest received on municipal bonds is free of federal income taxes and is not included in gross income.

FEDERAL RESERVE NOTES. U.S. paper money, also called dollar bills.

FEDERAL RESERVE SYSTEM. Established as the Central bank for the United States by the federal reserve act of 1913.

FEE-BASED FINANCIAL SERVICES. Financial services, like insurance and ATM services, for which prices are started in dollars or other currency units.

FEED-FORWARD CONTROL. A control system that attempts to identify future deviations from plans, early enough to take action before the deviations occur, by developing a model of system or process inputs, monitoring these inputs, and taking action in time to percent undesired of unplanned system outputs.

FIAT MONEY. Paper money, money does not represent a claim to any physical commodity. Fiat money is money which has a face value (or value as money) that exceeds its value as a commodity. Examples include U.S. federal reserve notes.

FIELD THEORY OF MOTIVATION. Psychologist Lwin's theory that motivation depends on organizational climate and must be looked upon as an element in a larger field restraining and driving forces.

FILL-OR-KILL (FOK). Must be executed immediately upon receipt by the broker or be automatically cancelled. It is a combination of two orders entered at the same time, with one contingent or the other. On-the-opening, order is executed during the opening period of the trading session. On-the-closing, order is executed during the closing period.

FILTERING. Screening out negative information by the sender of a communication and sending in only favourable information.

FINANCE LEASE. A financing device whereby a user can acquire use of an asset for most of its useful life. Rentals are net to the lessor and the user is responsible for maintenance, taxes and insurance. Rental payments over the life of the lease are sufficient to enable the lessor to recover the cost of the equipment plus a return on its investment.

FINANCIAL ACCOUNTING. It is concerned mainly with how accounting can serve external decisions, as distinguished from Management Accounting.

FINANCIAL ACCOUNTING STANDARD (FASB). The primary regulatory body over accounting principles and practices. It is an independent creature of the private sector.

FINANCIAL ANALYSIS. Financial Analysis is the process of identifying the strengths on weaknesses of the firm by properly establishing relationships between the items of balance sheet and profit and loss account.

FINANCIAL BUDGET. That part of the master budget that is composed of the capital budget, cash budget, budgeted balance sheet, and budgeted statement of changes in financial position.

FINANCIAL CAPITAL MAINTENANCE. The quantity of financial resources (usually historical costs), as distinguished from physical resources or operating capability, to be recovered before income emerges.

FINANCIAL DISTRESS. Financial distress occurs when the firm finds it difficult to honour the obligations of creditors. The extreme form of financial distress is insolvency. The firm may have to sell its assets at "distress" price. More important consideration is the inflexibility of raising funds when needed and non-availability of funds on acceptable terms.

FINANCIAL FLOWS. Financial flows include interest dividends lease rentals repayments of debt etc.

FINANCIAL INSTITUTION REFORM, RECOVERY, AND ENFORCEMENT ACT OF 1989 (FIRREA). This act was directed at the problem facing the savings and loan industry during the late

1980's. It abolished the federal saving and loan insurance corporation and the federal home loan bank board which had regulated the savings and loan industry.

FINANCIAL INTERMEDIARY. A financial institution that accepts funds from savers. Transforms them, and lends them to borrowers.

FINANCIAL LEASE. Long term, non-cancellable lease contracts are known as financial lease. Financial leases are very popular with high cost and high-technology equipment. Financial leases amortizes the cost of the asset over the term of lease. They are, therefore, also called capital or full pay-out leases. Most financial leases are direct leases.

FINANCIAL MARKET. An institution or arrangement that facilitates the purchase and sale of financial instruments such as corporate stocks and bonds, government bonds, and more exotic things such as options and futures contracts.

FINANCIAL SERVICE MARKETS. Markets in which individuals and firm purchase services that enhance the working of debt and equity markets.

FINANCING DECISION. Financing decision is to decide when, where and how to acquire funds to meet the firm's investment needs. The mix of debt and equity is known as the firm's capital structure.

FINEX. Financial instruments exchange NEW YORK.

FIRST LIEN. The first claim against an asset.

FIRST-IN FIRST-OUT. The stock of merchandise or material that is acquired earliest is assumed to be used first; the stock acquired latest is assumed to be still on hand.

FISCAL POLICY. Government spending or tax policy.

FISCAL TERMITES. The fiscal termites help wealthy people and multinational corporations plan their tax strategies. There are other, less interesting words for these tax consultants : tax minimization, tax defense, tax planning, or tax optimization. In addition, while the termites munch in increasingly complex pattern, they are finding it easier, faster and there are more of them than ever. Eventually, just like the termites in our houses, they bring the whole thin down.

FISHER EQUATION. The equation that sets the nominal interest rate equal to the real interest rate plus the expected inflation rate.

FIX CONNECTIVITY. Connectivity makes it easier to trade by reducing keystrokes. FIX stands for financial information exchange (FIX) protocol. It is a "language" that was developed specially for the communication of securities transactions and is a public domain specification owned and maintained by FIX Protocol Organization.

FIXED ASSETS. Tangible assets or physical items that can be seen and touched, often called property, plant, and equipment of plant assets.

FIXED COST. A cost that, for a given period of time and range of activity called the relevant range, does not change in total but become progressively smaller on a per-unit basis as volume increases.

FIXED EXCHANGE RATES. Exchange rates in which a country or group of countries pledge to keep the exchange rate within a narrow band of a target level.

FIXED PRICE PURCHASE OPTION. A purchase option where the price a lesser would have to pay to become equipment owner or lease termination is established at the start of the lease, and may be nominal. Such options have so far been most common in Continental Europe, but will be permissible in US Finance Leases in 1984. All purchase options are forbidden in a UK Lease.

FLEET INSURANCE. It is a motor insurance policy that covers a group of vehicles from one organization.

FLEXIBILITY PRINCIPAL. The more that flexibility (the ability to change direction without undue cost, embarrassment, of friction) can be built into plans, the less the danger of losses incurred by unexpected

FLEXIBLE BUDGET. A budget, often referring to overhead costs only, that is prepared for a range, rather than for a single level, of activity — that can be automatically geared to changes in the level of volume. Also called variable budget. Direct material and direct labour are sometimes included in the flexible budget.

FLEXIBLE EXCHANGE RATES. The exchange rate is determined strictly by the intersection of private supply and demand, without any government intervention.

FLEXIBLE-BUDGET VARIANCES. Difference between actual amounts and the flexible-budget amounts for the actual output achieved.

FLEXIBLE-CONTROL-BUDGET VARIANCES. Same as flexible budget variances.

FLEX-TIME. It refers to variations in starting and quitting times, but assumes that a number of hours (usually eight) is worked each day.

FLEX-TIME. A plan that allows employees limited control over scheduling their own hours of work, usually at the beginning and end of the work day.

FLIMSIES. The hand written newsletters delivered by messenger to subscribers in the wall Street area were known as 'flimsies' in 1882.

FLOATING EXCHANGE RATE. A country's decision to allow its currency value to change freely. The currency is not constrained by Central bank intervention and does not have to maintain its relationship with another currency in a narrow band. The currency value is determined by trading in the foreign exchange market.

FLOATING POLICY. It is an insurance policy that covers goods of different values and at different locations in marine insurance, it covers a ship's cargoes for a stated number of voyages.

FLOATING RATE NOTE. A debt instrument that pays interest based on a changing (floating) rate of interest.

FLOATING RENTAL RATE. Rental which is subject to upward or downward adjustments during the lease term. Floating rents sometimes are adjusted in proportion to prime interest rate or commercial paper rate changes during the term of the lease.

FLOATING STOCK. The amount of securities believed to be available for immediate purchase.

FLOOR. A series of European interest rate put options, often used by a party that has purchased a floating rate note. The floor ensures that the effective interest rate received from the note never falls below a fixed level.

FLOOR LET. One of the component interest rate put options in a floor.

FLOOR TRADERS. A member of an exchange who trades on the floor of the exchange.

FOLLOW-ON OFFERING. The company will have an underwritten public offering in the foreign country, timing of the issue depends on the time taken for getting necessary approvals in India and in the foreign country.

FOREIGN CORRUPT PRACTICES ACT. A federal law that requires adequate internal controls, among other requirements.

FOREIGN CORRUPT PRACTICES ACT OF 1977. A federal law that regulates questionable payments of United States firms operating in other nations.

FOREIGN CURRENCY DERIVATIVE. A derivative security written on foreign currency spots exchange rates.

FOREIGN CURRENCY FORWARDS PRICE. The forward price of a foreign currency.

FOREIGN CURRENCY FUTURES. A futures contract written on a foreign currency spot exchange rate.

FOREIGN CURRENCY FUTURES OPTION. An option written on a foreign currency futures.

FOREIGN CURRENCY OPTION. An option written on foreign currency spot exchange rate.

FOREIGN CURRENCY SWAP. An exchange of payments converting a series of cash flows in one currency to series of cash flows in another currency.

FOREIGN CURRENCY. Active futures trading at foreign currencies dates back to the inception at freely floating exchange rates in the early 1970's. Contracts as US dollars, Canadian dollar, Japanese Yen, British pound, the Swiss franc, German marc, French franc, Dutch guilders etc.

FOREIGN EXCHANGE MARKET. The market where different currencies are bought and sold.

FOREIGN SERVICE CORPORATION. An offshore special service corporation which is used by US companies to invest in a equipment which is utilized in foreign service under certain guidelines. Through such it US investors pay less tax on rentals and revenues derived from the assets.

FORMAL ORGANIZATION. The planned structure of a business in which individuals are given authority and responsibility to perform the specific tasks assigned to them.

FORTRAN. Formula Translation, a computer language.

FORWARD CONTRACT. A deferred contract in which two parties agree to buy and sell an asset at some future time under condition that are mutually agreeable. In contrast to futures contracts forward contracts are not standardized nor are they marked to market.

FORWARD EXCHANGE RATE. An exchange rate and quantity of currency contracted for today, but the actual exchange takes place at a specific future date.

FORWARD MARKET. Forward markets are contracts for deferred delivery.

FORWARD OPTION. An option on a forward contract.

FORWARD PRICE. The delivery price written in a forward contract such that the initial value of the forward contract is zero.

FORWARD RATE AGREEMENT. A contract written on LIBOR that requires a cash payment at maturity based on the difference between a spot rate and a forward rate of interest.

FORWARD RATE. The interest rate one can contract for today for riskless borrowing at a future date.

FORWARD SWAP. An interest rate swap in which the swap rate is set but the swap does not commence until a later date.

FOSSIL FUEL. Fuel derived from the ancient fossilized remains of plants and animals that were deposited many years ago; coal, petroleum, and natural gas are examples.

FOUR-FIFTHS ($4/5^{TH}$) RULE. It states that discrimination generally occurs if the selection rate for a protected group is less than 80 per cent of the selection rate of the majority group.

FRACTIONAL RESERVE BANKING. A banking system in which bank reserves equal only a fraction of outstanding demand deposits.

FRANCHISE. A privilege granted by a government, manufacturer, or distributor to sell a product or services in accordance with specified conditions.

FRANCHISE. It is a licence to manufacture or market a product with an established trade name or to operate a service, the equipment or supplies, which are manufactured by a monopoly producer. Franchises are often given for a particular area. The franchisee (or the holder of the licence) make an initial payment of pays a royalty.

FRANCHISEE. The firm that receives the franchise.

FRANCHISER. The parent company that franchises firms to sell their products.

FRANCHISING. An arrangement where one firm licenses another firm with exclusive rights to sell its products in a specified territory.

FRAUD. Intentional misrepresentation of the truth to deceive another.

FREE ASSET RATIO. In insurance the ratio of an insurer's free assets (at market value) to its liabilities.

FREE BANKING SYSTEM. A system begun in Michigan (1837) and New York (1838) to make entry into the banking industry less difficult by simplifying the process of obtaining a state charter and to make bank notes more safe : anyone could open a bank and issue notes so long as that person provided the requisite collateral.

FREE CASH FLOW. It is the cash flow available to service both creditors and shareholders who have provided funds to financial investments.

FREE ENTERPRISE IDEOLOGY. A set of beliefs about an ideal way to organize economic life, including individualism, freedom, private property, profit, equality of opportunity, competition, the work ethic, natural laws, and a limited government.

FREE ENTERPRISE SYSTEM. An economic system based on the free market, with an accompanying free enterprise ideology that explains why the fire market is an ideal way to organize economic life.

FREE MARKET. The ideal form of an economic system based on voluntary and free exchange among buyers and sellers. Competition regulates prices in all market exchanges.

FREE RESERVES. The difference between the total earnings to date and the total amount of dividends to date is known as reserves and surplus. It represents total undistributed earnings.

FREEDOM. An ability to make one's own decisions and take responsible actions without restrictions.

FREE-MARKET ECONOMIES. An economic system in which the government does not interfere in any way with business activity. There are no price controls, no permits, no kickbacks, no trading restrictions nor foreign exchange controls. India is making hesitant moves towards this economy.

FREE-REIN LEADERSHIP. Emphasizes a leadership style of "the less supervision the better".

FREIGHT FORWARDER. *See* Foreign freight forwarder.

FRICTIONAL UNEMPLOYMENT. Unemployment which occurs as people seek their first jobs, as people quit one job to seek another, or as people are displaced from jobs due to technical change and must seek another job.

FRICTIONLESS MARKETS. Markets where there are no restrictions nor costs to trading assets.

FRINGE BENEFIT. Any employee benefit other than salary, wages and cash bonus.

FRIVOLITY THEORY. It says that future market trends can be predicted by looking at the amount of money the citizens of a country spend on food. If the amount is above 36 per cent of a household's income, the market will drop.

FSC. *See* Foreign Sales Corporation.

FTZ. *See* Foreign trade zone.

FULL BODIED MONEY. A commodity money in which the commodity itself circulates as money.

FULL COST. It has two commonly used meanings.

First, it is often a synonym for absorption cost. Second, it often means absorption cost plus an allocation of non manufacturing cost.

FULL PAY-OUT LEASE. *See* Finance Lease.

FULL-BODIED MONEY. Gold money that is worth its face value as a commodity.

FULL-SERVICE WHOLESALER. Provides a full line of services such as taking title to merchandise maintaining a sales force, and extending credit to customers.

FUNCTIONAL ANALYSIS. An analytical approach that helps society match social needs to the organizations most capable of meeting those needs.

FUNCTIONAL APPROACH. *See* Functional Costing.

FUNCTIONAL AUTHORITY. The right or power inherent in a position to issue instructions of approve actions of persons in position not reporting directly to the person holding such authority; normally it is a limited line-type of authority applicable only to specialized areas and representing a delegation to a specialist by a superior manager with authority over both the position given functional authority and the position subjected to this authority. For example, a company controller is ordinarily given functional authority to prescribe the system of accounting throughout the company but this specialized authority is really a delegation from the chief executive.

FUNCTIONAL COSTING. Classifying cost by allocating them to the various functions performed, such as manufacturing, warehousing, delivery, and billing.

FUNCTIONAL CURRENCY. The currency of the primary economic environment in which an entity operates.

FUNCTIONAL DIVISION. An organization structure in which each function in foreign countries (*e.g.* marketing or production) reports separately to a counterpart functional group at headquarters.

FUNCTIONAL MODEL. Description of aspects of a system that transforms values using functions, mappings, constraints and functional dependencies.

FUNCTIONAL ORGANIZATION. An organization plan which uses specialized authority. This type of organization has characteristics of both line and staff.

FUNCTIONAL REGULATION. Regulations aimed at a particular function of business, such as competition or labour relations.

FUNCTIONALISM. The ideal that social functions should be performed by the institutions that can carry them out most efficiently.

FUNCTIONS OF MANAGEMENT. The activities a manager must perform to do his job. Management functions include planning, organizing, directing, controlling and coordinating.

FUND. A specific amount of cash or securities earmarked for a special purpose.

FUND MANAGER. A professional investment manager appointed by the AMC to invest money in accordance with the stated objectives of the scheme.

FUNDED METHOD. It provides pension benefits over a long period from funds accumulated ahead of time.

FUNDS PROVIDED BY OPERATIONS. The excess of revenue over all expenses requiring working capital.

FUNDS STATEMENT. A statement of sources and applications of working capital or cash.

FUTURE CONTRACT. Future contracts can be traded only in organized exchanges. Forward contracts are traded off exchange. The quantity and quality of the commodity to be delivered in accordance with a forward contract is usually not standardized but is negotiated between the parties at the time of contract.

FUTURE COST. The cost that would be incurred if the firm were to raise capital from each source at the present time, or in the near future. The historical costs that were incurred in the past in remaining capital are not relevant in financial decision making.

FUTURE MARKET. In the future market standardized contractual agreements are bought and sold, not the actual commodities. A futures contract is very specific as to quantity and date but it does not involve immediate transfer of ownership of the commodity. One can buy and sell commodities in a future market regardless of whether or not one owns the particular commodity.

FUTURE SHOCK. A human reaction to rapid technological change where individuals experience difficulty in coping with the new conditions of life brought on by new technology.

FUTURE VALUE. The value at some future date, given the prevailing interest rate of a present amount.

FUTURES COMMISSION MERCHANT (FCM). An individual or organization legally authorized to solicit or accept orders to buy or sell futures under the rules of a contract market. An FCM also accepts payments from customers and holds the margin deposits or whose orders are accepted. An FCM must be registered with the commodity futures trading commission. Futures Commission Merchant does the function similar to a broker in the stock market.

FUTURES CONTRACT. A deal made now to take place at a specified future date, at a price and quantity specified today. A future contract is defined as a commitment to buy or sell at specified future settlement date and a designated quantity of a commodity or financial asset. It is a legally binding contract by two parties to make or take delivery of the commodity at certain point of time in future. It is legal commitment between a buyer and a seller in which they agree to exchange something at a specified price, at the end of a designated period of time the buyer agrees to take delivery of something and the sellers agrees to make delivery.

FUTURES CONTRACT. A financial contract that obligates the owner to purchase some underlying asset for fixed price at a fixed future date. The financial contract is marked-to-market.

FUTURES OPTION. An option on a futures contract.

FUTURES PRICE. The delivery price written in a futures contract.

G

GAMMA. The change in the options delta for a unit change in the underlying asset's price.

GAMMA NEUTRAL. A portfolio position that has a zero gamma.

GAMMA STOCKS. Stocks of small, new, poorly financed or loss making companies, which are infrequently traded. They are also referred to as cats and dogs.

GANTT CHART. A technique for planning and control developed by Henry L. Gantt showing by bars on a chart the time requirements for the various tasks, or 'events', of a production or other programme.

GARNISHMENT. It is a court action in which a portion of an employee's wages is set aside to pay a debt owed a creditor.

GARN-ST. GERMAIN ACT OF 1982. Legislation designed to make depository institutions more competitive with money market mutual funds.

GENERAL AGREEMENT ON TARIFFS AND TRADE. The General Agreement on Tariffs and Trade (GATT) was drawn up by 23 countries in 1948. Most of the rounds deals with tariff reduction only. The Kennedy Round (1964-1967) came to an agreement on anti-dumping. And the Tokyo Round went further; dealing with subsidies and countervailing measures, technical arrears to trade, import licensing procedures, government procurement and other non-tariff areas of concern. The most recent round, the Uruguay Round, was the most comprehensive of any, lasting over seven years and creating a legal institution — the World Trade Organization to replace the provisional GATT.

GENERAL PARTNER. A partner who must maintain an active part in the business and who has unlimited liability.

GENERAL STORE. A store which usually sells a wide range of goods but in limited amounts of selections.

GENERALIZED SYSTEM OF PREFERENCES. Preferential import restrictions extended by industrial countries to developing countries.

GENERALLY ACCEPTED ACCOUNTING PRINCIPLES (GAAP). A technical term including both broad concepts or guidelines and detailed practices. It includes all conventions, rules, and procedures that together make up accepted accounting practice at a given time.

GENERALLY ACCEPTED ACCOUNTING PRINCIPLES (GAAP). The accounting standards accepted by the accounting profession in each country as required for the preparation of financial statements for external users.

GENERIC. Any of a class of products, rather than the brand of a particular company.

GEOCENTRIC. Operations based on an informed knowledge of both home and host country needs.

GEOCENTRIC BUSINESS. A company whose business standards and policies are worldwide in outlook including multinational ownership, management, markets, and operations.

GEOGRAPHIC DIVISION. An organizational structure in which a company's operations are separated for reporting purpose into regional area.

GEOGRAPHY. A science dealing with the earth and its life, especially with the description of land, sea, air, and the distribution of plant and animal life.

GILT FUND. Funds that invest only in government securities and treasury bills. They provide investors an opportunity to buy risk-free government securities. These funds generally provide a slightly higher yield than a money market fund. They are good for investors who desire safety or principal.

GLASS-STEAGALL ACT (1933). Also known as the banking act of 1933. This legislation made fundamental changes in the structure of the banking industry. Among other things, it created the federal deposit insurance corporation or FDIC.

GLOBAL BOND. A combination of domestic bond and Eurobond that is issued simultaneously in several markets and must be registered in each national market according to that market's registration requirements.

GLOBAL COMPANY. A company that integrates operations located in different countries.

GLOBAL SOURCING. The acquisition on a worldwide basis of raw materials, parts and sub-assemblies for the manufacturing process.

GLOBALLY INTEGRATED COMPANY. *See* Global Company.

GNMA. Government National Mortgage Association.

GO-GO-FUND. A mutual fund invested in highly speculative shares, with investors looking for huge short-term profits.

GOAL CONGRUENCE. Sharing of the same goals by top managers and their subordinates.

GOD-FATHER OFFER. A takeover offer so attractive that the target company cannot reject.

GOING CONCERN CONVENTION. An entity that it is assumed will continue indefinitely or at least will not be liquidated in the near future.

GOING CONCERN VALUE. It is the amount that a company could realize if it sells its business as an operating business.

GOLD CERTIFICATES. Paper claims that are redeemable for a specified amount of gold.

GOLD STANDARD. International fixed exchange rate system in which currencies are pegged to specified amounts of gold. Gold Standard : Before World War I, the world economy operated under the gold standard, which means that the currency of countries was convertible directly into gold. American dollar, for example, could be turned into the U.S. Treasury and exchanged for approximately 1/20 ounce of gold.

GOLDEN PARACHUTE. Term in contract of employment whereby the employer is bound to pay the employee a substantial sum of money in the event of dismissal or redundancy.

GOLDEN PARACHUTE. A provision in a corporate executive's contract that guarantees all or some portion of the executive's salary and / or benefits if discharged.

GOLDI-LOCKS. It is an economic scenario in which both corporate earnings and overall economy stay not too hot and not too cold.

GO-NO-GO DECISION. A decision such as on foreign investments, that is based on minimum threshold criteria and does not compare, different opportunities.

GOOD ACCOUNTS. It is financially strong customer.

GOODWILL. An intangible asset, the good name and reputation of the business firm that attracts customers.

GOOD-BAD-DELIVERY. A share certificate together with its transfer form which meets all the requirements of the title transfer from seller to buyer is called a good delivery in the market. Delivery of a share certificate, together with a deed of transfer, which does not meet requirements of title transfer from seller to buyer is called a bad delivery in the market.

GOVERNMENT AND BUSINESS PARTNERSHIP. A subtype of socio-economic system in which government and business work cooperatively to solve social problems.

GOVERNMENT BUDGET CONSTRAINT. The restriction that the government cannot purchase goods and services without having a source of funds to pay for these purchases.

GOVERNMENT OWNERSHIP. Exists when government owns and controls business firms.

GOVERNMENT PAPER. Government securities are called government paper *e.g.*, 182 days treasury bills.

GOVERNMENT PURCHASES. Goods and services demanded by government.

GOVERNMENT SECURITIES. Long-term debt instruments issued by the U.S Treasury bonds and notes.

GOVERNMENTAL POLITICS. Activities undertaken by business and other interest groups to influence government policies, forthcoming legislation, and the actions of regulatory agencies.

GRADE. The measured quality of a commodity.

GRANDCHILD SUBSIDIARY. An operation that is under a tax haven subsidiary also called a second tier subsidiary.

GRANTBACK PROVISIONS. Stipulations requiring that licences provide licensors with the use of improvements made on the technology originally licensed.

GRAPEVINE. A kind of informal organization network over which information tends to flow usually regularly, between persons who know and trust each other.

GRASS-ROOTS CAMPAIGN. A method of influencing government action from the bottom up.

GRAVELLED. It is the London equivalent to bottoming out. This occurs when a stock's price starts up after it hits a low, which then sparks interest in the security because of its low price.

GREED INDEX. It is a system of grading portfolio managers. The lower the score, the more bearish, thus more preferable. A manager can receive up to 10 points in each of the 10 categories which includes, institutional activity, preference of stocks to bonds, money manager of personal investment, investment for aggressive growth, etc.

GREEKS. The options partial derivatives with respect to its input parameters.

GREEN BAIZE DOOR. Also called Chinese wall, it is an artificial barrier erected between the underwriting and brooking departments in a brokerage firm. The purpose of a Chinese wall is to prevent insider trading.

GREEN CARD. It is the International Motor Insurance card which is issued to a holder of motor insurance, certifying that the cover provided is at least the statutory minimum period required by the foreign country or countries named.

GREENBACKS. Fiat currency used during the civil war that was not backed by gold or otherwise redeemable.

GREENHOUSE EFFECT. A rise in the average temperature of the earth's atmosphere caused by increased amounts of carbon dioxide that is a by-product of the burning of fossil fuels.

GREENMAIL. It is a procedure whereby a person with a sufficient shareholding in a company seeks a sum of money, or the repurchase of his shares by the company at a very high price, in order to induce him to refrain from making a takeover bid.

GRESHAN'S LAW. The theory states that if a country has two forms of currency, the citizens will hoard the currency with higher intrinsic value, thus forcing the other currency out of circulation.

GREY KNIGHT. In a takeover situation, a third party acting as counter bidder whose intentions towards the target company are not at all clear. Grey knights are not normally welcome to both the target and the original raider.

GREY MARKET. Grey market refers to the players who do not belong to the organized sector, and sell personal computers that are locally assembled.

GREY WAVE. The term is normally used in venture capital circles to describe a company or new industry that shows potential but whose realization is a long way in the future.

GRIEVANCE. It is a specific formal notice of dissatisfaction expressed through an identified procedure.

GRIEVANCE PROCEDURE. It is a format channel of communication used to resolve formal complaints (grievance).

GROSS BOOK VALUE. Carrying amount of an asset before deducting any related amounts (such as accumulated depreciation).

GROSS DOMESTIC PRODUCT (GDP). The total of incomes earned by residents of a country, regardless of where the productive assets are located.

GROSS MARGIN. Also called gross profit. Excess of sales over the cost of goods sold, that is, over the cost of the merchandise inventory that is acquired and resold.

GROSS NATIONAL PRODUCT. The total of all goods and services produced by the nation.

GROSS PROFIT. The amount of money received from the sale of products after the costs of the product are deducted. General and selling expenses are not included.

GROSS PROFIT. The difference between sales revenue and the cost of inventories sold.

GROSSING UP. The practice of adjusting pre-tax profits and tax charge by an amount of national tax benefits on non-taxable Region Development Grants in the UK. This practice is also recommended by the Equipment Leasing Association UK in dealing with the problem of pre-tax losses on leases which are profitable after tax during the transitional period.

GROUP OF 7 (G-7). A group of developed countries that periodically meets to make economic decisions, this group consists of Canada, France, Germany, Italy, Japan, the United Kingdom and the United States.

GROUP OF THIRTY. An international financial policy organization, the members of which include representatives of central banks, international banks, and securities firms.

GROWTH FIRM. Growth firms are those firms which expand rapidly because of ample investment opportunities yielding returns than the opportunity cost of capital. These firms are able to reinvest earnings at a rate which is higher than the rate expected by the shareholders. They will maximize the value per share if they follow a policy of retaining all earnings for internal investment.

GROWTH STOCK. The stock of a company that reinvests profits back into the firm in order to generate growth in earnings.

GSP. *See* Generalized system of preference.

GTC. A good, till cancelled order will remain in the system until it is cancelled by the trading member.

GTD. A good, till day's order allows the trading members to specify the days upto which the order should stay in the system. At the end of this period the order will get flushed out from the system.

H

HALF-YEAR CONVENTION. A widely used custom of regarding all depreciable assets placed in service during the year as if they had been placed in service at the year's midpoint.

HAND DELIVERY. Delivery and payment within the time or on the date stipulated when entering into the bargain, which item of date shall not be more than fourteen days following the date of the contract.

HARD CURRENCY. A currency that is freely traded without many restrictions and for which there is usually strong external demand; often called a freely convertible currency.

HARDSHIP ALLOWANCE. A supplement to compensate expatriates for working in dangerous or adverse conditions.

HARD-TO EMPLOY. Individuals who have never worked, who have been unemployed for long periods of time.

HARDWARE. The mechanical and electronic processing equipment.

HAZARDOUS WASTE. Waste materials from industrial, agricultural, and other activities capable of causing death or serious health problems.

HEALTH. It refers to a general state of physical, mental and emotional well-being.

HEALTH MAINTENANCE ORGANISATION (HMO). It is a form of health care which provides services for a fixed period on a prepaid basis.

HEATH-JARROW-MORTON MODEL. A model for pricing interest rate derivatives.

HEDGE. To attempt to protect foreign currency holdings against an adverse movements of an exchange rate.

HEDGE FUNDS. A hedge fund is an investment vehicle for individuals and institutions. By limiting investment to a select few, these funds are not subject to same regulations as that of a standard mutual fund. They are sometimes referred to as high risk/high return mutual funds. They employ speculative and complex investing strategies.

HEDGE RATIO. The number of

future or option contracts required to achieve a certain hedging objective.

HEDGERS. Those who go to the forward market to buy or sell currency now in order to protect against fluctuations in exchange rates.

HEDGING. Buying and selling in the futures commodity market in order to shift the risk to speculators.

HETERARCHY. An organizational structure in which management of an alliance of companies is shared by so-called equals rather than being set up in a superior subordinate relationship.

HICKENLOOPER AMENDMENT. A U.S. act requiring cessation of aid to country that nationalizes assets of U.S. citizens or has moved to abrogate contracts without taking appropriate means of settlement within a reasonable period of time.

HIERARCHY OF NEEDS. A well-known motivation theory stating that there is a hierarchy of needs and that people must fulfil the lower order needs sufficiently before they will be motivated by the higher order ones. Psychologist Abrahma Maslow's theory the basic human needs.

HIGH POWERED MONEY. Currency in the hands of the public plus commercial bank reserves, also called the monetary base.

HIGH-CONTEXT CULTURE. A culture in which most people consider that peripheral and hearsay information are necessary for decision making because they bear on the context of the situation.

HIGH-NEED ACHIEVER. One who will work very hard to achieve material or career success, sometimes to the detriment of social relationships or spiritual achievements.

HIGH-PAY-OUT CLIENTELE. Investors who prefer near dividends to future dividends are high-pay-out clientele. They prefer dividends than capital gains. They wish firms to pay higher dividends than retention of profits.

HIGH-VALUE ACTIVITIES. Activities that either produce high profits or are done by high salaried employees such as managers.

HIRE PURCHASE. Hire purchase contract involves regular payments for acquiring (owning) an asset.

HIRED GUN. An expert who is hired by a takeover target to fight off a predator.

HISTORIC VOLATILITY. The volatility estimated from using past observations of the underlying asset's price.

HISTORICAL COST. *See* Sunk cost.

HISTORICALLY PLANNED ECONOMY (HPE). The World Bank's term for second world countries in transition to market economies.

HISTORY. A branch of knowledge that records and explains past events.

HOLD OVER. To defer settlement of a deal on the stock exchange until the next settlement day.

HOLDING COMPANY. It may be anywhere from a small fraction to 100 per cent of another company.

HOLDING GAINS. Increases (or decreases) in the replacement cost (or other appropriate measure of current value) of the assets held during the current period.

HOLDING-OF-THE-REGISTER OF MEMBERS DATE. It is the date which is taken as a basis for sending letters of rights to the existing shareholders of the company when it issues rights.

HOME-COUNTRY NATIONALS. Expatriate employees who are citizens of the country in which the company is headquartered.

HOMEO-STATIS, DYNAMIC. The characteristic of a system whereby it is constantly in motion, with a tendency to seek equilibrium at various changing levels.

HOMOGENEOUS EXPECTATIONS. All investors have the expectations about the expected return and risk of securities.

HOMOGENEOUS RISK CLASSES. Firms can be grouped into homogeneous risk classes. Firms would be considered to belong to a homogeneous risk class if their expected earnings have identical risk and characteristics. It is generally implied under the M-M hypothesis that firms within same industry constitute a homogeneous class.

HORIZONTAL EXPANSION. Any foreign direct investments by which a company produces the same product it produces at home.

HORIZONTAL OPTION SPREAD. Buying and selling call or put options with the same strike price but different expiration dates.

HORSE AND PENNY INSURANCE. A specialist form of insurance cover, which can be an extension to a household policy or sand-alone. Compensation is provided in the event of the death, injury, and loss by theft. Extensions to the basic cover can be provided to cover equipment and third party liability.

HOST COUNTRY. Any foreign country in which an international company operates.

HOURLY RATE. Payments to workers on an hourly basis.

HOWEVER. Where preferred stock exists, the preferred dividend must be deducted in order to compute the net income applicable to common stock.

HPE. *See* Historically Planned Economy.

HULL INSURANCE. Insurance of vessel and its machinery. A policy that is generally taken out during construction which covers the ship for the whole of its useful life.

HUMAN ASSET ACCOUNTING. Programmes attempting to measure the value, and its changes, of investment in human assets of an enterprise.

HUMAN CAPITAL. The skills and training an individual acquires that makes her a productive employee or entrepreneur.

HUMAN RELATIONS SKILL. The ability of a manager to deal effectively with people.

HUMAN RESOURCE ACCOUNTING. It is a specialized personnel audit that continually attempts to quantify the value of organizational human resources.

HUMAN RESOURCE DEVELOPMENT. It focuses on increasing the capabilities of employees for continuing growth and advancement in the organization.

HUMAN RESOURCE INFORMATION SYSTEM (HRIS). It is an integrated computerized system designed to provide information to be used in making personnel decisions.

HUMAN RESOURCE PLANNING. It consists of analyzing and identifying the need for and the availability of the human resources required for an organisation to meet its objectives.

HURDLE RATE. Minimum desired rate of return. Also called required rate of return.

HYGIENE FACTORS IN MOTIVATION. Psychologist Hezberg's theory that certain human needs motivate and others merely cause dissatisfaction if they are not met; in other words, the meeting of this latter class of needs is a 'maintenance' or 'hygiene' factor; these are such factors in a work situation as salary, company policy and administration, quality of supervision working conditions, interpersonal relations, status, and job security.

HYPERINFLATION. An extended period in which inflation exceeds 100 per cent per year.

I

IAS 17 INTEREST RATE IMPLICIT IN A LEASE. The discount rate which, when applied to minimum lease payments (excluding executor costs paid by the lessor) and unguaranteed residual value, causes the aggregate present value at the beginning of the lease term to be equal to the gain value at the beginning of the lease term to be equal to the fair value of the leased property at the inception of the lease, minus any investment tax credit retained by the lessor and expected to be realized by him. The international accounting standard on treatment of losses, published by the International Accounting Standard Committee in London, September 1982. The standard is not binding on individual lease transactions but is expected to serve as a model for mandatory rules adopted by national organizations in future.

ICC. International Clearing Corporation.

ICCH. International Commodities Clearing House Limited.

IDEAL CAPACITY. The absolute maximum number of units that could be produced in a given operating situation, with no allowance for work stoppages or repairs. Also called theoretical capacity.

IDEALISM. Trying to determine principles before settling small issues.

IDEOLOGY. The systematic and integrated body of constructs, theories, and aims that constitute a society.

IDEOLOGY. A set of basic beliefs that define an ideal way of living for an individual, an organization, or a society.

IDLE TIME. A classification of indirect labour that constitutes wages paid for unproductive time due to circumstances beyond the worker's control.

IFE. *See* International Fisher Effect.

IFS ALLIANCE (Interactive Financial Services Alliance). This is an alliance formed between members of leading financial institutions and IBM in the Asia Pacific Region. The mission of this alliance is to promote the usage of the IFS platform for e-business within the Asia Pacific Region. The alliance will also work to providing inputs and direction to IBM on the functionality and content of its platform. It will work with regulatory bodies, provide input to national and international agencies concerning e-commerce.

ILLIQUID. The description of a bank that lacks enough liquid assets to meet the immediate demands of its creditors and depositors.

ILO. *See* International Labour Organization.

IMF. *See* International Monetary Fund.

IME. International Monetary Exchange.

IMITATION LAG. A strategy for exploiting temporary monopoly advantages by moving first to those countries most likely to develop local production.

IMMEDIATE CONFIRMATION. It indicates that people learn best if reinforcement is given as soon as possible after training.

IMMEDIATE OR CANCEL ORDER (IOC). It allows a trading member to buy or sell a security as soon as the order is released into the market failing which the order will be removed from the market.

IMMEDIATE RECOGNITION. According to this principle, the costs which will not provide any future benefits should be recognized immediately. The examples of such costs are selling, administration expenses and losses.

IMPERFECT INFORMATION. In the loan market, when banks do not know for certain which borrowers will and will not repay loans, but only that some borrowers are more likely to repay than others.

IMPLEMENTATION LAGS. The time between when a policy action is needed and the time when the action occurs.

IMPLICIT TRANSACTIONS. Events (like the passage of time) that are temporarily ignored in day-to-day recording procedures and that are recognized via end-of-period adjustments.

IMPLICIT VOLATILITY. The volatility implied from option prices.

IMPLIED REPO RATE. The interest rate implicit in a forward contract.

IMPLIED VOLATILITY. The future price volatility of an asset that the market currently expects based on the current price of a particular option contract.

IMPORT. A good or service made overseas but purchased

by a U.S. resident. A product that is brought in from another nation for sale in the nation.

IMPORT BROKER. An individual who obtains various government permissions and other clearances before forwarding necessary paperwork to the carrier that will deliver the goods from the dock to the importer.

IMPORT DEPOSIT REQUIREMENT. Government requirement of a deposit price to the release of foreign exchange.

IMPORT LICENSING. A method of government control of the exchange rate whereby all recipients exporters and other who receive foreign exchange are required to sell to the Central bank at the official buying rate.

IMPORT SPECIE POINT. Point in the variation of exchange rates at which it becomes cheaper for a nation on the gold standard to import gold rather than buy foreign currency.

IMPORT SUBSTITUTION. An industrialization policy whereby new industrial development emphasizes products that would otherwise be imported.

IMPORT TARIFF. A tax placed on goods entering a country.

IMPULSE BUYING. A purchase made without preplanning.

IN-THE-MONEY. A term referring to a call (put) option when the market value of the asset on which the option is written is greater (less) than the strike price.

IN THE MONEY OPTION. An option is in-the-money if it has intrinsic value. A call option is in the money if the current asset price is above the options strike price; a put option is the money if the current asset price is below the options price.

INCENTIVE. Those informal and formal performance measures and rewards that enhance goal congruence and managerial effort.

INCENTIVES. They are rewards designed to encourage and reimburse employees for efforts beyond normal performance expectations.

INCEPTION OF A LEASE. The date the lease commitment or lease agreement is signed, provided the property to be leased has been constructed or has been acquired by the lessor; otherwise, the property is acquired by the lessor.

INCOME. A flow of earnings over some given time interval.

INCOME AND GROWTH PLANS. An income plan pays annual or other such periodic income in the form of dividends to the investors, while a growth plan reinvests the earnings. Investors who want an income prefer the former, while growth plans are suited for those who prefer capital appreciation.

INCOME BOND. A bond which has characteristics of both non cumulative preferred stock and bonds.

INCOME EFFECT. The fact that a higher return on assets leaves a person with more income which normally leads to the purchase of more assets.

INCOME PERCENTAGE OF REVENUE. Income divided by revenue.

INCOME STATEMENT. A statement that evaluates the operating performance of the corporation by matching its accomplishments (revenue from customers, which usually is called sales) and efforts (cost of goods sold and other expenses).

INCOME STATEMENT. An accounting statement that is a measure of income, expenses and profit over a specific period of time.

INCOME STOCK. The stocks of companies that have a low level of retained earnings and thus pay most of their earnings to shareholders as dividends.

INCORPORATE STOCK HOLDING. It exists when a corporation holds stock in other corporations and is unlawful when it injures competition.

INCREMENT. *See* Incremental.

INCREMENTAL. The change in total results (such as revenue, expense, or income) under a new condition comparison with some given or known condition.

INCREMENTAL APPROACH. A method of determining which of two alternative courses of action is preferably calculating the present value of the difference in net cash inflow between one alternative and the other.

INCREMENTAL BORROWING RATE. The interest rate which a person would expect to pay for a certain loan at a certain time.

INCREMENTAL CASH FLOWS. Cash flows from an investment when compared to a hypothetical zero-cash-flow project.

INCREMENTAL COST. The difference in total cost between two alternatives. Also called differential cost.

INDEMNITY AGREEMENT. In a leveraged lease, an agreement whereby the owner participates and the lease indemnify the trustees from liability as a result of ownership of the leased equipment. In a leveraged lease, an agreement whereby the owner participants and the lessee indemnity the trustees from liability as a result of ownership of the leased equipment.

INDEMNITY CLAUSE. Although lease documentation contains various indemnities, the indemnity clause actually refers to the tax indemnity clauses whereby the lessee indemnifies the lessor from loss of tax benefits.

INDENTURE. An indenture is a legal agreement between the company issuing debentures and the debenture trustee, who represents the debenture holders. It is the responsibility of the trustee to protect the interests of debenture holders by ensuring that the company fulfils the contractual obligations.

INDENTURE TRUSTEE. In a leveraged lease, the indenture trustee holds the security interest in the leased equipment for the benefit of the lenders. In the event of default, the indenture trustee exercises the rights of a mortgagee. The indenture trustee is also responsible for receiving rent payments from the lessee and using such funds to pay the amounts due the lenders with the balance being paid to the owner trustee. The indenture trustee verifies that correct filings are made to protect the security interest of the lenders. The bond register is maintained by the indenture trustee, who also acts as transfer agent.

INDEPENDENCE. An extreme situation in which a country would not rely on other countries at all.

INDEPENDENT EVENTS. The occurrence of one event has no effect on the occurrence of the other event.

INDEPENDENT LESSOR. Any leasing company investing in leases, also brokers without funds to invest in leases sometimes prefer to call themselves "independent lessors" rather than "brokers". Any leasing company investing in lease without funds to invest in leases sometimes prefer to be called themselves "independent lessors" rather than brokers.

INDEPENDENT MONETARY POLICY. A policy conducted through open market operations with the goal of changing the money supply without changing taxes or spending.

INDEPENDENT OPINION. *See* Auditor's report.

INDEX AMORTIZED SWAP. An interest rate swap for which the notional principal is amortized over the life of the swap. The rate of amortization is related to the level of interest rates.

INDEX ARBITRAGE. Process of selling stocks at the same time as buying stock index futures, or *vice versa.* It is a form of programme trading.

INDEX NUMBER. A ratio of two numbers expressed as a percentage.

INDEX OPTIONS. Optional contracts written on a stock index.

INDIGENIZATION. The process of introducing elements of an outside culture.

INDIRECT FINANCE. Finance that involves a middleman a third party linking the borrower and lender.

INDIRECT LABOUR. All factory labour that is not direct labour.

INDIRECT MANUFACTURING COSTS. All manufacturing costs other than direct material and direct labour.

INDIRECT QUOTE. An exchange rate given in terms of the number of units of the foreign currency for one unit of the domestic currency.

INDIRECT SELLING. A sale of goods by an exporter through another domestic company as an intermediary.

INDIVIDUAL BRAND. A manufacturer's policy of distributing each of his products under different brand names.

INDIVIDUAL RETIREMENT ACCOUNT (IRA). Allows an employee to set aside in a special account funds which are tax-deferred until the employee retires.

INDIVIDUALISM. A belief that each individual person has an inherent worth and dignity and possess basic human rights that should be by society. Each person is presumed to be a free agent capable of knowing and promoting his or her own self-interest.

INDIVIDUALLY VALIDATED LICENCE (IVL). A special export licence under which certain restricted products need to be shipped.

INDUCTIVE STATISTICS. The making of predictions, forecasts, and generalizations about a larger set of data based on information derived from a smaller set of data.

INDUSTRIAL GOODS. Goods which are used in producing another product or expended in connection with carrying on a business operations.

INDUSTRIAL SOCIETY. A society in which the building and mechanical processing of material goods dominates work and employs the largest proportion of the labour force.

INDUSTRIAL SOURCE BASE. The minerals, energy sources, water supplies, skilled labour force, and human knowledge necessary for industrial production.

INDUSTRIAL UNION. Union whose membership is determined by the nature of the industry, such as a auto workers.

INDUSTRIAL UNION. A union whose members, regardless of their skills or craft, work in a particular industry, such as automobile manufacturing or the chemical industry.

INDUSTRIALIZATION ARGUMENT. A rationale for protectionism that argues that the development of industrial output should come about even though domestic prices may not become competitive on the world market.

INDUSTRY ANALYSIS. To determine the financial condition and performance of a firm, its ratios may be compared with average ratios of the industry of which the firm is a member. This sort of analysis is known as the industry analysis; helps to ascertain the financial standing and capability of the firm *vis-à-vis* other firm in the industry.

INDUSTRY-SPECIFIC REGULATION. Regulations aimed at specific industries, such as telephone service or railroad transportation, involving control of rates charged, customers served, and entry into the industry.

INELASTIC (PRODUCT DEMAND). A condition in which sales are likely to increase or decrease by a percentage that is less than the percentage change in income.

INFANT-INDUSTRY ARGUMENT. The position that holds that an emerging industry should be guaranteed a large share of the domestic market until it becomes efficient enough to compete against imports.

INFLATION. Depreciation in the purchasing power of money.

INFLATION. A persistent, general rise in the average price of all goods.

INFLATION PREMIUM. The part of the nominal interest rate that is over and above the real interest rate. This compensates for the decline in purchasing power due to inflation.

INFLATION RATE. The rate of change in the price level stated as a percentage change on an annual basis.

INFLATION RISK. Risk that the actual inflation rate will differ from that expected by borrowers and lenders.

INFLATIONARY EXPECTATIONS. Expectations or educated estimate of the inflation rate.

INFO-PRENEURE. He is a person who makes out a living by collecting and selling information to interested parties.

INFORMAL ORGANIZATION. Generally, patterns of human behaviour and relationships coexisting with, or lying outside, the formal organization structure. According to professor Keith Davis it is a network of personal and social relations not established or required by the formal organization but arising spontaneously as people associate with one another. Structured around people and based on the interpersonal relationships of workers which exists within the framework of the formal organization.

INFORMATION LAGS. Lags in the availability of information about the state of the economy.

INFORMATION RETRIEVAL. The furnishing of information rapidly to the place where it is needed.

INFRASTRUCTURE. The underlying foundation of a society such as roads, schools, and so forth, that allows it to function effectively.

INFRASTRUCTURE. The internal social, educational, political, and economic conditions that affect a nation.

INITIAL DIRECT COSTS. Direct costs incurred by a lessor in negotiating and consummating a lease, such as commissions and legal fees.

INITIAL MARGIN. Initial Margin is the amount a trader must deposit before trading futures. This margin approximately equal the maximum daily price fluctuations permitted for the contract being traded. The amount of money that customers must put up while establishing a futures or options position to guarantee their contract obligations.

INITIAL MARGIN. The initial margin that is required in a margin account.

INITIATING A POSITION. This implies knowing that the types of orders and types of markets in the futures industry is all good and fine but knowing how to apply that knowledge is usually best left to the professionals.

INITIATING STRUCTURE. They refers to task-oriented efforts on the part of the leader to get the job done.

INJUNCTION. A court order obtained by management to prohibit the union from performing some act.

INJURY TAX. A tax levied against an organization, based on the number and severity of job-related injuries suffered by its employees. Institutional investor — a financial institution, insurance company, endowment fund, or similar organization that invests its accumulated funds in the securities offered for sale on stock exchanges.

INPUT. Putting data into the computer which are to be processed.

INPUT-OUTPUT TABLE. A tool used widely in national economic planning to show that resources utilized by different industries for a given output as well as the interdependence of economic sectors.

INQUIRY WINDOW. It is this window that the inquiries such as market by order, market by price, previous trade, order log, outstanding order and the shape quote as regarding the various orders available in the system can be viewed.

INSOLVENT. The description of a bank with total liabilities that exceed the value of its assets.

INSPECTION. Checking for defective products in the quality control process.

INSTALMENT SALES CONTRACTS. Contracts in which a customer agrees to pay for a purchase by paying a certain amount of money each month for a specific number of months.

INSTANT CROSSING. Instant crossing is an after-hours equity trading product designed to lower transaction costs by providing a passive trading environment. In this environment, instant customers reap the benefits of anonymity, neutrality and confidentiality while relying on benchmark prices. These benchmark prices are the last sale on the primary exchange and the midpoint of the closing inside bid and offer for OTC securities.

INSTITUTIONAL ADVERTISING. Advertising with the purpose of building a positive image for the company.

INSTRUMENT. In terms of monetary policy, variables the policy maker can control.

INSTRUMENT INSTABILITY. It rises when a change in the instrument affects the targeted variable over a number of future periods. Leading to ever widening swings in the instrument in order to stabilize the targeted variable.

INSURANCE COMPANIES. Business that calculate the risk of any loss and insure against that loss for the payment of premiums. Financial institutions that help protect individuals against certain risks. Such as risks to health, disability, and life.

INSURANCE OMBUDSMAN. Official in-charge of service set up by insurance companies in 1981, to arbitrate the disputes between insurance companies and policy holders.

INSURED PLAN. It is one administered through insurance companies or similar institutions which buy retirement annuity policies.

INSURED VALUE. A schedule included in a lease which

states the agreed value of equipment of various times during the term of the lease, and establishes the liability of the lessee to the lessor the event the leased equipment is lost or rendered unusable the lease term, due to a casualty.

INTANGIBLE ASSETS. Rights are economic benefits that are not physical in nature. Examples are franchises, patents, trademarks, copyrights, and goodwill.

INTANGIBLE ASSETS. Assets that have no form but do have value such as goodwill and patents.

INTANGIBLE FIXED ASSET. Represents the firm's rights and include patents, copyrights, franchises, trademarks, trade names and goodwill. Patents are the exclusive rights granted by the government enabling the holder to control the use of an invention. Copy rights are the exclusive rights to produce and sell literary musical and artistic works.

INTANGIBLE PROPERTY. *See* Intellectual property rights.

INTANGIBLE REWARD. Exists in the form of recognition plaques, etc. it has little or no money value.

INTEGRATED SYSTEM. A system for taxation of the corporate income aimed at preventing double taxation through the use of the split rates or tax credits.

INTELLECTUAL PROPERTY RIGHTS. Ownership rights to intangible assets, such as patents, trademarks, copy rights and know-how.

INTER COMMODITY SPREAD. A spread between two future contracts written on different but related commodities.

INTERACTIVE MODEL OF BUSINESS. The combined primary and secondary interactions that business has with society.

INTERACTIVE SYSTEM. The closely inter-twined relationships between business and society.

INTER-BANK MARKET. The market for foreign-exchange transactions among commercial banks.

INTER-BANK TRANSACTIONS. Foreign-exchange transactions that take place between commercial banks.

INTER-CORPORATE DEPOSITS. Inter-corporate lending/borrowing or deposits (CDs) is a popular short-term investment alternative for companies. Generally, cash surplus companies will deposit their funds in sister or associate companies or with outside companies with high credit standing. In practice, companies can negotiate inter-corporate borrowing or lending for very short periods. The risks of default are high, but returns are quite attractive.

INTER-CORPORATE FUNDS MARKET. Inter-corporate loans have been a traditional feature of corporate financing in India. These loans are generally made by corporate units with seasonal surplus funds to other companies whether directly or through brokers. The loans are generally for short periods and may be secured.

INTERDEPENDENCE. The existence of mutually necessary economic relations among countries.

INTEREST AGGREGATION. The collection of interests in the political system.

INTEREST ARBITRAGE. Investing in debt instruments in different countries and earning a profit due to interest-rate and exchange-rate differentials.

INTEREST ARTICULATION. The process by which politicians, individuals, business and interest groups make their desires known in the political process.

INTEREST COVERAGE RATIO. Interest coverage ratio or the times-interest-earned is used to test the firm's debt servicing capacity. The interest coverage ratio is computed by dividing earnings before interest and taxes (EBIT) by interest charges. The interest coverage ratio shows the number of times the interest charges are covered by funds that are ordinarily available for their payments.

INTEREST EARNING ASSETS. Futures trading, an interest bearing assets started in 1975, but the growth at this market has been phenomenal. Contracts are traded on treasury bills, euro-dollars, deposits municipal bonds, etc.

INTEREST ELASTICITY OF DEMAND FOR LOANS. The percentage change in the quantity demanded of loans divided by the percentage change in the interest rate.

INTEREST RATE ADJUSTMENT ACT (1961). Extended the glass-steagall interest rate limits to thrifts.

INTEREST RATE CEILING. A specified amount above which the interest rate is not permitted to rise.

INTEREST RATE DERIVATIVE. A derivative security the value of which depends on the evolution of the term structure of interest rates.

INTEREST RATE DIFFERENTIAL. An indicator of future changes in the spot exchange rate.

INTEREST RATE FLOOR. A feature of many financial instruments that prevent the interest from falling below some specified amount.

INTEREST RATE IMPLICIT IN A LEASE. The discount rate which, when applied to minimum lease payments (excluding execution costs paid by the lessor) and unguaranteed residual value, causes the aggregated present value at the beginning of the lease term to be equal to the fair value of the beginning of the lease term to be equal to the fair value of the leased property at the inception of the lease, minus any investment tax credit retained by the lessor and expected to be realized by him.

INTEREST RATE PARITIES. A theory stating that the forward premium or discount on one currency in terms of another currency is directly related to the short-term interest rate difference between the two countries.

INTEREST RATE PARITY. An arbitrage relations that holds between foreign currency spot prices and interest rates.

INTEREST RATE RISK. The risk of a change in the overall level of interest rates, and the resulting change in the bond prices.

INTEREST RATE SWAP. A swap based on interest rates.

INTEREST TAX SHIELD. The profit after tax figure excludes interest on borrowing. Interest is tax deductible and therefore a firm which pays more interest pays less taxes. Tax saved on account of payment of interest is called interest tax shield.

INTERFACES. They are areas of contact between the personnel unit and other managers in an organization that occur in personnel activities.

INTER-FIRM ANALYSIS. The analysis of the financial performance of all firms in an industry and their comparison at a given point of time is referred to the cross-sectional analysis or the inter-firm analysis.

INTERIM RENT. Daily rental accruing from delivery, acceptance and/or funding until a later starting debate for a basic lease term, often used when equipment delivers over a period of time.

INTERLOCKING DIRECTORATES. Exists when a person is a member of the board of directors of more than one corporation. It is unlawful when the firm are in competition.

INTERMEDIATE TARGET. This target is a value for a variable that the policy maker tries to achieve not because it is desirable in its own right, but become it helps achieve the final target.

INTERMEDIATE-TERM ASSETS. Assets in the debt market which mature between one and ten years from the date of issue.

INTERMITTENT PRODUCTION. Also called job lot production. Orders are produced to each customer's specifications.

INTERNAL ACCOUNTING CONTROL. Methods and procedures that are mainly concerned with the authorization of transactions, safeguarding of assets and accuracy of the financial records.

INTERNAL DATA. Data collected by a firm from its own records and reports.

INTERNAL DEBT. Government borrowing within the country.

INTERNAL MEASURE. Ratio assesses a firm's ability to meet its regular cash expenses, is the internal measure. It relates liquid assets to average daily operating cash outflows.

INTERNAL RATE OF RETURN. The rate of interest at which the present value of expected cash inflows from a particular project equals the present value of a expected cash outflows of the same project also called time adjust rate.

INTERNALIZATION. Control through self-handling of foreign operations, primarily because it is less expensive to deal with in the same corporate family than to contract with an external organization.

INTERNATIONAL ACCOUNTING STANDARDS COMMITTEE (IASC). The international private sector organization that sets financial accounting standards for worldwide use.

INTERNATIONAL BALANCE OF PAYMENTS. The net effect or balance of all payments made by a nation, all payments received by that nation in its trading and investments relationships with other nations. A favourable balance exists when net payments received are greater than net payments made; an unfavourable balance occurs when net payments made exceed net payments received.

INTERNATIONAL BUREAU FOR THE PROTECTION OF INDUSTRIAL PROPERTY RIGHTS (BIRPI). A multilateral agreement to protect patents, trademarks and other property rights.

INTERNATIONAL BUSINESS. All business transactions involving private companies or government of two or more countries.

INTERNATIONAL DIVISION. An organizational structure in which virtually all foreign operations are handled within the same division.

INTERNATIONAL FISHER EFFECT (IFE). The theory that the

relationship between interest rates and exchange rates implies that the currency of the country with the lower interest rate will strengthen in the future.

INTERNATIONAL LABOUR ORGANIZATION (ILO). A multilateral organization promoting the adoption of humane labour conditions.

INTERNATIONAL LENDING SUPERVISORY ACT OF 1983. Legislation which addressed the issue of bank capitalization and authorized the federal reserve system, the FDIC, and the comptroller of the currency to set and enforce minimum capital requirements.

INTERNATIONAL MONETARY FUND (IMF). A multigovernmental association organized in 1945 to promote exchange rate stability and to facilitate the international flow of currencies.

INTERNATIONAL MONETARY MARKET (IMM). A specialized market located in Chicago and dealing in select foreign currency futures.

INTERNATIONAL ORGANIZATION OF SECURITIES COMMISSIONS (IOSC). An international organization of securities regulators that wants the IASC to establish more comprehensive accounting standards.

INTERNATIONAL STANDARD OF FAIR DEALING. The concept that investors should receive prompt, adequate, and effective compensation in cases of expropriation.

INTERNATIONAL TRADE ADMINISTRATION (ITA). A branch of the U.S. department of commerce offering a variety of services to U.S. exporting companies.

INTERNATIONAL TRADE. Buying and selling products between nations.

INTERNATIONAL UNION. An affiliation of local unions and membership in Canada, Mexico and Central America as well as in the United States.

INTERPERIOD TAX ALLOCATION. Accounting procedures that account for timing differences between revenues and expenses reported to income tax authorities and to others.

INTERSTATE COMMERCE COMMISSION. A federal agency which regulates common carriers engaged in interstate transportation by rail and pipelines which move oil or other commodities (except water and gas) in interstate commerce.

INTERVENTION CURRENCIES. The currencies in which a particular country trades the most.

INTERVIEW METHOD. Information gathering technique, mainly using personal interview, telephone and mail questionnaire.

INTERVIEW. The face-to-face contact between the company representative and the applicant.

IN-THE-MONEY. The call option is said to be 'in the money' if the actual market price is higher than the exercise price.

INTRA-COMMODITY SPREAD. A spread between two futures contracts written on the same commodity but wit different delivery months.

INTRA-ZONAL TRADE. Trade among countries that are part of a trade agreement, such as the E.U.

INTRINSIC VALUE. For a call option the difference of the asset price less the strike price if positive zero otherwise. For a put option, the difference of the strike price less the asset price if positive zero otherwise.

INVENTORY APPROACH TO MONEY DEMAND. Pioneered by William baumol and James tobia in the 1950s provides a microeconomic justification for including interest rates a determinant of money demand.

INVENTORY CONTROL. The process that strives to maintain adequate materials while minimizing inventory carrying costs.

INVENTORY MANAGEMENT. Management of stocks of raw materials, stocks available for sale or in the process of being made ready for sale.

INVENTORY TURNOVER. Cost of goods sold divided by average inventory for a specific period.

INVESTING. Purchasing stock with the intent of holding it a rather long period of time with the anticipation of appreciation in value.

INVESTMENT BANKS. Financial institutions that purchase large blocks of stock from issuing companies and resell them in the market in small lots.

INVESTMENT CANADA. A Canadian act whose intent is to persuade foreign companies to invest in Canada.

INVESTMENT CENTRE. An area of responsibility for costs, revenues and related investment.

INVESTMENT DECISION. It involves the decision of allocation of capital or commitment of funds to long term assets that would yield benefits in the future.

INVESTMENT GOODS. Goods and services demanded by businesses for use as capital inputs into productions.

INVESTMENT PERFORMANCE. This has been calculated using the internal rate of return method the return calculated have been adjusted for rights, bonuses and dividends for the period of existence of the scheme. It takes the face value of the scheme as the initial outflow and the latest net asset value as the inflow. The formula takes into account any rights, bonus, or dividends during the period under consideration and makes suitable adjustments for the same. All returns have been annualized.

INVESTMENT PERIOD METHOD. Lessor accounting method, which apportions profit earned on a lease to those periods where lessor has an after tax, net investment in the lease.

INVESTMENT TAX CREDIT. Direct reductions of income taxes arising from the acquisition of depreciable assets.

INVESTMENTS IN AFFILIATES. Often used to describe investments in voting stock that represents 20% to 50% ownership.

INVESTMENTS IN ASSOCIATES. Often used as synonym for investments affiliates.

INVISIBLE. *See* Services.

INVISIBLE HAND. A phrase derived from Adam Smith to describe market competition as the regulator of a free market economy.

INVOICE PRICE. The actual price that a long pays to a short at delivery after all adjustments.

IPE. International Petroleum Exchange.

IPO. Initial Public Offering of equity shares.

IRDA ACT. An Act to provide for the establishment of an Authority to protect the interests of holders of insurance policies, to regulate, promote and ensure orderly growth of the insurance industry and for matters connected therewith or incident thereto and further to amend the Insurance Act, 1938, the Life Insurance Corporation Act, 1956 and the General Insurance Business (Nationalization) Act, 1972.

IRON LAW OF RESPONSIBILITY. The iron law of responsibility states that in the long run those who do not use power in a way that society considers responsible will tend to lose it.

IRREVOCABLE LETTER OF CREDIT. A letter of credit that cannot be cancelled or changed without the consent of all parties involved.

ISDA. International Swaps and Derivatives Association.

ISLAMIC LAWS. A system of theocratic law based on the religious teachings of Islam; also called Muslim law.

ISO 9000. A quality standard

developed by the international standards organization in Geneva that requires companies to document their commitment to quality at all levels of the organization.

ISSUES MANAGEMENT. Identifying, analyzing, developing recommendations, and implementing policies concerning issues that have special meaning and importance for a company.

IVL. *See* Individually validated licence.

J

JAJO. It represents January, April, July and October, which are expiration months of successively offered option contracts. It also represents payments that are due quarterly.

JAMAICA AGREEMENT. A 1976 agreement among countries that permitted greater flexibility of exchange rates, basically formalizing the break from fixed exchange rates.

JAMES BOND. It is the nickname for a US Treasury bond, that matures in the year 2007, so named because the maturity date is James Bond's agent number in the popular series of movies.

JEFFERSONIAN IDEAL. The preferences, usually attributed to Thomas Jefferson, for a society composed of many small-scale procedures, a representative political system, widespread dispersal of power, and individual freedom and responsibility for all citizens.

JELLY ROLL SPREAD. A long and short position in the same index option with different classes; a put and a call, which have different expiration dates.

JEOPARDY CLAUSE. It is a situation in the Euro-currency agreement that guarantees that certain actions will be taken to protect the market if some events curtail the lender's activities or Euro market operations.

JIT. *See* Just-in-time system.

JOB. It is a grouping of similar positions.

JOB ANALYSIS. A systematic collection of all information about a job to determine its requirements.

JOB DEPTH. It is the amount of planning and control responsibilities in a job.

JOB DESCRIPTION. The description of the requirements of the job.

JOB DESIGN. The structuring of a job in terms of content, function, and relationships. It may focus on individual positions or on work groups.

JOB ENLARGEMENT. It is the concept of broadening the scope of a job by expanding the number of different tasks to be performed.

JOB ENRICHMENT. Programmes of building into jobs a high sense of meaning, challenge, and potential for accomplishment.

JOB EVALUATION. It is the systematic determination of the relative worth of jobs within an organization.

JOB LOT. Collection of stocks or goods sold together, perhaps to somebody who wants only some of them.

JOB ORDER. A document that shows the costs allocated to a specific batch of product.

JOB ORDER COSTING. The method of allocating costs of products that receive varying attention and effort.

JOB REDESIGN. Restructuring the work of employees to allow a more direct connection between an employee's personal effort and the tangible results of that work effort.

JOB ROTATION. It is the process of shifting a person from job to job.

JOB ROTATION. A plan that allows employees to move periodically from one job to another within an office or plant, as one way to reduce boredom and monotony and improve the quality of work life.

JOB SCOPE. It refers to the number and variety of tasks performed by a job holder.

JOB SPECIFICATION. A detailed list of the personal qualifications needed for each job.

JOINT PRODUCT COSTS. Costs of two or more manufactured goods, of significant sales values, that are produced by a single process and that are not identifiable as individual products up to a certain stage of production, known as the split-off point.

JOINT STOCK COMPANIES. Now called limited company. Although a limited company has quite a few characteristics, the 'limited' refers to the liability of the members, which is confined to the face value of shares they have bought. A limited company is a legal entity, *i.e.*, it can enter into contracts as a person, independent of its members. Most of the large companies, public or private, are limited by shares, the number of which is stated in its memorandum of association. A public limited company needs a certificate of incorporation from the Registrar of Companies.

JOINT VENTURE. Two or more people joining together in co-ownership for a specific limited purpose.

A specialized form of a partnership.

JONES TOWN DEFENSE. Any form of defensive tactics against a hostile take over bid that is so extreme as to appear suicidal.

JUMBO CERTIFICATE. A jumbo certificate is a single composite share certificate issued by consolidating/ aggregating a large number of market lots.

JUNIOR STOCKS. Stocks offered to executives of companies at below market price. Initially they have a low dividend rate.

JUNK BONDS. Bonds that have a relatively high risk of default.

JUNK MAIL. Unselected mail not wanted by the receiver.

JUNK TELEPHONE CALL. An unsolicited telephone call not wanted by the receiver.

JUST IN TIME. A system of inventory control that concentrates on the final manufacturing process and then looks backward throughout the preceding processes. The earlier processes produce only enough quantities to replace those withdrawn by the subsequent processes.

JUST-IN-TIME (JIT) INVENTORY SYSTEM. A system that decreases inventory costs by having components and parts delivered as they are needed in production. The supplier delivers the components and parts to the production line 'just in time' to be assembled. Other names for this or similar methods are 'zero inventory' and 'stockless production'.

JUSTICE. A concept used in ethical reasoning that refers to the fair distribution of benefits and burdens among the people in a society, according to some agreed-upon rule.

K

KANGAROO. Stock exchange's nickname for shares in Australian companies, especially those dealing in tobacco, property and mining.

KAPPA. *See* Vega.

KC. Kansas City Board of Trade.

KCBOT. Kansas City Board of Trade.

KEIRETSU. A corporate relationship linking certain Japanese companies, usually involving a non controlling interest in each other, strong high level personal relationship among managers in the different companies and interlocking directorship.

KEOGH PLAN (H.R. 10 PLAN). It allows self-employed individuals to establish an individualized pension plan.

KEY INDUSTRY. Any industry that might affect a very large segment of a country's economy or population by virtue of its size or influence on other sectors.

KEYMAN INSURANCE. In order to see that any loss of personnel due to unforeseen incidents like ill-health or accidents does not adversely influence the profitability, venture capitalists ensure that management writes a 'keyman insurance policy', under this, the core employees of the organization are insured.

KEYNESIANS. Followers of John Maenad keenness who view the economy as unstable and in need of government intervention and control. They tend to argue that the interest elasticity of money demand is/or can be high.

KNOWLEDGE SOCIETY. A society in which the use and electronic manipulation of knowledge and information dominate. Work and employ the largest proportion of the labour force.

KNOWN DIVIDEND MODEL. An extension of the Black-Scholes model for pricing European options which the underlying asset pays dividends.

L

L MONETARY AGGREGATE. M3 + short-term Treasury securities + commercial paper + saving bonds + banker's acceptances.

L.C.L. LOT. Less than carload lot. The rate charges for shipping less than a full rail car of freight.

LABOUR MARKET. The mix of available workers and labour costs available to companies.

LABOUR UNION. An association or workers intended to promote and protect the welfare interests and rights of its members, primarily by collective bargaining.

LAG EFFECT. A functional relationship between one variable in the current time period and another variable in the previous time periods. Thus it might be postulated that the increase in current consumer spending is the effect of a bull run in the stock markets in the previous year.

LAG STRATEGY. An operational strategy that involves delaying collections of foreign currency receivables if the currency is expected to strengthen or delaying payment of foreign-currency is expected to weaken; the opposite of a lead strategy.

LAISSEZ FAIRE. The concept of minimal government intervention is a society's economic activity.

LAISSEZ FAIRE. A French phrase meaning to let alone used to describe an economic system where government intervention is minimal.

LAMBDA. A measure of the change in an option premium with respect to a unit change in the price volatility of the options underlying asset.

LAND. In the economic terms, it represents any natural resources.

LAST IN FIRST OUT. A cost-flow assumption that the stock acquired earliest is still on hand; the stock of merchandise or material acquired latest is used first.

LATIN AMERICAN FREE TRADE ASSOCIATION (LAFTA). A free-trade area formed by Mexico and the South America countries in 1960; it was replaced by ALADI in 1980.

LATTICE. A tree describing the evolution of an asset price or interest rate over time. The branches in the lattice recombine. If the branches do not recombine, the lattice is usually called a bushy lattice.

LAUNDER. Transfer of funds to conceal their origin.

LAUNDERING. It is a method of disguising the origin of funds by moving them rapidly from one account or country to another, making it difficult to trace their origin, movements and the ultimate destination, counterfeit or stolen money may be laundered.

LAW OF DEMAND. A law of economics which states that as the price of a good or service rises, consumers will purchase less of it.

LAW OF DIMINISHING MARGINAL RETURNS. Economic principal which states that as the amount of one input increases and all other inputs remain constant, the marginal product of the input eventually begins to decline.

LAW OF LARGE MEMBERS. Implies that if individual withdrawal decisions are independent and the number of depositors gets closer and closer to the probability that one depositor withdraws his deposits.

LAW OF PERSISTENT UNDERDEVELOPMENT. Severe environmental constraints tend to perpetuate low development in a nation.

LAW OF SUPPLY. More goods or services are provided when the price is high than when it is low.

LAW. A rule of action or conduct created and enforced by an organized government.

LEAD COUNTRY STRATEGY. A strategy of introducing a product on a test basis in a small-country market that is considered representation of a region before investing to serve larger country markets.

LEAD STRATEGY. An operational strategy that involves collecting foreign currency receivables early when the currency is expected to weaken expected to strengthen; the opposite of a lag strategy.

LEAD SUBSIDIARY ORGANIZATION. A foreign subsidiary that has global responsibility (serves as corporate headquarters) for one of a company's products of functions.

LEAD TIME. The time interval between placing an order and receiving delivery.

LEAD TIME. Lead time is the time normally taken in replenishing inventory after the order has been placed.

LEADERSHIP CONTINUUM. The concept advanced by Tannenbaum and Schmidt in which leadership is seen as involving a variety of styles ranging from highly boss-centred to highly subordinate-centred, depending on situations and personalities.

LEADERSHIP, DEFINITION OF. Influence, or the art or process of influencing people so that they strive willingly and enthusiastically toward the accomplishment of group goals.

LEADING. The function of managers involving the process of influencing people so that they will contribute to organization and group goals.

LEAPS. Long Term Equity Anticipation Securities (long term options on the S&P 500 index).

LEARNING CURVE. A concept used to support the infant industry argument for protection it assumed that costs will decrease as workers and managers gain more experience.

LEASE. Lease is a contract between a lessor, the owner of the asset and a lessee, the user of the asset. Under the contract, the owner gives the right to use the asset to the user over an agreed period of time for a consideration called the lease rental. The lessee pays the rental to the lessor as regular fixed payments over a period of time at the beginning or at the end of a month, quarter, half-year or year. Thus the ownership of the asset is retained by the lessor but the right of the use of the asset is given to the lessee for an agreed period of time in return for a series of rentals paid by the lessee to the lessor.

LEASE LINE. A lease line of credit similar to a bank line of credit which allows a lessee to add equipment, as needed, under the same basic terms and conditions without negotiating a new lease contract.

LEASE PURCHASE. As an alternative to outright purchase where the company regards eventual ownership as desirable. Legally hire purchase but with a different rental stream.

LEASE RATE. The equivalent simple annual interest rate implicit in minimum lease rentals. Not the same as interest rate implicit in a lease.

LEASE RENTAL. Lessee pays lease rentals to the lessor periodically for the use of the asset.

LEASE TERM. The fixed non-cancellable term of the lease, includes for accounting purposes, all period covered by fixed-rate renewal options which for economic reasons appear lively to be exercised at the inception of the lease and for tax purposes, all periods covered by fixed-rate renewal options.

LEASE UNDERWRITING. An agreement whereby a packager commits firmly to enter into a lease on certain terms and assumes the risk of arranging any financing.

LEASE. A contract between a lessor and a lessee for the hire of a specific asset. The ownership of the asset is retained by the lessor but the right to the use of the asset is given to the lessee for an agreed period of time in return for a series of rentals paid by the lessee to the lessor.

LEDGER. A group of accounts.

LEGAL FORM. A contract may be written or verbal depending upon its nature and provisions and the state in which it is enacted.

LEGAL PURPOSE. A requirement of valid contracts which means that the contract must call for action that is legal under law.

LEGAL RESERVES. Vault cash and reserve deposits at federal Reserve banks.

LEGAL VALUE. Par or stated value that is almost always far below the actual cash invested by a stockholder.

LEGISLATIVE LAGS. Lags in the enactment of the appropriate legislation needed for a policy action to occur.

LEGITIMACY OF ORGANIZATIONAL INFLUENCE. Acceptance by others of an organization's authority to require a specific standard of performance from them.

LENDER. He makes money available to the firm on a lending basis and retains title to the funds lent.

LENIENT CREDIT POLICY. Credits once granted for longer periods even to those customers whose credit worthiness is not fully known or whose financial position is doubtful.

LEONTIEF PARADOX. A surprising finding by Wassily Leontief that over all U.S. exports were less capital intensive and more labour intensive than U.S. imports.

LESS DEVELOPED COUNTRY (LDC). *See* Third world country.

LESSEE. A person who pays the rent for an asset or property from another person for an agreed period of time. The user of the equipment being leased.

LESSEE'S INCREMENTAL BORROWING RATE. The interest rate which the lessee, at the inception of the lease, would have incurred to borrow over a similar term the funds necessary to purchase the leased assets. In a leveraged lease, the rate on the bonds is normally used.

LESSOR. The owner of the equipment which is being leased to a lessee or user.

LETTER OF CREDIT. A precise document by which the import's bank extends credit to the importer and agrees to pay the exporter.

LEVEL PAYMENTS. Equal payments over the term of the lease.

LEVERAGE LEASE. A lease which meets the definition criteria for a direct financing lease or a capital lease, plus all of the following characteristics: (a) At least three parties are involved; a lessee, a lessor, and a long-term creditor; (b) The financing provided by the creditor is substantial to the transaction and without recourse to the lessor; (c) The lessor's net investment typically declines during the early years of the lease and rises during the late years of the lease.

LEVERAGE. A portfolio position using borrowing to finance a purchase.

LEVERAGE. An amount borrowed. A lease is sometimes referred to as 100 per cent leverage for the lessee. In a leveraged lease, the debt portion of the funds used to purchase the asset represents leverage of the equity holder.

LIABILITIES. Probable future sacrifices of economic benefits stemming from present legal, equitable, or constructive obligations of a particular enterprise to transfer assets or provide services to other entities in the future as a result of past transactions or events affecting the enterprise.

LIABILITIES. Liabilities are debts payable in the future by the firm to its creditors. They represent economic obligations to pay cash or to provide goods or services in some future period. Liabilities are two types. (1) current liabilities (2) long-term liabilities. Debts of an individual or business firm.

LIABILITY OF FOREIGNNESS. Foreign companies lower survival rate than local companies for many years after they begin operations.

LIBID. London Interbank Bid Rate. The rate at which a bank is willing to lend Eurodollars.

LIBOR. London Interbank Offer Rate. The rate at which a bank is willing to lend Eurodollars.

LIBOR. *See* London Inter-bank offered rate.

LICENCE. Formal or legal permission to do some specified action a governmental method of fixing the exchange rate by requiring all recipients exporters and others that receive foreign exchange to sell it to the Central bank at the official buying rate.

LICENSING AGREEMENT. A procedure that requires potential importers or exporters to secure permission from governmental authorities before they conduct trade transactions.

LIE DETECTOR. (*See* Polygraph.)

LIFETIME EMPLOYMENT. The Japanese custom that workers are effectively guaranteed lifetime employment with the company and that workers seldom leave for employment opportunities with other companies.

LIFFE. London International Financial Futures Exchange.

LIFO INCREMENT. *See* LIFO layer.

LIFO LAYER. A separately identifiable additional segment of LIFO inventory.

LIFO POOL. *See* LIFO layer.

LIFO RESERVE. The amount of "cushion" or "under-statement" of current inventory values that the LIFO method produces in relation to FIFO.

LIFO. *See* last-in, first-out.

LIMITED BRANCHING. Restrictions that limit the ability of banks to open offices within the state's boundary.

LIMITED LIABILITY. Corporate creditors ordinarily have claims against the corporate assets only. Therefore the stockholders as individuals have no liability beyond their original investment in the corporation.

LIMITED LIABILITY. Usually refers to limited partners and corporations it means the owner may lose only his investment and not other assets.

LIMITED PARTNER. A partner who may or may not be active in the business, but who has limited liability. May be silent, secret, dormant or nominal partner.

LIMITED-FUNCTION WHOLESALER. Specializes in one or only a few lines of trade and serves particular customers needs.

LIMITING FACTOR. The item that restricts or constrains the production or sale of a product or services.

LIMITING FACTOR, PRINCIPLE OF. In choosing from among alternatives, the more individuals can recognize and solve for those factors which are limiting or critical to the attainment of the desired goal, the more clearly, accurately, and easily they can select the most favourable alternative.

LINE. An authority relationship in organizational positions where one person (a manager) has responsibility for the activities of another person (the subordinate). It is commonly, but erroneously, though of as a department or a person, and not a relationship; it is also commonly, but inaccurately, thought of as the major departments of an enterprise believed to be most closely contributing to the achieving of enterprise objectives, such as marketing and production in a manufacturing company.

LINE AND STAFF ORGANIZATION. An organization plan which adds specialists or staff personnel who give advice and make recommendations to line managers.

LINE AUTHORITY. Authority that is exerted downward over subordinates.

LINE CHART. A chart useful in presenting data covering longer periods of time.

LINE OF CREDIT. An amount of credit a bank determines it will lend without security being pledged.

LINE ORGANIZATION. The oldest and simplest form of organization plan which is especially suitable for small organizations. Line managers have total and direct authority, and subordinates report to a single supervisor.

LINEAR PROGRAMMING. A technique for determining the optimum combination of limited resources to obtain a desired goal, it is based on assumption that a linear relationship existing between variables and that the limits of variables can be determined.

LIQUID ASSET. An asset is liquid if it can be converted into cash immediately or reasonably soon without a loss of value.

LIQUIDATION VALUE. It is the amount that a company could realize if it has sold its assets, after having terminated its business.

LIQUIDITY (SETTLING) OF FUTURES POSITION. Under the futures contract, the traders have an obligation to take delivery (a long position) or to make delivery (a short position) the underlying commodity. Three ways at liquidating a futures position are : Physical delivery, by making an off setting futures transaction (called offsetting) and by engaging in an exchange for physicals (called an EEP) settlement by cash delivery. The relative ease with which an asset may be converted into the medium of exchange without substantially losing value.

LIQUIDITY PREFERENCE. A theory that helps explain capital budgeting and when applied to international operations means that investors are willing to take less return in order to be able to shift the resources to alternative users.

LIQUIDITY PREMIUM. The additional interest rate lenders must receive to compensate them for liquidity risk.

LIQUIDITY RISK. Risk due to the possibility that it will be necessary to liquidate a bond or other debt instrument prior to maturity, with some probability that the price received in such a situation will be less than favourable.

LLCs. Limited Liability Companies.

LLPs. Limited Liability Partnerships.

LME. London Metal Exchange.

LME. London Metals Exchange.

LOAD FUND. A mutual fund for which the investor pays a commission.

LOAD. A charge by fund when an investor buys (entry load) or sells (exit load) units in the fund. The charge is used to discourage investors from taking short-term positions in the fund's units. As a fund has to sell holdings to pay investors, if too many of them cash this can eat into the fund's overall returns. Most short term funds, like guilt funds and Monday funds, charge no loads. Loads are limited by SEBI regulations to 7% a fund cannot quote a difference of more than 7% between the sale and repurchase price of its units.

LOAN GUARANTEE. An agreement usually by the federal government, to repay a bank loan if a borrower cannot repay it. The borrower pays a fee to the government for this guarantee.

LOAN PARTICIPANT. A lender in a leveraged lease, a holder of debt in a leveraged lease evidenced loan certificates or bonds issued by the owner trustee.

LOAN VALUE. The amount of cash that can be borrowed on a life insurance policy.

LOAN-ABLE FUNDS. Funds supplied by lenders and demanded by borrowers. The prices of these financial services are stated as an interest rate.

LOBBYIST. An individual who participates in advancing or otherwise securing passage of legislation by influencing public officials before and during the legislation process.

LOCAL CONTENT. Costs incurred within a given country, usually as a percentage of total costs.

LOCAL UNION. The primary organizational unit for labour groups.

LOCALLY RESPONSIVE COMPANY. Synonym for multi domestic company.

LOCALS. Citizens of the country in which they are working.

LOCATION ADVANTAGE. The competitive advantage that accrues to a firm when customers value the convenience of utilizing a firm located in close proximity to where they live.

LOCK-IN-PERIOD. The period between the grant of options and vesting of option (at least one year). The company has the freedom to specify the lock-in-period for the shares issued pursuant to exercise of option. The employee does not have right to receive any dividend or to vote or in any manner.

LOCKOUT. Employees are locked out of the firm until a settlement of the labour dispute is reached.

LOG-NORMAL DISTRIBUTION. A probability distribution for a random variable × such that the natural logarithm of × follows a normal distribution.

LONDON INTER-BANK OFFERED RATE (LIBOR). The interest rate for large inter-bank loans of Euro-currencies.

LONDON INTERNATIONAL FINANCIAL FUTURES AND OPTIONS EXCHANGE (LIFFOE). It specializes in futures on financial instrument.

LONDON STOCK EXCHANGE (LSE). A stock exchange located in London and dealing in Euro-equities.

LONG HEDGE. A future or option position to protect against a possible increase in prices.

LONG LIVED ASSETS. Resources that held for an extended time, such as land, buildings, equipment, natural resources, and patents.

LONG POSITION. A position in an asset that has been purchased.

LONG TERM ASSETS. Assets in the debt market which mature more than ten years from the date of issue.

LONG TERM INVESTMENTS. Represents the firm's investments in debentures, shares, bonds of other firms or government bodies for profits and control. These investments are held for a period of time greater than the accounting period. Usually long-term investments are shown at the original cost but the current market price may also be indicated.

LONG-RUN AGGREGATE SUPPLY CURVE (I.R.A.S). Characterizes the supply side of the macroeconomy in the long run *i.e.* summarizes the total quantity of goods and services that an economy will produce at various price levels, after allowing the prices of inputs and prices expectations to adjust to any changes in the price level.

LONG-TERM LIABILITIES. Liabilities (debts) that are not

payable for one year or more.

LOOP. Circular chain of shareholding, *e.g.* A owns 20 per cent of stock of B, B owns 20 per cent of the stock of C, C owns 20 per cent of the stock of D, and D owns 20 per cent of the stock of A.

LOSSES. Losses (or other appropriately descriptive terms) are decreases in owners' equity (net assets) from peripheral or incidental transactions of an enterprise and from all other transactions and other events and circumstances affecting the enterprise during the period excepts those that result from expenses or distributions by the enterprise to owners.

LOW BALL BID. A bid to perform a lease transaction purposely priced below market or with terms not acceptable from a tax or accounting stand point, with a view to renegotiating of a higher price and/ or more expensive terms at a late date once the bid is awarded the low ball bidder and the other interested lessor are no longer available. Typically the low ball bidder raises the price when it is too late for the lessee to seek other leasing sources.

LOW LOAD FUND. Mutual fund that charges a low initial fees.

LOW PAY-OUT CLIENTELE. Investors in high-tax brackets desire the company to declare low dividends and retain more, as to avoid tax burden.

LOW-CONTEXT CULTURE. A culture in which most people consider relevant only information that they receive firsthand and that bears very directly on the decision they need to make.

LOWER OF COST OR MARKET. The superimposition of a market-price test on an inventory cost method.

LUDDITIES. Groups of early nineteenth century English workers who believing that machines took away jobs from workers destroyed factory machinery.

LUXURY TAX. It is the tax assessed against non-essential items, such as built-in swimming pools, etc.

M

$M^S = [(1+C^D)/(RR+E^D+C^D)] \times M\,B$(14).

M1 MONEY AGGREGATE. Currency + demand deposits + traveller's cheque + other checkable deposits.

M1. This is a symbol used to represent the money supply. M1 represents the narrow version of money, comprising the total value of bank notes and coins in circulation together with national currency and bank deposits on current account.

M2 MONEY AGGREGATE. M1 + savings deposits + small time deposits + money market deposit accounts + money market mutual shares (not owned by institutions) + overnight repurchase agreement + overnight Eurodollars.

M2 MONEY SUPPLY. It is defined as notes and coins in circulation plus non-interest bearing bank deposits, building society deposits and National Savings accounts.

M3 MONEY AGGREGATE. M2 + large denomination time deposits + money market mutual shares (institutional) + term repurchases agreements + term Eurodollars. This represents a broader version of money supply comprising in addition to M1, interest bearing deposit accounts (including deposits in any currency held by the citizens of the concerned country) and certificates of deposits.

MAASTRICHT TREATY. The leaders of the 12 European Community (EC) nations — Great Britain, France, Germany, Italy, Belgium, Denmark, Netherlands, Spain, Portugal, Greece and Luxembourg — reached an agreement in December, 1991 on a former plan to create a closure economic and political Union. The treaty on European Union was finalized at a summit at Maastricht in the Netherlands, and it came to be known informally as the Maastricht Treaty. The treaty and its provisions were binding on the existing EC members as well as post-communist nations in Eastern Europe that sought to join the Union. The

Maastricht Pact created a new common European entity, the European Union (EU), which would have greater powers than the old EC over matters that had previously been the jurisdiction of national governments. The EU was intended to pursue a common foreign policy and defence policy and coordinated economic agenda. The treaty took effect on November 1st, 1993.

MAASTRICHT [TREATY OF]. The treaty approved in December 1991 that was designed to bring the EU to a higher level of integration and is divided into Economic and Monetary Union (EMU) and political union.

MACRO POLITICAL RISK. Negative political actions affecting a broad spectrum of foreign investors.

MACRO-PRUDENTIAL INDICATORS. Indicators of the health and stability of the financial system.

MAGNETIZING THE DEFICIT. Paying for government spending by printing money.

MAIL ORDER HOUSE. Selling by means of catalogue orders.

MAIN FRAME COMPUTER. A full-scale computer that is capable of handling huge amounts of data. Some of these "supercomputers" are used for engineering, simulation, and the manipulation of large.

MAINTENANCE MARGIN. Maintenance margin is an additional margin required by the broker from the client. When there has been a price decline or advance on the loss in the margin account, the client should deposit just enough money to bring the amount of margin back to the original margin then the client can continue trading. The call for then maintenance margin is a variation call because a change in the market price required the additional margin.

MAINTENANCE MARGIN. The minimum amount of margin that must be kept in a margin account after its initiation.

MALONEY ACT. Provides for setting up the National Association of securities dealers, a self-regulating agency or over the counter dealers.

MANAGED COSTS. *See* Discretionary costs.

MANAGEMENT ACCOUNTING. Concerned mainly with how accounting can serve internal decision makers. Defined as the process of identification, measurement, accumulation, analysis, preparation interpretation, and communication of information that assists executives in fulfilling organizational objectives.

MANAGEMENT AS A SCIENCE. Organized knowledge — concepts, theory, principles, and techniques — underlying the practice of managing science systematically explains phenomena in managing as it does in any field.

MANAGEMENT AS AN ART. The use of underlying knowledge and application of it to realities in a situation, usually with blend or compromise, to obtain practical results : managing is an art but management is more properly used to refer to the body of knowledge — science — underlying this art.

MANAGEMENT AUDITING. Auditing the quality of managers through appraising them as individual managers and appraising the quality of the total system of managing in an enterprise.

MANAGEMENT BY EXCEPTION. The practice by the executive of focusing his or her attention mainly on significant deviations from expected results. It might also be called management by variance.

MANAGEMENT BY OBJECTIVES (**MBO**). Joint formulation by a manager and his or her superior of a set of goals and of plans for achieving the goals for a forthcoming period.

MANAGEMENT BY OBJECTIVES. A performance appraisal plan in which each subordinate sets his own goals as the basis for improving his own performance.

MANAGEMENT CONTRACT. An arrangement whereby one company provides management personnel to perform general or specialized management functions to another company for a fee.

MANAGEMENT DEVELOPMENT. Programmes designed to provide managers with opportunity to improve their managerial skills and also to provide training for potential managers.

MANAGEMENT INFORMATION SYSTEM. A formal system to gather, integrate compare analyze, and disperse information internal and external to the enterprise in a timely, effective, and efficient manner.

MANAGEMENT INVENTORY. A technique usually by use of chart, whereby managers in an enterprise are designated as promotable now. Promotable in one year. Have potential for future promotion are satisfactory but not promotable or should be terminated. Another term for "inventory chart" is "management replacement chart".

MANAGEMENT TECHNIQUES. Ways of doing things in managing.

MANAGEMENT THEORY JUNGLE. The term applied by Harold Koontz in 1961 identify the existence of a variety of schools of, or approaches to, management theory and knowledge. He found just six such schools or approaches in 1961, but in 1979 identified eleven. He found that the school or approaches tended to vary in their semantics and their view of management, and approached the theory of management from different specialists points of view.

MANAGEMENT TRAINING. The provision of opportunities through various approaches and programmes to improve a person's knowledge of, and proficiency in, the managerial task.

MANAGEMENT. The process of designing and maintaining environment in which individuals work together in groups accomplish efficiently selected aims.

MANAGER. One who gets things done through others. He oversees work.

MANAGER DEVELOPMENT. The progress a person makes in learning how to manage effectively.

MANAGERIAL APPRAISAL. Evaluating the performance of managers in their positions, ideally evaluating performance in setting and achieving verifiable objectives and performance as a manager.

MANAGERIAL EFFORT. Exertion toward a goal. Includes all actions (such as watching or thinking) that result in more efficiency and effectiveness.

MANAGERIAL GRID. A way of analyzing leadership styles, developed by Blake and Mouton whereby leaders are classified on a grid with the two dimensions of concern for people and concern for production.

MANAGERIAL KNOW-HOW. Managerial knowledge applied effectively in practice; it includes both knowledge of the science underlying managing and the artful ability to apply it to realities.

MANAGERS. Those who undertake the tasks and functions of managing, at any level in any end of enterprise.

MANAGERS, FUNCTION OF. To so planning, organizing, staffing, leading, and controlling.

MANAGERS, GOAL OF. To so establish and maintain an environment for performance that individuals will contribute to group objectives with the least cost — whether money, time, effort, materials, discomfort, or dissatisfaction — to create a surplus value, or 'profit'.

MANAGERS, TASK OF. The design and maintenance of an environment for the effective and efficient performance of individuals working together in groups toward the accomplishment of reselected missions and objectives.

MANAGING BY OBJECTIVES. Programmes of basing much of managerial planning, operation, and appraisal on having each manager set objectives in verifiable terms (with the superior's approval) and assessing his or her performance against the achievement of these objectives. Sometimes called management by objectives or 'MBO'. More recently, MBO is seen as a system of managing that includes key manorial activities in planning, organizing, staffing, leading, and controlling.

MANUFACTURER'S AGENT. Represents more than one manufacturer simultaneously and sells only a part of the manufacturer's goods in a limited geographical area.

MANUFACTURER-OWNED STORE. A retailing outlet owned by the manufacturing.

MANUFACTURING AUTOMATION PROTOCOL (MAP). A network of machines and various office devices looked together. General motors, for example, has been very active in linking robots with numerically controlled machine tools.

MANUFACTURING EXPENSES. *See* Factory overhead.

MANUFACTURING INTERCHANGE. A process by which various plants produce a range of components and exchange them so that all plants assemble the finished product for the local market.

MANUFACTURING OVERHEAD. *See* Factory overhead.

MAQUILADORA. An individual operation developed by the Mexican and U.S. governments in which U.S. sourced components are shipped to Mexico duty free assembled into final products and re-exported to the United States.

MAREVA INJUNCTION. Injunction that prevents the transfer of funds overseas until a case concerning them has been heard in the UK courts.

MARGIN. The Dollar amount of cash or securities used as collateral to purchase some derivative security or asset.

MARGIN CALL. A demand made by clearing house to a clearing member, or by a brokerage firm to a customer, for additional funds.

MARGIN CASH FLOWS. The members at an exchange are classified as clearing members and non-clearing members. Non-clearing member must clear his/her trades through a clearing member. The clearing house demands margin deposits for clearing member to cover all future positions that are carried out by that clearing member.

MARGIN REQUIREMENT. The percentage of down payment required by the federal reserve on stock and other securities.

MARGINAL ACCOUNT. The customer with moderate financial health and risk.

MARGINAL COST. The change in total cost caused by a one dollar change in the amounts of loans.

MARGINAL COST OF CAPITAL. The weighted average cost of new or incremental capital is termed as the marginal cost of capital.

MARGINAL COSTING. *See* Contribution margin.

MARGINAL PRODUCT. The change in total product (or total output) that results from a one-unit change in the usage of a variable input. Holding the quantities of other inputs constant.

MARGINAL PROPENSITY TO IMPORT. The tendency to purchase imports with incremental income.

MARGINAL RESOURCE COST OF DEPOSITS. The change in a bank's cost of deposits arising from a one dollar change in its deposits.

MARGINAL REVENUE. The change in total revenue caused by a one dollar increase in the amount of loans.

MARGINAL REVENUE PRODUCT OF DEPOSITS. The marginal product of deposits multiplied by the marginal revenue of a loan indicates the additional revenue earned by a bank if it attracts another $1 in deposits.

MARGINAL SOCIAL COST. The cost of an additional unit of production to society as a whole, taking into account external economies and diseconomies so that optimal conditions can be formulated by a programme of taxes and subsidies, an attempt can be made to alter the marginal costs of individual firms until they equal the marginal social cost causing an increase in welfare for society as a whole.

MARGINAL UTILITY OF MONEY. It indicates that an investor always prefers a higher return to a lower return and that each successive identical increment of money is worth less to him than the preceding one.

MARKET BY ORDER. The purpose of market by order is to enable the trading member participant to view outstanding orders in the trading books in the order of price/ time.

MARKET BY PRICE. The purpose of market by price is to enable the trading members or participants to view aggregate outstanding orders in the trading book at different prices.

MARKET CAPITALIZATION. A common measure of the size of a stock market which is computed by multiplying the total number of shares of stock listed on the exchange by the market price per share.

MARKET ECONOMY. An economic system in which resources are allocated and controlled by consumers who "vote" by buying goods.

MARKET ENVIRONMENT. The environment that involves the interactions between households (or individuals) and companies to allocate resources free from governmental ownership or control.

MARKET FRICTIONS. Conditions in the market that make trading costly or restrict trading.

MARKET LOT. Market lot is the minimum number of shares of a particular security that must be transacted on the exchange. Multiples of the market lot may also be transacted. In demat scrips the market lost is 'l' share.

MARKET TO BOOK RATIO. Market price of a share divided by book value per share.

MARKET VALUE. A bond/ debenture may be traded in a stock exchange sold or bought is called the market value of the bond/debenture.

MARKET VALUE ADDED (MVA). It is the excess of the market value of the company over the value of investors capital. In other words, current market value of debt plus equity, minus economic book value (the sum of share capital, free reserves and debt).

MARKET VALUE TO BOOK VALUE (MV/BV RATIO). It is the ratio of market price of share to the book value per share. Note, the book value per share is the net worth divided by the number of shares outstanding.

MARKET VALUE WEIGHTS. Weighted cost of capital computed using market value weights is known as market value weights.

MARKET VALUE-TO-BOOK VALUE (MV/BV RATIO). It is the ratio of market price of share to the book value per share. Note, the book value per share is the net worth divided by the number of shares outstanding.

MARKET WATCH WINDOW. The market watch window is the main focus for a trading member. The purpose of market watch is to view market information at preselected securities that are of interest to the trading member.

MARKETABLE SECURITIES. Any notes, bonds, or stocks that can readily be sold via public markets. The term is often used as a synonym for short-term investment.

MARKETING FUNCTIONS. Activities that must be performed for goods and services to move from producer to consumer. Marketing functions include selling, buying transportation, storage, risk bearing, standardization and grading, financing, and market programme.

MARKETING MANAGER. Makes the management decision about the firm's marketing programme.

MARKETING STRATEGY. Identifying the customers to whom the firm will appeal and deciding upon the activities needed to satisfy the customers in the market segment.

MARKETING VARIANCE. Synonym for sales volume variance.

MARKETING. The performance of business activities that direct the flow of goods and services from producer to consumer or user.

MARKOV EXPECTATIONS HYPOTHESIS. Asserts that individuals expect the future to be like the most recent past.

MARK-TO-MARKET. The process to record daily price changes in the futures markets and to debit or credit accounts.

MARTINGALE. A stochastic processes the expected value of which equals the current value.

MARTINGALE PRICING. A pricing method that used martingale probabilities to compute present values.

MARTINGALE PROBABILITIES. The probabilities used in the risk neutral valuation techniques.

MARXIST THEORY. This theory is about political and economic system largely based on theories developed by Karl Marx, in which the State makes the major economic decisions, owning the capital assets being responsible for production and distribution.

MASS PRODUCTION. Large scale production employing standardized parts.

MASTER BUDGET. The budget that consolidates the organization's overall plans.

MASTER BUDGETED SALES. The expected sales employed in formulating the master budget for the period.

MASTER LEASE. A lease line of credit which allows a lessee to add equipment under the same basic terms and conditions without negotiating a new lease contract.

MATCHING. Establishing a relationship between efforts (expenses) and accomplishments (revenues).

MATCHING AND COST RECOVERY. The procedure of accrual accounting whereby expenses are either directly attributed to related revenues (matching) of a given period or are otherwise regarded as costs that will not be recovered from revenue in future periods. In short, cost recovery is the justification for carrying un-expired costs as assets rather than writing them off expenses.

MATCHING PRINCIPLE. It requires the expenses be reflected in the same period as the revenues to which they are related.

MATERIALITY. The accounting convenient that justifies the exclusion of insignificant information from financial reports. Whether an item is material (significant) is a matter of professional judgment.

MATIF. Marche a Terme International deFrance.

MATRIX. A method of plotting data on a set of vertical and horizontal axes, in order to compare countries in terms of risk and opportunity.

MATRIX ORGANIZATION. A form of organization in which two or more basic types of departmentation are combined; in engineering and marketing this is likely to be a combination of project (or product) and functional departments with one overlaying the other; often referred to as 'grid' organization structures, 'project' or 'product' management.

MATRIX STRUCTURE. An organizational structure in which foreign units report (by product, function, or area) to more than one group each of which shares responsibility over the foreign unit.

MATURITY DATE. The date on which a derivative security contract matures.

MATURITY FACTORING. Implies that payment will be made to the client on maturity.

MATURITY. It refers to the time period over which interest and principal are to be made.

MAY TAKE the form of an outlay cost or an opportunity cost.

MBO. Symbol for management by objectives.

MCE. Mid America Commodity Exchange.

McFADDEN ACT [1927]. Legislation introduced to allow states to write laws regulating branch banking within their boundaries, and gave states the power to impose these rules on national banks and banks chartered in other states.

ME. Montreal Exchange Canada.

MEDIA. The means by which advertising messages are conveyed.

MEDIAN. The value which divides an arrayed list of figures in half.

MEDIATION. The third party the mediator can make specific recommendations for the settlement of a labour management dispute.

MEDIUM OF EXCHANGE. Whatever is commonly accepted as payment for goods and services, or to repay debts. The distinguishing feature of money.

MEGA-CORPORATION. One of the very largest business corporations.

MEGA-GROWTH. A company that has the ability to offer more services than any similar firm that has capital totalling at least $25 bn.

MEGALOPOLIS. A continuous and very extensive city development that occurs when urban and suburban populations expand and merge geographically.

MEMORY. The computer's storage bank.

MENTAL ABILITY TEST. A test of general verbal ability reasoning ability, visualizing ability, and social perceptions.

MENTOR. A person at headquarters who looks after the interests of an expatriate employee.

MERCANTILISM. An economic philosophy based on the beliefs that a country's wealth is dependent on its holdings of treasure, usually in the form of gold, and that countries should export more than they import in order to increase wealth.

MERCHANDISE ACCOUNT. A part of the current account that consists of exports and imports of goods and services, or to repay debts. The distinguishing feature of money.

MERCHANDISE IMPORTS. Goods brought into a country.

MERCHANDISE TRADE ACCOUNT. The part of a country's current account that measures the trade deficit or surplus, its balance is the net of merchandise imports and exports.

MERCHANDISE TRADE BALANCE. The difference between merchandise exports and merchandise imports.

MERCOSUR. A major subregional groups composed of Argentina, Brazil, Paraguay and Uruguay, which spun off from ALADI in 1991 with the goal of setting up a customs union and common market.

MERGER. The acquisition of one company by another.

MEZZANINE BRACKET. An underwriter, who is next to the major underwriters, subscribes to the next largest portion of the issue.

MEZZANINE FINANCE. Money lent to a small and growing, but financially viable company. It is so-called because the risk of making the loan falls between that of advancing venture capital and the safer course of putting the finance into established debt markets.

MFA. *See* Multifibre arrangement.

MFN. *See* Most-favoured nation clause.

MGE. Minneapolis Grain Exchange.

MICRO POLITICAL RISK. Negative political actions aimed at specific rather than most foreign investors.

MICROCOMPUTER. Smaller than the minicomputer; may be a desk computer, home computer, personal computer, portable computer, or a computer for a small business system.

MICRO-HEDGE. A hedge that reduces the risk involved in owning a security or an asset.

MICROPROCESSOR. A small silicon chip capable of a very large number of computational operations (*See* Semiconductor silicon chips).

MIDDLE EAST. The countries on the Arabian peninsula plus those bordering the eastern end of the Mediterranean; sometimes also including other adjacent countries, particularly Jordan, Iraq, Iran and Kuwait.

MILESTONE BUDGETING. Budgeting by breaking down a programme or project into identifiable and controllable pieces, or 'milestones'.

MINICOMPUTER. Small than the mainframe computer but more powerful than the microcomputer. This kind of computer is often connected with peripheral equipment.

MINIMUM FILL. Minimum fill order allows the trading member to specify the minimum amount by which an order should be filled for example an order of 1000 with minimum fill of 200 will require that each trade be for at least 200.

MINIMUM LEASE PAYMENTS FOR THE LESSOR. The payments considered minimum lease payments for the lease plus any guarantee by a third party of the residual value payments beyond the lease term.

MINIMUM-RISK HEDGE RATIO. The number of futures or option contracts that results in the maximum possible reduction in the variability of the value of the total hedged position.

MINISTRY OF INTERNATIONAL TRADE AND INDUSTRY (MITI). The Japanese government agency responsible for coordinating overall business direction and helping individual companies take advantage of global business opportunities.

MINORITY ENTERPRISE PROGRAMME. A programme to provide assistance in making business opportunities available to minority group members.

MINORITY INTEREST. The total shareholder interest (other than the parent's) in a subsidiary corporation.

MINORITY. A racial or religious group that is different from the majority group.

MINORITY-INTEREST. The portion of the equity that is not owned by the consolidator or holding company is shown as a 'minority-interest' liability on the balance sheet. Net income on the statement of income is reduced by the portion accruing to minority interests.

MIRROR PRINCIPLE. A human relations concept that contends that people react in the same manner as they receive action.

MISSION STATEMENT. A long range strategic intent.

MISSION, OR PURPOSE. The basic function or task of an enterprise or agency or any department of it.

MISSION. What the company will seek to do and become over the long term.

MISSIONARY SALESPERSON. Works with middlemen and their customers and assists in setting up promotional displays or training sales force.

MIXED COST. A cost that has both fixed and variable elements.

MIXED ECONOMY. An economic system characterized by some mixture of market and command economics and public and private ownership.

MIXED STATE AND PRIVATE ENTERPRISE. A socioeconomic system in which government owns and key industrial and financial enterprises but most business are owned and operated by private individuals and corporations.

MIXED VENTURE. A special type of joint venture in which a government is in partnership with a private company.

MNE. *See* Multinational enterprise.

MODE. The point of greatest concentration.

MODEL. A depiction of interrelationships of recognized factors in a real situation.

MODEL MIS SPECIFICATION. The error in a given mode.

MODERN QUANTITY THEORY OF MONEY DEMAND. Model of money demand developed by Milton Friedman that builds on the simple quantity theory by phasing the unique property of money as the medium of exchange.

MODIFICATIONS. A form of synthetic process in which materials are altered to form a product.

MODIFIED DURATION. Duration divided by one plus the bond's yield.

MONETARY AGGREGATES. Ways of adding up the quantity of different assets in the economy into a measure of the money stock.

MONETARY BASE. Currency in the hands of the public plus commercial bank reserves also called high powered money.

MONETARY ECONOMY. An economy in which money is used in most transactions, such as buying or selling goods and services.

MONETARY-ITEMS. A claim receivable or payable in a specified number of dollars; the claim remains fixed regardless of changes in either specific or general price levels.

MONETARY POLICY. A tool of general macro-economic policy under the control of monetary authorities that seeks to attain government's economic objectives by influencing money supply and/or rate of interest and therefore credit. The use of interest rates and controls on the money supply by the government or Central Bank to influence the methods of monetary policy include setting of interest rates changed by the Central Bank, sales or purchases of securities to control the money supply and changes in the required reserve ratios of banks and other financial institutions.

MONETARY POLICY ACTIONS. Government actions directed at the money supply.

MONETARY POLICY GAME. A situation where strategic interactions between the fed and the private sector make the payoffs resulting from their actions interdependent.

MONETARY UNION. A group of nations that have agreed on exchange rates so as to make their currencies interchangeable.

MONETIZATION. Financing the national debt by printing new money, which causes inflation as a result of a larger money supply.

MONEY. Anything that is widely and generally accepted as a medium of exchange.

MONEY MARKET. The financial market in which the most liquid, short term debt obligations are traded. Typically this term refers to the market for financial instruments that mature in one year or less.

MONEY MARKET ACCOUNT. An investment that earns interest at the spot rate of interest.

MONEY MARKET INSTRUMENTS. Money markets are for borrowing and lending money for one year or less. The securities in a money market can be Government Bonds, Treasury bills and commercial paper from banks and companies.

MONEY MARKET MUTUAL FUND (MMMF). A fund that invests in short term debt, such as treasury bills, or short-term commercial paper. Their goal is to preserve principal while yielding a modest return. They are favoured by investors looking for low risk of investment avenues and who prefer instant liquidity. Mutual funds that sell shares of the fund to savers and invests in short term. Safe asserts such as treasury bills, large bank certificates of deposit, commercial paper, and banker's acceptance.

MONEY ORDER. A check purchased at a post office or express office which is payable at another post office or express office.

MONEY STOCK. The total amount of money in the economy.

MONEY SUPPLY. The total amount of currency and demand deposits in circulation in the United States at any time.

MONEY SUPPLY CURVE. The amount of money that suppliers are willing and able to supply at various interest rates.

MONEY SUPPLY EQUATION. A relation that indicates how much money is created in the economy for a given monetary base. M^s = [(1+c^d)/(rr+ e^d+c^d)] × MB(14).

MONISM. A social system with one centralized power structure that governs all human affairs.

MONOCHRONIC CULTURE. A culture in which most people prefer to deal with situations sequentially (especially those involving other people), such as finishing with one customer before dealing with another.

MONOPOLIES AND RESTRICTIVE TRADE PRACTICES (MRTP) ACT.

MONOPOLY. The market structure in which there is only one seller for the entire market.

MONOPOLY. An industry or market with one producer or seller.

MONOPOLY ADVANTAGE. The perceived supremacy of foreign investors in relation to local companies, which is necessary to overcome the perceived greater risk of operating in a different environment.

MORAL SUASION. The Fed's ability to persuade depository institutions and other financial institutions to be have in what it regards as the public's best interest.

MORAL HAZARD. A situation created by ex-post asymmetric information that induces one party to take an action that is undesirable from the other part's perspective, for instance reduces the incentive for individuals to guard themselves against risk.

MORALE. The mental attitude of employees concerning their work environment.

MORALITY. A situation in which the most fundamental human values are preserved and allowed to shape human thought and action.

MORBIDITY. The term refers to the probability or the risk of disability.

MORTGAGE. A debt instrument used to finance the purchase of homes and other forms of real estate when the underlying real estate serves as collectoral for the loan.

MORTGAGE BOND. A bond secured by the real property of the firm (plant, equipment).

MOST–FAVOURED-NATION (MFN) CLAUSE. A GATT requirement that a trade concession that is given to one country must be given to all other countries.

MOTIVATION. It is derived from the word "motive" and is an emotion or desire operating on a person will and causing that person to act.

MOTIVATION. The reasons people have for doing things. Most motivations are the result of reward or punishment.

MOTIVATIONS RESEARCH. A technique designed to discover the underlying motives of consumer behaviour.

MOTIVATORS. Forces that induce individuals to act or perform; forces that influence human behaviour.

MOTIVES. The drives, desires, needs, wishes, and similar forces that channel human behaviour toward goals.

MOTOR CARRIER ACT. Regulates motor and water carriers engaged in interstate or foreign transportation of passengers or property.

MOVING AVERAGE. A moving average is an average of the current and a given number of lagged values of a variable. Each time we add another observation we delete the observation furthest in the past when we calculate the moving average.

MPLS. Minneapolis Grain Exchange.

MULTI-DOMESTIC COMPANY. A company with international operations that allows operations in one country to be relatively independent of those in other countries.

MULTI-FIBER ARRANGEMENT (MFA). *See* Arrangement regarding international trade in textiles.

MULTILATERAL AGREEMENT. An agreement involving more than two governments.

MULTILATERAL INVESTMENT GUARANTEE AGENCY (MIGA). A member of the World Bank Group that encourages equity investment and other direct investment flows to developing countries by offering investors a variety of different services.

MULTINATIONAL CORPORATION. A company that conducts business in two or more nations, usually employing citizens of various nationalities.

MULTINATIONAL CORPORATIONS (MNC). Corporations headquartered usually in one country, but having operations (usually at least manufacturing and market) in other countries.

MULTINATIONAL ENTERPRISE (MNE). A company that has an integrated global philosophy encompassing both domestic and overseas operations; sometimes used synonymously with multinational corporation or transnational corporations.

MULTIPLE DEPOSIT EXPANSION. The process whereby depository institutions create money in the form of checkable deposits that are multiple of the monetary base.

MULTIPLE EXCHANGE-RATE SYSTEM. A means of foreign exchange control whereby the government sets different exchange rates for different transactions.

MULTIPLIER EFFECT. A situation in which one event leads to more than one other related event.

MULTI-STEP PROFIT AND LOSS ACCOUNT. This gives more useful information. It makes a distinction between operating revenue and the non-operating revenue.

MUNICIPAL BONDS. A bond issued by state or local governments in finance building highways, schools, etc.

MUSAHI LEASE. A Japanese leasing structure using foreign currencies.

MUSLIM LAW. *See* Islamic law.

MUSTER LEASE. Muster Lease provides for a period longer than the asset's life and holds the lessor responsible for providing equipment in good operating condition during the lease period.

MUSTER ROLL. Register of the holders of the security.

MUTUAL ASSETS. Requirements of a valid contract specify all parties must agree to the contract of their own free will.

MUTUAL FUNDS. Companies that sell their own stock to obtain money which they invest in the securities market.

MUTUAL SAVINGS BANKS. A depository institution designed to promote mortgage lending, much like savings and loans, but owned cooperatively by members with a common interest, such as employees of a company, union members, or members of a church.

N

NAA. *See* National Association of Accountants.

NAKED OPTION POSITION. An option position with no associated position in the underlying asset.

NASD. National Association of Securities Dealers, a self-regulating agency of over the counter dealers.

NASDAQ (**National Association of Securities Dealers Automated Quotations**). The automated system which reports over the counter trading activity.

NATIONAL ADVANTAGE. Some factors that gives one nation an advantage in producing a cheaper product than other nations.

NATIONAL ASSOCIATION OF ACCOUNTS. The largest US processional organization of accounts whose major interest is management accounting.

NATIONAL BANKING ACT OF 1863. Created a new banking system with charters issued by the federal government.

NATIONAL BANKS. Banks with charters issued by the comptroller of the currency.

NATIONAL BRAND. A brand owned by a manufacturer and advertised and sold in all or nearly all sections of the country.

NATIONAL FUTURES ASSOCIATION. National futures association (NFA) is established at the law in USA contemplated for institution of more than a single self-regulatory body. The NFA is responsible for screening futures.

NATIONAL RESPONSIVENESS. Readiness to implement operating adjustments in foreign countries in order to reach a satisfactory level of performance.

NATIONAL SECURITIES CLEARING CORPORATION LIMITED. Settlement is on a physical basis requiring the delivery and receipt of documents. NSE has set up a clearing house *i.e.*, National Securities Clearing Corporation Limited (NSCCL) is for managing settlement of securities. There are no sub-groups or sections and all securities are handled by the NSCCL.

NATIONALISM. The feeling of pride and/or ethnocentrism

focused on an individual home country or nation.

NATIONALIZATION. The transfer of ownership to the state.

NATIONALIZATION. Government taking ownership and control of private property with or without pay.

NATURAL LAW. A belief, originating in ancient greece, the human affairs are governed by laws of nature. Some eighteenth century philosophers, including Adam Smith, applied the idea to the economic system and developed the "natural laws of supply and demand".

NATURAL ADVANTAGE. Climatic conditions, access to certain natural resources or availability of labour which gives a country an advantage in producing some product.

NATURAL MONOPOLIES. High-fixed-cost industries where duplication is a waste or increases costs, such as utilities, railroads, telephone companies etc.

NATURAL RATE OF EMPLOYMENT. The level of employment that occurs when there is only frictional unemployment.

NATURAL RATE OF OUTPUT. The level of output that corresponds to the long-run supply curve, *i.e.* the amount of goods that can be produced with available technology and the full employment of an economy's capital and labour resources.

NAV DATE. Gives the date for which the NAV figures have been published.

NAVIGATIONAL CHANGE, PRINCIPLE OF. The more planning decision commit for the future, a person can look back with certainty and determine whether or not it has been accomplished; goals or objectives may be verifiable either I expressed quantitatively (*i.e.*, in numbers) or qualitatively (a programme with certain specific characteristics to be put into effect by a certain date).

NCCL. National Clearing Corporation of India Limited.

NEARBY CONTRACT. A futures contract calling for delivery in a month that is nearby in time.

NEARBY FUTURE. Futures contracts that are closest to maturity date.

NEED HIERARCHY. *See* Hierarchy of needs.

NEED HIERARCHY. Need hierarchy in the view that human needs exist in some order of priority.

NEGATIVE REINFORCEMENT. It is action taken to repel the person from the undesired action.

NEGATIVE VOLUME ISSUES TRADED INDEX.

NEGOTIABLE INSTRUMENTS. Stocks, bonds, promissory notes etc., that may have their ownership transferred from one party to another party.

NEGOTIATED MARKET PRICE. A transfer price negotiated by the buying and selling segments when here is no market mechanism to fix a price clearly relevant to the situation.

NEIGHBOURHOOD SHOPPING CENTRE. A small shopping centre with from several to a dozen stores.

NEO-MERCANTILISM. The approach of countries that apparently try to run favourable balance of trade in an attempt to achieve some social or political objective.

NET ADVANTAGE OF LEASING. It denotes the incremental advantage over the NPV of buying the assets through normal financing channels.

NET ASSET VALUE. Represents the net assets on a per unit basis. It is equal to the net assets divided by the number of outstanding units.

NET ASSETS. It is the sum total of the market value of all investments plus accrued income minus the liabilities and expenses for a given scheme.

NET BOOK VALUE. Carrying amount of an asset, net of any related accounts (such as accumulated depreciation).

NET CAPITAL FLOW. Capital inflow minus capital outflow, for other than import and export payment.

NET CASH FLOWS. In addition to the initial cash outlay, a project may require some reinvestment of cash flows for maintaining its revenue generating ability during its life. As a consequence, net cash flows will be reduced by cash outflow for additional cash expenditure, thus net cash flows will be equal to after tax operating income plus depreciation minus increase in networking capital and minus capital expenditure.

NET CONVENIENCE YIELD. The convenience yield less the spot rate of interest.

NET EARNINGS. The payment to the entrepreneur for undertaking the risk of business. It is also referred to as pure profit. It is the amount that is left of the producer's income after all the payments have been made.

NET EXPORT EFFECT. Export stimulus minus export reduction.

NET EXPORTS. The net foreign demand for U.S. goods and services, calculated as exports minus imports.

NET IMPORT CHANGE. Import displacement minus import stimulus.

NET INCOME. The excess of all revenues and gains for a period over all expenses and losses.

NET INCOME ON INVESTMENTS. The net flow of investment income such as dividends, interest income and royalties.

NET INTEREST. Any interest paid on deposit or investment after deduction of income tax at source.

NET LEASE. In a net lease, the net rentals are payable to the lessor. All costs in connection with the use of the equipment are not a part of the rental. For example, taxes, insurance, and maintenance are paid directly by the lessee. Most capital leases and direct financing leases are not leases.

NET MONETARY POSITION. Total monetary assets minus total monetary liabilities.

NET PRESENT VALUE METHOD. A method of calculating the expected utility of a given project by discounting all expected future cash flows to the present, using some predetermined minimum desired rate of return.

NET PROFIT. The amount that remains after all income and expenses are computed.

NET REALIZABLE VALUE. Estimated selling price of a product in the ordinary course of business, less reasonably predictable cost of completion and disposal.

NETWORK ADVERTISING. Messages beamed to a large audience covering a wide territory simultaneously.

NETWORK ORGANIZATION. A situation in which a group of companies is interrelated and in which the management of the interrelation is shared among so-called equals.

NET WORKING CAPITAL GAP. The difference between current assets and current liabilities is called networking capital gap.

NET WORTH. A synonym for owner's equity; no longer widely used.

NETTING. A contractual agreements to aggregate all payments between two counter parties. The transfer of funds from subsidiaries in a net payable position to a central clearing account and from there to the accounts of the net receiver subsidiaries.

NETTING BY NOVATION. A single agreement to combine the obligations of multiple contracts with a single counter party all of which are denominated in the same currency.

NEW DEAL. The popular name given to president Franklin D. Roosevelt's economic programmes to combat the Great Depression of the 1930's.

NEWLY INDUSTRIALIZING COUNTRY. A third world country in which the cultural and economic climate has led to a rapid rate of industrialization and growth since the 1960's.

NFA. National Futures Association.

NO-COMPETITION AGREEMENT. This agreement is undertaken to protect the venture capitalist and the promoter, under this agreement, certain key employees are bound not to start parallel business in the event of their leaving the organization.

NO-BRAINER. Fund that tracks the performance of a stock index. Its manager buys all the stock listed on a major index and hence no discretionary management is required.

NOISE POLLUTION. High levels of sound that are harmful to humans and nature.

NO-LOAD FUND. Mutual fund which employ no sales persons and charge no commission.

NOMADIC SOCIETY. A society in which food gathering hunting and fishering, dominate work and where human groups move as necessary to find such food.

NOMINAL DOLLARS. Those total are not restated for fluctuations in the general purchasing power of the monetary unit.

NOMINAL INTEREST RATE. The interest rate started in the loan contract.

NOMINAL LEASE. Earlier, parlance for a tax benefit transfer.

NOMINAL OUTPUT. The current dollar value of the final goods and services produced in the economy in one year.

NOMINAL PARTNER. A person who lends his name to business firm but who is not actually a partner.

NOMINAL WAGE RIGIDITY. Nominal wages that are slow to adjust to changes in demand or supply of labour.

NON-CALLABLE BONDS. This refers to a bond which cannot be redeemed before its maturity.

NON-CLEARING MEMBER. He should clear his trades through a clearing member.

NON CONTRIBUTORY PLAN. It is one in which the employer provides all the funds.

NON-CONVENTIONAL INVESTMENT. Non-conventional investments one whose cash outflows are not restricted to the initial period, but are interspersed with cash inflows throughout the life of the project.

NON-DEPOSITORY FINANCIAL INSTITUTIONS. Financial institutions that do not accept deposits, but that serve various functions ranging from financial intermediation to selling insurance against risk.

NON-DIRECTIVE COUNSELLING. An approach in which the counsellor uses broad, open-end questions.

NON-DURABLE GOODS. Tangible goods which are expected to last only a short time as they are used up in one or a few uses.

NON-OPERATING REVENUES. Revenues which are incidental or indirect to the main operations of the firm are called non-operating revenues, example — dividend and interest income from tem-porary investments.

NON-PERFORMING ASSETS. That part of a bank's assets, currently yielding no return, and on which nothing is expected.

NONSIGNER'S CLAUSE. Exists when one retailer agrees to sell an item above an agreed price and the manufacturer and all other retailers in the state are bound by that agreement.

NORMAL ACTIVITY. The rate of activity needed to meet average sales demand over a period long enough to encompass seasonal and cyclical fluctuations.

NORMAL COST SYSTEM. *See* Normal costing.

NORMAL COSTING. The method of allocating costs to products using actual direct materials, actual direct labour, and predetermined overhead rates.

NORMAL DISTRIBUTION. The standard bell-shaped, symmetric probability distribution.

NORMS. Norms are expected standards of behaviour, usually unwritten and often unspoken, that are generally understood by all members of a group.

NOT HELD ORDER. This order gives the broker additional discretion and the customer relies on the floor broker market judgment in determining when to buy or sell.

NOTATION. Discharge of one contract in favour of another. Example : A builder may contract to start work on a certain day, and later notifies the client that he or she will be unable to do so. In this case the client may discharge the contract and sign another on same terms, with a second builder.

NOTES PAYABLE. Promissory notes that are evidence of a debt and state the terms of payment.

NRF. It is a performance indicator *i.e.*, BSE, National Index Relative Factor. It is a measure of percentage change in the NAV of a particular scheme over a specific period of time *vis-à-vis* the percentage change in the 100 shares BSE national index over the period. The NRF factor considers only the BSE sensex. Theoretically, it is not applicable to income schemes as these schemes invest their corpus in debt instruments. Same is applicable to income-*cum*-growth schemes where the corpus is split into debt and equity markets.

NSDL. National Securities Depository Limited.

NSE. National Stock Exchange.

NYCE. Net York Cotton Exchange.

NYFE. New York Futures Exchange subsidiary of NEW YORK Cotton Exchange.

NYFE. New York Futures Exchange.

NYM. New York Mercantile Exchange.

NYMEX. New York Mercantile Exchange.

NYSE. New York Stock Exchange.

O

OBJECT OF COSTING. *See* Cost objective.

OBJECTIVE. The goals of the firm such as profit and service.

OBJECTIVE FUNCTION. Goal that can be quantified, often expressed as a maximization (or minimization) of some form of profit (of cost).

OBJECTIVES OF FUTURE CONTRACTS. The main objectives of the futures contracts are pledging or speculation, price, discovery allocation of resources, etc.

OBJECTIVITY. Accuracy supported by convincing evidence that can be verified by independent accounts.

OBSERVATION METHOD. Direct observation technique used to gather statistical data, such as counting auto traffic on a certain street.

OCC. Options Clearing Corporation.

ODD LOT. A number of shares that are less than the market lot are known as odd lots. Under the scrip based delivery systems, these shares are normally traded at a discount to the prevailing price for the marketable lot. Trading in shares of stock in lots of less than one hundred.

OFF-AT-A-SPECIFIC-TIME-ORDER. This is a day order with a time contingency. It remains in effect only until the time indicated, when it will be cancelled if not executed.

OFFER. The price at which a person is willing to sell a security.

OFFER FOR SALE. Principal method whereby new issues of equities are marketed.

OFFER OF RIGHTS DATE. It is the date on which letter of rights is sent.

OFFER RATE.

OFFICE MANAGER. Plans, organizes, directs, controls and coordinates all activities of the office to carry out its purpose of service.

OFFICIAL LIST. The list, issued by stock exchange authorities, containing the name of whose securities are permitted to be traded in the stock exchanges.

OFFICIAL RESERVES.

OFFICIAL SETTLEMENTS BALANCE. That part of the balance of payments that measures the change in official U.S. reserves.

OFFSET. The liquidation of a futures or option contract through the purchase or sale of an identical contract.

OFFSET POLICY. A pollution control plan that permits excess pollution from one source if another polluting source reduces its emissions by an equal or greater amount.

OFFSET TRADE. A form of counter trade in which an exporter sells goods for cash but then helps businesses in the importing country find opportunities to earn hard currency.

OFFSETTING. The most common way of liquidation in open futures position is to effect an offsetting futures transaction, in effect, to reverse the initial transaction which established the futures position. In the process, initial buyer of future contract liquidates his position by selling an identical future contract. Similarly, the initial seller liquidates his position by buying an identical contract.

OFFSHORE FINANCIAL CENTRES. Offshore finance centre is, at its simplest, the provision of financial services by banks and other agents to non-residents. These services include the borrowing of money from non-residents and lending to non-residents. This can take the form of lending to corporate and other financial institutions, funded by liabilities to offices of the lending bank elsewhere, or to market participants. It can also take the form of taking of deposits from individuals, and investing the proceeds in financial markets elsewhere.

OFFSHORE FUND. Generally used to refer to a fund in the channel islands.

OFFSHORE MANUFACTURING. Manufacturing outside the borders of particular country.

OLIGOPOLY. The market structure in which a few firms compete for customers with each other.

ON BALANCE VOLUME (OBV).

ON-STOP (OR STOP-LOSS) ORDER. It allows the trading member to place an order, which gets activated only when the market place of the relevant security crosses a threshold price. Until then the order does not.

ON-THE-JOB TRAINING. This type of training occurs while the worker is actually performing the job.

ONE-MAN-BUSINESS. It is the business where a single owner bears the full responsibility for running the business.

ONE-WAY OPTION STOCK. Stock with no firm date for redemption, redeemable at the option for the borrower only.

OPEC. Organization of Petroleum Exporting Countries.

OPEC OPEN ACCOUNT.

OPEN ACCOUNT. Buying or selling on credit usually by just an 'authorized signature' of the buyer.

OPEN ACCOUNT. Conditions of sale under which the exporter extends credit directly to the importer.

OPEN CONTRACT. Contract that has been bought or sold on the financial futures market, but has not been closed by making an offsetting transaction or taking delivery of the financial instrument involved.

OPEN ECONOMY MODEL. A model of an economy that is open to international trade.

OPEN-ENDED LEASE. A lease which contains a provision for the extension of the lease of predetermined terms after the end of the fixed period.

OPEN GENERAL LICENCE. In general, the import and export of goods into and out of a country, require licences. For goods on which there are no restrictions, open general licences are available.

OPEN INTEREST. The total number of options contracts outstanding in the market at any given point of time.

OPEN MARKET OPERATIONS. Buying and selling of banks securities by the Federal Reserve to control the money supply.

OPEN MARKET PURCHASE. The purchase of U.S. government securities by the fed.

OPEN MARKET SALE. The sale of U.S. government securities by the fed.

OPEN ORDER. A order to purchase or sell a security at a specified price. Such order is valid till it is executed or cancelled.

OPEN OUTCRY. Buyers and sellers begin a trade by contacting their FCM which in turn directs the customers order to a floor broker on the exchange floor who executes the trade. The orders are executed on the floor of the exchange. The rules of the exchange requires all bids and offers be exposed to other traders in the pit in order to assure execution of orders at competitive prices. This is called open outcry system.

OPEN SHOP. Workers have the right to decide if they desire to become members of the union.

OPEN SYSTEM. It is a living entity which takes energy from its environment processes it, and returns output to the environment.

OPEN-ENDED FUND. In such funds, investors are free to enter or exit the scheme at any point of time. The investor can purchase or sell units of mutual funds from/through the mutual fund trust. The price at which the units are purchased/sold depends on the NAV of the fund at that point of time, as specified by the fund.

OPEN-ENDED LEASE. A lease which contains a provision for the extension of the lease of predetermined terms after the end of the fixed period.

OPERATING CYCLE. The time span during which cash is used to acquire goods and services.

OPERATING BUDGET. Budget of the income statement together with supporting schedules.

OPERATING CASH FLOWS. Earnings before depreciation minus taxes. Measures the cash generated from operations, not counting capital spending or working capital requirements.

OPERATING LEASE. For financial accounting purposes a lease which does not meet the criteria of a capital lease or direct financing lease. Also, used generally to describe a short-term lease whereby a fraction of the useful life of the asset, the lessor may provide services in connection with the lease such as maintenance insurance and payment of personal property taxes. Short term cancellable lease agreements are called operating lease, convenience and instant services are the hallmark of operating lease.

OPERATING MARGINS. Operating profit expressed as a proportion of price.

OPERATING PROCEDURE. A combination of intermediate targets and procedures for using the policy instruments to achieve the intermediate targets.

OPERATING RISK. Operating risk can be defined as the variability of EBIT (or return on total assets).

OPERATING TARGET. An immediate target of policy, a target for a variable that the fed can definitely control on a daily or weekly basis, such as a category of reserves or a short run interest rate.

OPERATION COSTING. System where distinctions are made between batches of product. Materials and conversion costs are computed for each operation undergone during production.

OPERATIONAL AUDIT. The regular and independent appraisal by a staff in internal auditors of the accounting, financial and other operations of an enterprise.

OPERATIONAL CENTRES. Offshore financial centres that perform specific functions such as the sale and servicing of goods.

OPERATIONAL SYNERGIES. Operational synergies result when companies combine their strength. In the process they could shed down overlapping operations, cut down the manpower, integrate procurement, etc. This leads to cutting down the costs of the company. Complementary operations could also result in obtaining operational synergies.

OPERATIONS MANAGEMENT. Activities necessary to produce and deliver a product or service.

OPERATIONS RESEARCH. The use of mathematical models to reflect the variables and constraints in a situation and their effect on a selected goal, ordinarily thought of as using optimizing models; the application of scientific method in a problem situation with a view to providing a quantitative basis for arriving at an optimum solution in terms of goals sought.

OPIC. *See* Overseas Private Investment Corporation.

OPINION LEADER. One whose acceptance of some concept is apt to be emulated by others.

OPPORTUNITY COST. The maximum alternative earning that might have been obtained if the productive good, service, or capacity had been applied to some alternative use.

OPPORTUNITY COSTS. The various opportunities that cannot be realized because money is spent for one purpose rather than for others.

OPTIMISM. A characteristic of an accounting system that implies that companies are more liberal in recognition of income.

OPTIMUM CAPITAL BUDGET. Means the availability of funds to invest in all profitable projects so that the NPV is maximized.

OPTIMUM-TARIFF THEORY. The argument that a foreign producers will lower its prices if an import tax is placed on its products.

OPTION. A foreign exchange instruments that gives the purchaser the right, but not the obligation, to buy or sell a certain amount of foreign currency at a set exchange rate within a specified amount of time.

OPTION. A contract granting the right to buy or sell on asset at a stated price over a specified period.

OPTION CLASS. All listed options of a particular type (call or put) on a particular underlying instrument — all sensex call options (or) all sensex put options.

OPTION CONTRACT. An instrument that gives the owner a right — but not obligation — to sell or buy an item at a prespecified price within a prespecified period of time. The right to buy or sell a specific quantity of a specific asset at a fixed price at or before a specified future date.

OPTION HOLDER. One who buys an option, which can be a call, or a put option. He enjoys the right to buy or sell the underlying asset at a specified price on or before specified time. His upside potential is unlimited while losses are limited to the premium paid by him to the option writer.

OPTION MARKETS. Markets where options are traded.

OPTION PREMIUM. In an option agreement, writer of the option grants the right (to purchase from or sell to the writer) to the buyer for a certain sum of money called the option premium. Thus it is the price paid by the buyer to the seller to acquire the right to buy or sell.

OPTION SELLER/WRITER. One who is obligated to buy (in case of put option) or to sell (in case of call option) the underlying asset in case the buyer of the option decides to exercise his option. His profits are limited to the premium received from the buyer while his downside is unlimited.

OPTION WRITER. The person who sells or grants an option in return for a premium, and who is obligated to perform if the option holder exercises his right under the option contract.

OPTION'S AGREEMENT. An option agreement is a contract in which the seller of the option grants the buyer of the option the right to purchase from or sell to the writer a designated instrument at a specified price or receive a cash settlement within a specified period of time.

ORDER-DRIVEN TRADING. It is a trading initiated by buy or sell orders from investors or brokers.

ORDER ENTRY WINDOW. Order entry mechanism enables the trading member to place orders in the market. The system accepts orders from all trading members and provides equal access to all trading members.

ORDER LOG. The order log shows the activities which have been performed as any order at the trading member such as whether the order has been traded against fully or partially. It has been modified or has been cancelled. It displays information only at these order in which some activity has taken place. It does not display orders which have entered the books but have been matched (fully or partially) or modified or cancelled.

ORDER-FILLING COST. A marketing cost incurred in the storing, packing, shipping billing, credit and collection, and in other similar aspects of selling merchandise.

ORDER-GETTING COST. A marketing cost incurred in the effort to attain a desired sales volume and mix.

ORDINARY INCREMENTAL BUDGET. Budget that usually considers the previous period's budget and actual results as a given. The budget amount is then changed in accordance with experience during the previous period and expectations for the next period.

ORGANIZATION. It is a goal-oriented system of co-ordinated relationships between people, tasks, resources, and managerial activities.

ORGANIZATION. A concept used in a variety of ways such as (1) a system or pattern of any set of relationships in any kind of undertaking, (2) an enterprise itself, (3) co-operation of two or more persons, (4) all behaviour of all participants in a group, and (5) the international structure of roles in a formally organized enterprise.

ORGANIZATION CULTURE. The general pattern of behaviour, shared beliefs, and values that members of an organization have in common.

ORGANIZATION DEVELOPMENT (OD). A systematic, integrated, and planned approach to improving the effectiveness of groups of people and of the whole organization; OD uses various techniques for identifying and solving problems.

ORGANIZATION FOR ECONOMIC COOPERATION AND DEVELOPMENT (OECD). A multilateral organization of industrialized and semi industrialized countries that helps formulate social and economic policies.

ORGANIZATION FOR EUROPEAN ECONOMIC COOPERATION (OEEC). A sixteen nation organization established in 1948 to facilitate the organization of aid from the Marshall Plan; it evolved into the EU and EFTA.

ORGANIZATION MANUAL. A handbook given to employees containing essential information on company policies and procedures.

ORGANIZATION OF AFRICAN UNITY (OAU). An organization of African nations that is more concerned with political than economic objectives.

ORGANIZATION OF PETROLEUM EXPORTING COUNTRIES (OPEC). A producer's alliance among twelve petroleum-exporting countries that attempt to agree on oil production and pricing policies.

ORGANIZATION STRUCTURE. The formal relationships among the individuals and segments within an organization.

ORGANIZATION STRUCTURE. The framework which shows the authority and responsibility relationships among people, the formal communication channels, and the relationship of each part of the company to the others.

ORGANIZATIONAL AUTHORITY. The degree of discretion in organizational positions conferring on persons occupying these positions the right to use their judgment in decision making.

ORGANIZATIONAL CHART. The formal, structural outline of the company.

ORGANIZATIONAL CLIMATE. It is a composite view of the characteristics of an organization as seen by employees.

ORGANIZATIONAL COMMITMENT. A stage in the development of social responsiveness within a company when social responses have become a normal part of doing business. Therefore, the entire organization is committed to socially responsible actions and politics.

ORGANIZATIONAL ROLE. An organizational position designed for individuals to fill; to be meaningful to people, it should incorporate (1) verifiable objectives, (2) a clear concept of the major duties or activities involved, (3) the availability of information and resources necessary to accomplish a task.

ORGANIZATIONAL SOCIETY. A society often technologically advanced where most areas of life are organized and largely controlled by big organizations such as labour unions, corporations, government agencies, universities, military units, churches and others.

ORGANIZING. The management function of arranging the people, tasks, and materials which are necessary for putting effective plans into operation to meet company objectives.

ORIENTATION. It is the planned introduction of employees to their jobs, their co-workers, and their organizations.

ORIGINAL MARGIN. The clearing house guards against the possibility of financial loss to any member. It must obtain some form of guarantee from its member firms each member deposit money for each contract that is cleared the performance money deposited by the member firms is called original margin.

OSE. Osaka Securities Exchange.

OTC DERIVATIVES. Derivative securities traded in the over-the-counter market.

OUT OF THE MONEY. The call option is said to be 'out of the money' if the actual market price is below the exercise price.

OUTCOMES. Consequences of the various possible combinations of actions and events.

OUTDATED TRANSFER DEEDS. The transferee who holds outdated transfer deeds has to fill in the prescribed form (form TC) and seek extension of time either from the registrar of companies (ROC) of the state in which the registered office of the company is situated or from the registrar of companies of the state in which he ordinarily resides.

OUT-GOER. A farmer who accepts financial inducements to turn his or her agricultural profession to another function.

OUTLAY COST. A ash disbursement, as distinguished from an opportunity cost.

OUT-OF-THE-MONEY. A term referring to call option when the market value of the asset on which the option is written is less than the strike price.

OUT-OF-THE-MONEY OPTION. An option that has no intrinsic value; a call option with a strike price above the current asset price, or a put option with a strike price below the current asset price.

OUTPUT. Data that have been processed.

OUTRIGHT FORWARD. A forward contract that is not connected to a spot transactions.

OUTSIDE STOCKHOLDERS' INTEREST IN SUBSIDIARIES. Synonym for minority interest.

OUTSOURCING. The use by a domestic company of foreign suppliers of components or finished products.

OUTSTANDING EXPENSES. They are also considered as current liabilities. The firm may owe payments to its employees and other at the end of the accounting period for the services received in the current year. These payments are payable within very short period, examples are wages payable, rent payable and commission payable.

OUTSTANDING ORDER. The purpose of outstanding order is to enable trading member to view his or her own outstanding buy or sell orders for a security descriptor. An outstanding order will be an order that was submitted by the trading member but which is not yet completely matched or cancelled.

OUT-TRADE. Floor brokers execute orders on the floor of the exchange. The rules of the exchange requires all bids and offers to be exposed to other traders in the pit in order to assure the execution of orders at open prices. The floor brokers then report all trades to the clearing house. If there is any disagreement as to exactly who executed which order at which price, the errors are corrected an exchange committee.

OVER ABSORBED OVERHEAD. *See* Over applied factory overhead.

OVER APPLIED FACTORY OVERHEAD. The excess of overhead applied to products over actual overhead incurred.

OVER LOADING. Sending too much information so those receiving messages cannot separate important and unimportant information.

OVERALL *vs.* SPECIFIC COST OF CAPITAL. The component costs are combined according to the weight of each component capital to obtain the average cost of capital. Thus, the overall cost is also called the weighted average cost of capital.

OVER-DRAFT. Under the over-draft facility, the borrower is allowed to withdraw funds in excess of the balance in his current account upto a certain specified limit during a stipulated period.

OVERHEAD. Costs that are not directly traced to a given cost objective. These indirect costs are usually divided into manufacturing.

OVERHEAD COSTS. The expenses of a business that are not attributable directly to the production or sale of goods.

OVERSEAS PRIVATE INVESTMENT CORPORATION (OPIC). A U.S. government agency that provides insurance for companies involved to international business.

OVER-THE-COUNTER MARKET. An off-exchange market between commercial and investment banks for trading in an asset.

OVER-THE-COUNTER MARKET. A market for trading securities which does not have a centralized location, dealers are spread throughout the country and transact their business by telephone.

OVER-THE-COUNTER-TRADING. Trading in those stocks which are not listed on a stock exchange.

OVERTIME PREMIUM. A classification of indirect labour costs, consisting of the wages paid to all factory workers in excess of their straight-time wage rates.

OWNER PARTICIPANT. The lessor or a group of lessors in a leveraged lease holding trust certificates evidencing their beneficial interest as owners under the owner trust. An owner participant is the same as an equity participant, trustee.

OWNER'S EQUITY. The interest of stockholders or other owners in the assets of an enterprise and, at any time, the cumulative net result of past transactions and other events and circumstances affecting the enterprise.

OWNER'S EQUITY. It is the residual in nature reflecting the excess of the firm's assets over its liabilities.

P

P/V CHART. A graph showing volume on the horizontal axis and net income on the vertical axis.

PACKAGER. A name used to describe the leasing company, investment banker or broker who arranges a leveraged lease.

PAC-MAN DEFENCE. It is a method of defending against a hostile take over whereby the target company makes a tender offer for the shares of the aggressor.

PACT FOR STABILITY AND GROWTH. The stability and growth pact accompanied the introduction of a single currency in the European Union as part of the third stage of economic and monetary union. It will govern the economic policies of the member countries, which have joined the single currency, and strongly constrain the policies of those who do not join.

PAID-IN CAPITAL. The owner's equity measured by the total amounts invested at the inception of a business and subsequently.

PAINTING THE TAPE. Method of creating any impression of activity around a share, by reporting fictitious transactions. Painting the tape is illegal.

PANDORA'S BOX. In Greek mythology, a box that when opened let loose all kinds of misfortunes on society.

PAPER COMPANY. Company established, usually with little capital, merely for financial purposes.

PAR BOND YIELD. The coupon that makes the price equal to its face value. The yield to maturity equals the coupon rate, given that the bond is selling at par.

PAR BOND YIELD CURVE. The graph of the paranoid yields for bonds of different maturates.

PAR SWAP RATE. The fixed rate on a plain vanilla interest rate swap that sets the value of the swap to zero.

PAR VALUE. The value printed on the face of the security certificate.

PAR VALUE. The state value on stock. It is an arbitrary

amount assigned to stock and has no relationship to either market value or book value. Exists for accounting purpose.

PARAMETER. A constant, such as a, or a coefficient, such as b, in a model or system of equations, such as y = a + bx.

PARITY OF AUTHORITY AND RESPONSIBILITY. *See* Authority, parity with responsibility.

PARLIAMENTARY GOVERNMENT. A form of government that involves election of representatives to form the executive branch.

PART-LOAD. Portion or a part of the share capital of open-ended investment companies not covered by the underlying assets.

PARTIAL CONTROLS. Controls designed to measure performance in a specific activity, such as quality, cash, production, or sales.

PARTIAL CROWDING OUT. Describes a situation in which crowding out is not complete, so the increase in government spending is greater than the resulting reduction in investment and consumption spending.

PARTICIPANT AGREEMENT. An agreement between the owner trustee, the lenders, the equity participants, the manufacturers, and the lessee which spells out the obligations of the parties under the leveraged lease. Also called financing agreement.

PARTICIPATE LEADER. This leader attempts to get people actively involved in decisions affecting them.

PARTICIPATION AGREEMENT. An agreement between the owner trustee, the lenders, the equity participants, the manufacturer, and the lessee which spells out the obligations of the parties under the leveraged lease. Also called financing agreement.

PARTICIPATION RATE. The percentage of eligible workers in a specific category, such as age group, who are employed.

PARTNERSHIP. A special form of organization that joins two or more individuals together as co-owners.

PARTNERSHIP. A business ownership comprised of two or more owners who operate under an agreement of the owners. It is not a legal entity form of ownership.

PARTY-AT-INTEREST. A person or persons having a vested interest in a business firm.

PASSIVE INCOME. Income from investments is tax haven countries or sales and services income that involves buyers and sellers in other than the tax heaven country, where either the buyer or the seller must be part of the same organizational structure as the corporation that earns the income also known as subpart income.

PASSIVE MONETARY POLICY. Situation where the fed does not increase the money supply in an attempt to bring down interest rates in times of economic up-heave.

PASSIVE RULE. A monetary policy rule that does not depend on the state of the economy. Such as keeping growth in the money supply constant.

PAST RATIO. Ratios calculated from the past financial statements of the same firm.

PATENT. A right to sole production of a product for 17 years.

PATENT COOPERATION TREATY. A multilateral agreement to protect patents.

PATENTS. Grants by the federal government to inventors giving them the exclusive right to produce and sell their inventions for a period of seventeen years.

PATH DEPENDENT OPTION. An option the value of which depends on the path of the price of the underlying asset over the life of the option.

PATH-GOAL APPROACH TO LEADERSHIP EFFECTIVENESS. An approach that sees as the main function of the leader clarifying and setting goals with subordinates, helping them to find the best path for achieving the goals, and removing obstacles.

PATRONAGE MOTIVES. The motives which influence a person to return repeatedly to a store to make additional purchases.

PAY. It is the basic compensation employees receive usually as a wage or salary.

PAY-BACK. The measure of the time needed to recoup, in the form of cash inflow from operations, the initial dollars invested. Also called payout and payoff.

PAY-BACK PERIOD. The number of years required to recover the initial outlay of investment.

PAY GRADES. Pay grades are used to group individual jobs having approximately the same job worth together.

PAYLATER OPTION. An option in which the premium is paid at expiration contingent on the option being in-the-money.

PAYOFF TABLE. *See* Decision table.

PAYOFFS. Synonym for outcomes.

PAY-ORDER. A Pay-order, as the name suggests, is an order which is valid for the day on which it is entered. If the order is not matched during the day, at the end of the trading day, the order gets cancelled automatically.

PAYOUT. *See* Pay-back.

PAYSOP. It is a payroll-based stock ownership plan.

PEER RATING. Appraising of managers by other managers at the same or similar organizational level.

PEG. To fix a currency's exchange rate to some benchmark, such as another currency.

PENETRATION STRATEGY. A strategy of introducing a product at a low price to induce a maximum number of consumers to try it.

PENSION FUNDS. Funds set up by company and employee contributions to provide retirement benefits. Funds that gather regular contributions from employees, usually by payroll deduction, to provide retirement income to employees covered by the pension plan.

PEPPERCORN RENTAL. The nominal rental paid during the secondary period of a finance lease.

PER CAPITA INCOME. Total income of the nation divided by the total population which produces the average income per person.

PERCENTAGE LEASE. Percentage lease provides fixed returns or some per cent of the previous year's gross revenue to be paid to the lessor. This ensures protection against inflation.

PERFORMANCE APPRAISAL. It is the process of determining how well employees do their jobs compared to a set of standards, and communicating that information to the employees.

PERFORMANCE REPORT. The comparison of actual results with the budget.

PERFORMANCE STANDARDS. The level of output expected of workers.

PERIOD COSTS. Those costs being deducted as expenses during the current period without having been previously classified as product costs.

PERIODIC BUDGETING. It involves the preparation of budget for the forthcoming year without providing for a comprehensive revision as the budget period passes.

PERPENDICULAR SPREAD. It is an investment strategy that includes using options with the same expiration dates with different strike prices. And this spread can be bullish or bearish.

PERPETUAL INVENTORY. An inventory control system which maintains a running account of materials on hand.

PERPETUITY. A loan that never matures; it consists of an infinite number of periodic interest payments, but no final payment of face value or principal.

PERQUISITES ("PERKS"). Perquisites are special benefits for executives that are usually non-cash terms.

PERSONALITY TEST. A test designed to aid in selecting managers or other personnel whose jobs require skills in interpersonal relations.

PERSONNEL AUDIT. It is a formal research effort to evaluate the current state of personnel management in an organization.

PERSONNEL GENERALIST. It is someone who has responsibility for performing a varied range of personnel activities.

PERSONNEL MANAGEMENT. It is a set of activities focusing on the effective use of human resources in an organization.

PERSONNEL RESEARCH. Analyzes past and present personnel practices through the use of collected data and records.

PERSONNEL SPECIALIST is someone who has in-depth knowledge and expertise in a limited area of personnel.

PERSONS ACTING IN CONCERT (PAC). PAC are individual(s) company(ies)/any other legal entity(ies) who are acting in concert for a common objective or for the purpose of substantial acquisition of shares or voting rights or gaining control over the target company either directly or indirectly. Inherent element in this action is an element of cooperation between the entities. This cooperation may either be direct or indirect, formal or informal. The concept of PAC assumes significance in the context of takeovers since it is possible that an acquirer can acquire shares or voting rights in a company "in concert" with any other person in a manner that the acquisitions made by him remain below the threshold limit, though taken together with the voting rights of persons acting in concert, the threshold may exceed. In the regulations, certain entities are presumed to be acting in concert, unless the contrary is established like companies with its holding company or subsidiary company; mutual funds with its sponsor/trustee/asset management company, etc.

PERT (PROGRAMME EVALUATION AND REVIEW TECHNIQUE). A time-event network analysis system in which the various events in a programme or project are identified, with the planned time for each, and are placed in a network showing the relationships of each event to other events; from the sequence of interrelated events, the path of those events in which there is zero (or the least) slack time in terms of planned completion is the 'critical path'; PERT/TIME systems deal only with time PERT/COST systems introduce costs of each event and are usually combined with elapsed time of each event of series of events.

PETER PRINCIPLE. Principle enunciated by Laurence J. Peter and Raymond Hall that managers end to be promoted until they reach the level of their incompetence.

PETRO-DOLLARS. They are the large dollar balances that oil-producing countries, earned through oil sales, have deposited in financial institutions worldwide.

PHANTOM SHARE. An executive incentive concept whereby an executive receives a bonus based on the market appreciation of the company's stock over a fixed period of time.

PHILADELPHIA STOCK EXCHANGE. A specialized market dealing in select foreign-currency options.

PHILANTHROPY (CORPORATE). Gifts and contributions made by corporations, usually from pretax profits, to benefit various types of non profit community organizations.

PHILOSOPHY OF MANAGEMENT. Establishes the primary, long-range objectives of a firm and provides the principles, practices, and ethical standards of a firm in its relationship with employees.

PHLX. Philadelphia Stock Exchange.

PHYSICAL CAPITAL. Economists' terminology for man made inputs into the production process.

PHYSICAL CAPITAL MAINTENANCE. The capacity to maintain previous levels of output of goods and services.

PHYSICAL DELIVERY. Liquidating a future position by making or taking physical delivery is usually the most cumbersome process to fulfil contractual obligation. But traders normally do not favour the settlement through physical delivery. However commercial firms settle through physical delivery and sometimes, it might be financially desirable to settle by physical delivery.

PI/I. Programming language I, a computer language.

PICKETING. The practice of workers marching at the entrance to a firm to protest some management practice.

PIE CHART. A chart in a circle divided into wedges frequently used to present data relating to percentages or dollar values.

PIECE CHART. Payment to workers on the basis of the

number of acceptable units of output produced.

PIGGYBACK. Combining motor and rail transportation services.

PIGGYBACK EXPORTING. Use by an exporter of another exporter as an intermediary.

PINK MOOD. When the price of a scrip is likely to shoot up, the scrip is said to be in pink mood.

PIRACY. The unauthorized use of property rights that are protected by patents trademarks or copyrights.

PLACE UTILITY. A good or service must be available at the place it is demanded to satisfy a want.

PLACING. The sale of a line of stock or shares by arrangement, direct to institution and others by the selling brokers without going through the market.

PLANNING. Selecting missions and objectives — and the strategies, policies, programmes, and procedures for achieving them; decision making; the selection of a course of action from among alternatives.... Thus the management function of formulating in advance the direction a firm to follow to reach its designed objectives.

PLANNING PREMISES, TYPES OF. premises may be external or internal to an enterprise, quantitative or qualitative or controllable, uncontrollable, or semi-controllable.

PLANNING PREMISES. The planning assumptions — the expected environment in which plans will operate; they may be forecasts of the planning environment in which plans will operate; they may be forecasts of the planning environment or basic policies and existing plans which will influence any given plan.

PLANNING PROCESS. A rational approach to setting and accomplishing an objective and evaluating alternatives in light of goals sought and against the environment of planning premises.

PLANS, TYPES OF. Purpose or missions, objectives, strategies, policies, procedures, rules, programmes, and budgets.

PLANT ASSETS. Assets, that are not easily converted into cash and have a long life such as building plant and land.

PLC. *See* Product Life Cycle theory.

PLEDGE. Under this agreement, the borrower is required to transfer the physical possession of the property offered as a security to the bank to obtain credit. The bank has a right of lien and can retain possession of the goods pledged unless payment of the principal interest and any other expenses is made. In case of default, the bank may either (a) sue the borrower for the amount due or (b) sue for the sale of goods pledged.

PLURAL EXECUTIVE. A committee, or group, which has the authority to execute, as a group, managerial functions. Pluralistic society : a society in which many organized groups present various interests. Each group has an impact on other groups, but no one group has an inordinate amount of power.

PLURALISM. A society in which numerous economic, political, educational, social artistic, and other groups are organized by people to promote their own interests.

PLURALISTIC SOCIETIES. Societies in which difficult ideologies are held by various segments rather than one ideology being adhered to by all.

PLUVIUS INSURANCE. Alternative name for weather insurance. It is an insurance against losses caused by inclement weather, available to farmers and organizers of outdoor events.

POINT. On stock market price quotations, a point is one dollar.

POLICIES. General statements or understandings which guide thinking in decision making; the essence of policies is the existence of discretion; within certain limits, in guiding decision making.

POLICY DECISION. A stage in the public policy process when government authorizes a course of action, for example, by passing a law issuing a court opinion, or adopting a new regulations.

POLICY EVALUATION. The final stage in the public policy process when the results of a public policy are judged by those who have an interest in the outcomes.

POLICY EVALUATION. The final stage in the public policy process when the results of a public policy are judged by those who have an interest in the outcomes.

POLICY FORMULATION. A stage in the public policy process when interested groups take a position and try to persuade others to adopt that position.

POLICY IMPLEMENTATION. A stage in the public policy process when action is taken to enforce a public policy decision.

POLICY INSTRUMENT. Variable that the policy maker can control.

POLICY TARGETS. Variable that the policy maker tries to influence.

POLITICAL ACTION COMMITTEE. A committee organized according to election law by any group for the purposes of accepting voluntary contributions from individual donors and then making contributions to candidates for election to public office.

POLITICAL FREEDOM. The right to participate freely in the political process.

POLITICAL RISK. Potential changes in political conditions that may cause a company's operating positions to deteriorate.

POLITICAL SCIENCE. A discipline that helps explain the patterns of governments and their actions.

POLITICAL SYSTEM. The system designed to integrate a society into a viable, functioning unit.

POLLUTION CHARGE. A fee levied on a polluting source based on the amount of pollution released into the environment.

POLLUTION TRADE-OFF. Accepting one form of pollution rather than another when it is not possible to eliminate both.

POLYCENTRIC BUSINESS. A company whose business standards are based on the customs, markets, and laws of two or a few different nations.

POLYCENTRISM. Characteristic of an individual or organization that feels that differences in a foreign country, real and imaginary great and small need to be accounted for in management decisions.

POLYCHRONIC CULTURE. A culture in which most people are more comfortable dealing simultaneously with all the situations facing them.

POLYGRAPHS. An operator administered instrument that is used to judge the truth or falsity of a person's statements by measuring physiological changes that tend to be caused by a person's conscience when lying.

POPULISM. The preference for a democratic political system, family-operated farms, small-size business firms, and small town life.

PORTABILITY. Allows employees to move their pension benefits rights from one employer to another.

PORTER DIAMOND. A diagram showing four conditions demand, factor endowments related and supporting industries, and firm strategy, structure, and rivalry that usually must all be favourable for an industry in a country to develop and sustain a global competitive advantage.

PORTFOLIO APPROACH TO MONEY DEMAND. (Also called the asset approach) Developed in the 1950s by James Tobin provides an alternative justification for Keynes' view that interest rates affect money demand.

PORTFOLIO INVESTMENT. An investment in the form of either debt or equity that does not give the investor a controlling interest.

POSITION. It is a collective of tasks performed by one person.

POSITIVE REINFORCEMENT. Psychologist Skinner's theory that people are best motivated by properly designing their work environment, giving them prompt feedback on performance, and including ways to help them and praise them for the good things they do.

POSITIVE VOLUME ISSUES TRADED INDEX (PVITI). It is summation of advances minus declines only on days when total volume of trading increases over that of the previous day.

POSITIVE-SUM GAIN. A situation in which the sums of gains and losses, if added together among participants, is positive especially if all parties gain from a relationships.

POSSESSION UTILITY. A good or service must be in the possession of an individual if it is to satisfy a want.

POST-INDUSTRIAL SOCIETY. A society combining the features of a service society and a knowledge society.

POWER. The ability of individuals or groups to induce or influence the beliefs or actions of other persons or groups. Several kinds of power may be identified such as legitimate power, expertness, referent power, reward power and coercive power.

POWER DISTANCE. A measurement of preference for consultative or autocratic styles of management.

PPP. *See* Purchasing-power parity.

PRACTICAL CAPACITY. The maximum level at which the plant or department can realistically operate most efficiently, *i.e.*, ideal capacity less allowances for unavoidable operating interruptions. Also called practical attainable capacity.

PRAGMATISM. Settling small issues before deciding on principles.

PRECAUTIONARY MOTIVE. The desire to hold money to meet unexpected expenditure requirements for emergencies or the proverbial rainy day.

PREFERENCE CAPITAL. Capital referring to preferred shares which give investors a fixed dividend from the company's earnings and entitle them to be paid before common shareholders.

PREFERENCE OR UTILITY THEORY. The theory that individual attitudes toward risk will vary from statistical probabilities, with some individuals being willing only to take lower risks than indicated by probabilities ('risk averters') and others taking greater risks ('gamblers').

PREFERENTIAL ALLOTMENT. Allotment entitled to payment before other debts and liabilities are met.

PREFERENTIAL FORM. Special application forms usually given to existing shareholders and employees when companies offer shares for public subscription and they are easily identifiable by their pink colour hence they are known as "Pink forms".

PREFERENTIAL HIRING. An employment plan that gives preference to minorities, women, and other groups that may be underrepresented in an organization's workforce.

PREFERENTIAL ISSUE. Preferential issue offers the shareholders preferential claims to the dividends, usually at a fixed rate and a prior claim to ordinary shareholders on the company's assets in the event of liquidation. The market price for the preferential shares tends to be more stable than that of the ordinary shares.

PREFERRED HABITAT HYPOTHESIS. Combines key features of both the expectation hypothesis and the segmented markets hypothesis. It says that while investors do have a preference for loanable funds of a given term, they are willing to substitute away from their preferred term — if they are compensated for doing so.

PREFERRED PROVIDER ORGANIZATION. It is a health care provider that contracts with an employer or an employer group to provide health care services to employees at competitive rates.

PREFERRED STOCK. Stock that has some priority over other shares regarding dividends or the distribution of assets upon liquidation.

PREFERRED STOCK. A certificate of ownership in a corporation which usually receives preferred payment but does not have voting rights.

PREMIUM (IN FOREIGN EXCHANGE). The difference between the spot and forward exchange rates in the forward market; a foreign currency sells at a premium when the forward rate exceeds the spot rate and when the domestic currency is quoted on a direct basis.

PREMIUM/DISCOUNT TO NAV. Gives the premium or discount to the NAV at which the funds units are traded on the bourses. A negative value indicates a discount while positive values indicates the extent to the premium.

PREPAID EXPENSES. Assets that exist because operating supplies and rights to services have been acquired in advance of use.

PREPAID EXPENSES. These are the expenses of future period paid in advance. Accrued incomes are the benefits which the firm has earned. But they have not been received in cash yet. They include items such as accrued dividend, accrued commission or accrued interest.

PRESENT VALUE. The current equivalent value of cash available immediately for a future payment or a stream of payments to be received at various times in the future. The present value will vary with the discount (interest) factor applied to the future payments.

PRESSURE GROUP. A group that tries to influence legislation or practices to foster its objectives.

PREVIOUS TRADES. This screen allows the trading members to view all previous trades that have taken place in the market.

PREVIOUS-DEPARTMENT COSTS. *See* Transferred-in costs.

PRICE BANK. The daily or weekly price limits within which price of a security is allowed to rise or fall.

PRICE ESCALATION. The process by which the lengthening of distribution channels increases a product's price by more than the direct added costs, such as transportation insurance, and tariffs.

PRICE INDEX. A single number that measures the average percentage change in price, volume, or value of a set or 'basket' of related items during the time between some elected base period and current period. In other words a price index measures the average percentage change in the prices of a given physical volume of commodities.

PRICE LEVEL. A measure of the average prices of goods and services in the economy.

PRICE LIMIT. The maximum price advance or decline permitted as a contract during one day or trading session under the rules of the exchange.

PRICE PERFORMANCE. The price performance indicates the net gain to the investor from a scheme on the basis of the latest market price. The price performance has also been calculated using the internal rate of return method and has been suitably adjusted for rights, bonus and dividends. Returns are on an annualized basis.

PRICE RIGGING. When a person or persons acting in concert with each other collude to artificially increase or decrease the price of a security, that process is called price rigging.

PRICE SPREAD. If a trade involves purchase of option and of sale option both on the same stock and expiring in the same month but exercise price of one is higher than the other, it is called price spread.

PRICE STABILITY. Measured by the stability of the inflation rate. And by the amount by which inflation exceeds a target level.

PRICE STABILIZATION RULE. A money policy rule that prescribes changes to the money supply in response to changes in aggregated supply or demand to keep the price level constant.

PRICE TO EARNINGS RATIO. Shows the multiple of earnings per share (adjusted for stock splits). Earnings per share for the P/E ratio are determined by dividing earnings for past 12 months by the number of common shares outstanding. Higher multiple means investors have higher expectations for future growth, and have bid up the stock's price.

PRICE VARIANCE. The different between the actual price and the standard price, multiplied by the total number of items acquired. The term price variance is usually linked with direct material the item rate variance which is conceptually similar to the price variance is usually linked with direct labour.

PRIMARY BUYING MOTIVES. The motives which influence the initial recognition of the need for a participate piece of merchandise.

PRIMARY DEFICIT. The amount the federal government spends on transfer payments and purchases over and above its current tax collections does not include interest payments on the debt.

PRIMARY INTERACTIONS OR INVOLVEMENT. The direct relationships a company has with those groups that enable it to produce goods and services.

PRIMARY MARKET. The market where newly issued securities are first offered.

PRIMARY NEEDS. Basic physiological needs of humans; food, shelter, clothing etc.

PRIMARY PERIOD. The period in a finance lease during which the lessor expects to recover the full capital cost of the asset, his money, costs and his profits.

PRIMARY SOURCE OF DATA. An agency which collects and publishes data.

PRIMARY SPENDING. Transfer payments and purchases of goods and services. Does not include interest payments on the debt.

PRIME COSTS. Direct material plus direct labour.

PRIME INTEREST RATE. The rate of interest banks charge their best customers, usually large corporation.

PRINCIPLE OF DELEGATION OF AUTHORITY. Decisions should be made at the lowest competent level in the company.

PRINCIPLE OF FLEXIBILITY. The company must be able to adjust to a changing environment both internally and externally.

PRINCIPLE OF FUNCTIONAL HOMOGENEITY. Activities within the company should be grouped on the basis of similarity.

PRINCIPLE OF LEVELS OF MANAGEMENT. The number of levels of management within a company should be kept to a minimum.

PRINCIPLE OF SPAN OF CONTROL. There is a limit to the number of people a worker can effectively supervise.

PRINCIPLE OF UNITY OF COMMAND. A worker should receive orders from and report to a single supervisor.

PRINCIPLE OF UNITY OF OBJECTIVES. Each part of the company must contribute to the accomplishment of overall objectives of the firm.

PRINCIPLE OF VALUE ADDITIVITY. Value added to capital as a result of incremental cash flows with the investment made in a project.

PRINCIPLES. Fundamental truths, or what are believed to be truths at a given tie explaining relationships between two or more sets of variables, usually an independent variable and a dependent variable; may be descriptive, explaining what will happen, or prescriptive (or normative), indicating what a person should do in the latter case, principles reflect some scale of values, such as efficiency, and therefore imply value judgments.

PRIOR INFORMED CONSENT. The concept of requiring each exporter of a banned or restricted chemical to obtain chemical to obtain through home country government the expressed consent of the importing country to receive the banned or restricted substance.

PRIORITY INCREMENTAL BUDGET. Similar to ordinary incremental budget. However, the budget request must be accompanied by a statement of what incremental activities or changes would occur if the budget were increased or decreased by a given amount or percentage.

PRIORITY OF HUMAN NEEDS. The concept that needs have a definite order of levels and each level must be satisfied before the person advances to the next one.

PRIVACY. (*See* Right of privacy.)

PRIVATE BRAND. A brand owned by a middleman (wholesaler or retailer) and usually advertised and sold in a smaller geographical area, such as a state or region.

PRIVATE CARRIER. A carrier which moves its own goods by using its own transportation system.

PRIVATE ENTERPRISE. Exists when private citizens, rather than the government, own business.

PRIVATE PROPERTY. A group of rights that gives control over physical and intangible assets to private owners, private ownership is the basic institution of capitalism.

PRIVATIZING. Selling of government owned assets to private individuals or companies.

PRO CYCLICAL POLICY. A policy that stimulates the economy during an expansion and restrains an economy during a recession.

PROBABILITIES. Likelihood of occurrence of events.

PROBABILITY. The chance or odds of something happening.

PROBLEM SOLVING. That function of the accountant's information-supplying task which expresses in concise, quantified terms the relative advantages and disadvantages to the firm of pursuing a possible future course of action, or the relative advantages of any one of several alternative methods of operation.

PROCEDURES. Plans that establish a required method of handling future activities. They are guides to action; they detail the exact manner in which certain activities must be accomplished.

PROCESS. A series of actions or operations leading to a definite end.

PROCESS COSTING. The method of allocating costs to the products resulting from the mass production of like units.

PROCESSING UNIT. The computer component in which the computer's arithmetic operations are performed.

PRODUCT COSTS. Costs that are identified with goods

produced or purchased for resale.

PRODUCT DIVISION. An organizational structure in which different foreign operations report to different product groups at headquarters.

PRODUCT LIABILITY. A legal responsibility of a person or firm for the harmful consequences to others stemming from use of a product manufactured, sold, managed, or employed by the person or firm.

PRODUCT LIFE CYCLE THEORY. The theory that certain kinds of products go through a cycle consisting of four stages (introduction, growth, maturity, and decline) and that the location of production will shift internationally depending on the stage of the cycle.

PRODUCT RECALL. An effort by a business firm to remove a defective or sometimes dangerous product from consumer use and from all distribution channels.

PRODUCT SAFETY. Products that are safe in use, free from contamination and safe for health.

PRODUCTION. The finished product ready for consumer consumption. In the economic sense, it also includes economic services.

PRODUCTION CONTROL. A function which ensures the orderly flow of work in manufacturing operations. It determines when, where and how production of a job will occur.

PRODUCTION MANAGEMENT. Those activities necessary to manufacture products or create services. It includes activities such as purchasing, warehousing, transportation, and other operations to procure raw materials until the product or service is bought by the customer.

PRODUCTION SWITCHING. The movement of production from one country to another in response to changes in cost.

PRODUCTION VOLUME VARIANCE. Difference between budgeted fixed factory overhead and the fixed factory overhead applied to products.

PRODUCTIVITY. The output ratio within a time period with due consideration for quality.

PRODUCTIVITY. The relationship between total inputs and total outputs. Productivity increases when the outputs of an organization increase faster than the inputs necessary for production.

PRODUCTIVITY AGENT ROLE. A role performed by management and others that seeks to use resources in ways that produce the most outputs (economic and social benefits) for each unit of input (economic and social costs).

PROFIT. The amount left to the business after all income is received and all expenses paid. The prime motivator in a private enterprise economic system.

PROFIT AND LOSS CONTROL. A control technique designed to measure a division or other part of a business enterprise by calculating the total profit or loss) performance of that entity.

PROFIT BEFORE DEPRECIATION INTEREST AND TAXES. It is equal to revenue minus all operating expenses except depreciation, interest and taxes.

PROFIT CENTRE. A segment of a business that is responsible for both revenue and expense.

PROFIT MAXIMIZATION. Profit maximization is an economic philosophy that business produces a public good of improved efficiency and reduced prices when it seeks to maximize its profits through competitive activity.

PROFIT PLANNING. The term profit planning refers to the operating decisions in the areas of pricing, costs, volume of output and the firm's selection of product lines.

PROFITABILITY ACCOUNTING. *See* Responsibility accounting.

PROFITABILITY INDEX. It is the ratio of the present value of cash inflows at the required rate of return, to the initial cash outflow of the investment.

PROFITS. The excess of revenues over expenses.

PROFITS. The revenues of a person or company minus the costs incurred in producing the revenue.

PRO-FORMA STATEMENTS. Forecasted financial statements.

PROGRAMME. The detailed instructions which transmit the calculations the computer is to make on a set of data.

PROGRAMME ANALYSIS. Future ratios are used as standards of comparison. Future ratios can be developed from the projected or Performa financial statements. The comparison of current and past ratios with future ratios shows the firms relative strengths and weaknesses in the past and the future. The future ratios indicate weak financial position and indicator of corrective actions to be initiated.

PROGRAMME BUDGETING. A budgeting approach, used primarily by government agencies, emphasizing goals, the programmes to achieve them, and budgetary allocations designed to support such programmes.

PROGRAMMED COSTS. *See* Discretionary costs.

PROGRAMMER. The person who writes the instructions for the computer.

PROGRAMMES. A complex of goals, policies, procedure, rules, task assignments, steps to be taken, resources to employed, and other elements necessary to carry out a given course of action and normally supported by capital and operating budgets.

PROMISSORY NOTE. A contract in which one party promises payment of funds borrowed plus interest to another party at some specific time.

PROMOTION. A change within the organization to a higher position with greater responsibilities and usually requiring more advanced skills and knowledge than the previous position. Thus an upward movement to a position of more authority, responsibility and salary.

PROMOTION. Normally brings greater status and increase in pay.

PROMOTION BASED ON OPEN COMPETITION. The policy of filling positions or making promotions from the most qualified people available whether from inside or outside a given enterprise.

PROMOTION FROM WITHIN. The practice of making all promotions in an enterprise from people within it if it is possible to do so.

PROPRIETORSHIP. A separate entity with a single owner.

PRORATION. It is a division of taxes, interest, insurance and similar charges that the seller and the buyer each pay the portion representing the period of his/her ownership.

PROSPECTUS. A booklet containing all information about a company that would affect the value of new securities it wants to issue.

PROTECTED GROUP MEMBER. It is an individual falls within a group identified for protection under equal employment laws.

PROTECTING A POSITION. Once an investor has initiated position and determines that the fundamental and technical factors for a particular commodity are inside and places an order with his broker, he should at the same time determine how far he is willing to let the market go against him before he abandons the position.

PROTECTIONISM. It is a policy that favours the use of tariffs, quotas or other import restrictions designed to make domestic products competitive with foreign imports.

PROTESTANT ETHIC. A theory that there is more economic growth when work is viewed as a means of salvation and when people prefer to transform productivity gains into additional output rather than into additional leisure.

PROVISIONS. These are other types of current liabilities. They include provision for taxes or provision for dividends. Every business has to pay taxes on its income. Usually it takes some time to finalize the amount of tax with the tax authorities. Therefore, the amount of tax is estimated and shown as provision for taxes or tax liability in the balance sheet. Similarly, provision for paying dividends.

PROXY. A legal instrument giving another person the right to vote the shares of stock of an absentee stockholder.

PROXY STATEMENT. A statement sent by a board of directors to a corporation's stockholders announcing the company's annual meeting, containing information about the business to be considered at the meeting, and enclosing a proxy form for stockholders not attending the meeting.

PUBLIC AFFAIRS FUNCTION. An organization's activities intended to perceive, monitor, understand, communicate with, and influence the external environment, including local and national communities, government relations, and public opinion.

PUBLIC INVESTMENT. Government investment. Occurs when the government purchases physical capital.

PUBLIC (OR SOCIAL) SERVICE LEAVE. A type of corporate gift consisting of a leave of absence granted to an employee to engage in community service work, usually with full or partial pay provided by the employee's business firm.

PUBLIC POLICY. A plan of action by government to achieve some broad purpose affecting a large segment of the public.

PUBLIC POLICY AGENDA. All public problems of issues that receive the active and serious attention of government officials.

PUBLIC POLICY PROCESS. All of the activities and stages involved in development carrying out, and evaluating public policies.

PUBLIC RESPONSIBILITY COMMITTEE. A committee of a corporation's board of directors with the function of identifying social and political issues that may have an influence on the company and making recommendations to the directors about appropriate actions.

PUBLIC TRUSTEE. A concept that a business owner or manager should base company decisions on the interests of a wide range of corporate stakeholders or members of the general public. In doing so the business executive acts as a trustee of the public interest.

PUBLICITY. Any type of information about a company or a product which has apparent news value and is reported in the indifferent media and is not paid for by the firm.

PUBLICLY HELD CORPORATION. A corporation whose stock is available for purchase by the general investing public.

PUISNE MORTGAGE. Mortgage issued despite the failure of the lender to take possession of the title deeds to the property offered as security for the loan. The lender may register the property with the Land Registrar, this ensures that any transaction concerning the property must have the approval of the lender.

PULL. A promotion strategy that sells consumers before they reach the point of purchase, usually by relying on mass media.

PUNCHED CARD. A method of recording instructions to computers by punching holes in the cards and feeding them into the input unit of the computer.

PUNISHMENT. It is action taken to repel the person from undesired action.

PURCHASE OPTION. An option to purchase leased property at the end of the lease term. In some jurisdictions (mainly UK) purchase options are impossible if the transaction is to quality as a lease in others (*e.g.*, the French system and its derivative), a purchase option is mandatory. In the US, if the tax characteristics of a true lease are to be protected, the purchase option may not be at a price less than the assets fair market value at the time the right is exercised (*see* also Fixed price purchase option).

PURCHASING. The process of acquiring materials and supplies.

PURCHASING POWER. What a sum of money actually can buy.

PURCHASING POWER PARITY. Theory which states that the equilibrium exchange rate makes the dollar cost of foreign and domestic goods identical.

PURE COMPETITION. The market structure in which a large number of well-informed buyers. No individual seller or buyer thinks that they can influence the market price.

PURELY COMPETITIVE DEPOSIT MARKET. Situation where individuals banks are small relative to the entire market for deposits and must pay the market rate on deposits.

PUSH. A promotion strategy that involves direct selling techinques.

PUT OPTION. Gives a buyer the option to sell a financial asset at a specified price, up to the expiration date of the option.

Q

QUALITATIVE FACTOR. A factor that is of consequence but cannot be measured precisely and easily in dollars.

QUALITY CIRCLE. A small group of supervision and workers who meet to discuss ways to improve the overall quality of work done in their unit.

QUALITY CIRCLES. They are small groups of employees that meet on a regular basis to discuss ways to improve productivity and to cut costs.

QUALITY CONTROL CIRCLES (OR QUALITY CIRCLES). Participation of workers in solving work-related problems. Often several people, usually rank and file workers, are involved in solving the problems.

QUALITY CONTROL. Inspecting and testing products to ensure only good products are sold to customers.

QUALITY OF WORK LIFE. The favourableness or unforgetableness of a job environment for an organization's employee.

QUALITY OF WORKING LIFE. Programmes representing a systems approach to job design and job enrichment which will make jobs more interesting and challenging. Programmes are closely associated with the socio-technical systems approach.

QUANTITY CONTROLS. Government limitations on the amount of foreign currency that can be used for specific purposes.

QUANTITY VARIANCE. Efficiency variance pertaining to materials or direct labour.

QUERY OPERATION. An operation that returns a computer a value without modifying any objects.

QUESTIONABLE PAYMENTS. Something of value given to a person or firm, which raises significant ethical questions of right or wrong in the host nation or other nations.

QUOTA. A limit on the quantitative amount of a product allowed to be imported into or exported out of a country in a year.

QUOTA SYSTEM. A commodity agreement whereby producing and/or consuming countries divide total output and sales in order to stabilize the price of a particular product.

QUOTAS. A restriction on the number of goods that can enter a nation.

QUOTAS (JOB, HIRING EMPLOYMENT). An employment plan based on hiring a specific number or proportion of minorities women, or other groups who may be under-represented in an organization's workforce.

QUOTE SHEET. An analysis of costs used as a basis for determining selling prices.

QUOTED CURRENCY. The currency whose value is not I when an exchange rate is quoted by relating one currency to another.

QUOTE-DRIVEN TRADING. Trading, where brokers/ market makers give buy or sell quote for a scrip simultaneously.

R

R SQUARED. Square of the correlation co-efficiency, the proportion of the variability in the series that can be explained by the variability of one or more other series.

RAIDER. Having positive effect on sensex.

RATE OF RETURN ON ASSETS. Total profit divided by total assets.

RATE VARIANCE. The difference between actual wages paid and the standard wage rate, multiplied by the total actual hours of direct labour used. *See* Price variance.

RATIFICATION. Occurs when union members vote to accept the terms of a negotiated labour agreement.

RATIO. A ratio is defined as the quotient of two mathematical expressions and as the relationship between two or more things.

RATIONAL BUYING MOTIVE. A decision to buy which involves conscious thought and deliberation.

RATIONAL EXPECTATIONS HYPOTHESIS.

RATIONALITY. Analysis enquiring a clear goal, a clear understanding of alternatives by which a goal can be reached, an analysis and evaluation of alternatives in terms of the goal sought, needed information, and a desire to optimize.

RATIONALIZATION. *See* Rationalized production.

RATIONALIZATION PRODUCTION. The specialized of production by-product or process in different parts of the world to take advantage of varying costs of labour, capital and raw material.

REAL ASSET. A firm requires real assets to carry on its business. Real asset can be tangible or intangible. Plant, machinery, office, factory, furniture and building are examples of tangible real assets while technical know-how, technological collaborations, patents and copy rights are intangible real assets.

REAL BILLS DOCTRINE. The view that loans made by the banking system that are ultimately used to fund the production of goods and services are not inflationary.

REAL EXCHANGE RATE. Exchange rate adjusted for inflation.

REAL INTEREST RATE. The nominal Interest rate (the interest rate stated in the loan contract) minus the expected rate of inflation.

REAL MONEY BALANCES. The nominal money stock divided by the price level. It provides a measure of the purchasing power of money.

REAL OUTPUT. The physical quantity of goods and services produced in the economy in one year.

REALISTIC JOB PREVIEW (RJP). It is the process of providing a job applicant with an accurate picture of a job.

REALIZATION. The recognition of revenue. Generally three tests must be met. First, the earning process must be virtually complete in that the goods or services must be fully rendered. Second, an exchange of resources evidenced by a market transaction must occur. Third, the asset received must be cash or convertible into cash with reasonable certainty.

REALLOCATION. Allocation of the costs of operating the service departments to the various production departments in proportion to the relative benefits or services received by each production department.

REAL-TIME INFORMATION. Information on events as they occur.

REAPPORTIONMENT. *See* Reallocation.

REAR-END LOADING. The practice of constructing a rental schedule where the larger payments are made towards the end of the lease.

RECIPROCAL QUOTE. The reciprocal of the direct quote; also known as the indirect quote.

RECOGNITION LAGS. Lags in the recognition of the monetary policy maker that a policy action is needed. Based in the information available to it.

RECORDS. Memory of the company.

RECOURSE. Actions available to a party to a contract when the other parties have not fulfilled their obligations.

RECRUITING. It is the process of generating a pool of qualified applicants for organizational jobs.

RECRUITMENT OF MANAGERS. Attracting candidates for managerial positions in order to meet the objectives of the enterprise.

RECYCLING. The process by which waste products are remanufactured to produce new products. Re-melting old bottles to produce new bottles is an example.

RED CIRCLE RATE. It is a job whose currents occupant's pay is out of grade or range.

REDEMPTION. When a closed-end fund completes its tenure, it is said to be due for redemption. Units are then redeemed at the existing NAV, and investors are refunded their money. If an investor chooses to say on his units are rolled over. As the redemption date nears the discount to the NAV generally tends to reduce.

REDEMPTION VALUE. The value which a bondholder/ debenture holder will get on maturity is called redemption value. A bond/debenture may be redeemed at par or at premium (more than par value) or at discount (less than par value).

REDISCOUNT RATE. The rate at which the federal reserve will discount paper for commercial banks who are member banks.

REDLINING. It is the improper practice of some financial institutions to refuse to make home-improvement loans or mortgages in a financially stressed area. The practice is called redlining.

RE-ENGINEERING. I aims to root-out needless work and get every process in the company pointed in the direction of customer satisfaction reduced cycle time, and total quality.

REFLEX RALLY. It is a price correction from an oversold position. The Security's price moves up, but does not change the price's established trend.

REGIONAL SHOPPING CENTRE. A large shopping centre with from 50 to 100 or more stores.

REGISTERED BOND. A bond that is registered to the owner.

REGRESSION. A statistical method showing relationships among variables.

REGRESSION ANALYSIS. The measurement of the average amount of change in one variable that is associated with unit increases in the mounts of one or more other variables.

REGULATION. Restricted the maximum interest rate that banks could pay on savings and time deposits.

REINVESTED EARNINGS. *See* Retained income.

REINVESTMENT. The use of retained earnings to replace depreciated assets or to add to the existing stock of capital.

REINVESTMENT ASSUMPTION. The cash flows generates by the project can be reinvested at its internal rate of return or at the opportunity cost of capital.

REINVESTMENT RATE. The interest rate a lessor earns on lease during the period following the investment period of a lease.

RELATED PARTIES. In leasing transactions under FAS 13, a parent and its subsidiaries, an owner and its joint ventures, an investor and its invests, provided the parent or investor has the ability to exercise significant influence over the financial and operating policies of the related party. Under the internal revenue code, 50 per cent ownership is a general test of a related party.

RELATIONSHIP ENTERPRISES. Networks of strategic alliances among big companies, spanning different industries and countries.

RELATIVE CASH FLOWS. The incremental cash-flows found out by comparison between two real alternatives can be called relative cash-flows.

RELEVANT DATA FOR DECISION MAKING. Expected future data that will differ among alternatives.

RELEVANT INFORMATION. *See* Relevant data for decision-making.

RELEVANT RANGE. The band of activity in which budgeted sales and expense relationships will be valid.

RELIABILITY. Refers to the consistency with which a test measures an item.

RENEGOTIATIONS. A process by which international companies and government decide on a change in terms for operations.

RE-ORDER POINT. The re-order point is that inventory level at which an order should be placed to replenish the inventory.

REPATRIATION. An expatriate's return to his or her home country.

REPLACEMENT VALUE. Replacement value is the amount that a company would be required to spend if it were to replace its existing assets in the current condition.

REPLACEMENT COST. Cost to replenish a given amount of an asset.

REPORT OF BOARD OF DIRECTORS. Directors' report provides a summary of profits made and appointed by the company and other relevant information such as industrial relations, investments, financing, reorganization, appointment of auditors and directors, etc.

REPRESENTATIVE DEMOCRACY. A type of government in which individual citizen elect representative to make decisions governing the society.

REPRESENTATIVE FULL-BODIED MONEY. Gold certificates. Money that is backed 100% by a commodity.

REPURCHASE AGREEMENT. An agreement between two

parties under which one party agrees to sell a security and to buy it back on an agreed-upon date and at an agreed-upon price. The difference between the original sale price and the subsequent repurchase price is in effect the interest on a loan which when expressed as an interest rate, is commonly known as the 'repo' rate.

REPURCHASE OF STOCK. Device to pay cash to firm's shareholders that provides more preferable tax treatment for shareholders than dividends. Treasury stock to the name given to previously issued stock that has been repurchased by the firm. A repurchase is achieved through either a Dutch auction open market, or tender offer.

REQUIRED RATE OF RETURN. Minimum desired rate of return.

REQUIRED RESERVES. The dollar amounts based on reserve ratios that banks are required to keep on deposit at a Federal Reserve Bank.

REQUIRED RETURN. The minimum expected return one would require to be willing to purchase the asset that is to make the investment.

REQUIRED YIELD. Generally referring to bonds, the yield required by the market place to match the available returns for financial instruments with comparable risk.

RESERVE. It has one of three meanings (1) a restriction of dividend-declaring power as denoted by a specific subdivision of retained income; (2) an offset to an asset; and (3) an estimate of a definite liability of indefinite or uncertain amount.

RESERVE. An accounting entry that property reflects the contingent liabilities.

RESERVE AGENT. It is trust company designated by a State bank department or a national bank located in a central reserve city which with the approval of the comptroller of the currency, could act as a reserve depository for a portion of the legal reserve requirements of bank.

RESERVE CULTURE SHOCK. The encountering of culture shock when returning to one's own country because of having accepted what was encountered abroad.

RESERVE CURRENCY. A foreign currency held by Central bank or monetary authority for the purpose of exchange, intervention and settlement of inter-Governmental claims.

RESERVE RATIOS. Specified percentages of deposits,

established by the Federal Reserve Board, that banks must keep in a non-interest bearing account at one of the 12 Federal Reserve Banks.

RESERVE REQUIREMENTS. The percentage of different types of deposits that member banks are required to hold on deposit.

RESERVES AND SURPLUS. *See* Reserve.

RESIDUAL ASSETS. Assets that remain after sufficient assets are dedicated to meet all senior debt holders' claims in full.

RESIDUAL CLAIM. Related to equity claim.

RESIDUAL DIVIDEND APPROACH. An approach that suggests a firm pay dividends if and only if acceptable investment opportunities for those funds which are currently not available.

RESIDUAL INCOME (RI). The net income of a profit centre or investment centre, less the imputed interest on the net assets used by the centre.

RESIDUAL INSURANCE. An insurance policy guaranteeing a certain residual value at the end of the lease term.

RESIDUAL INTEREST. The owners' equity in the entity's assets after deducting liabilities and any other claims with a higher priority.

RESIDUAL LEVEL. A price level above which it is supposedly difficult for a security or market to rise.

RESIDUAL LOSSES. Lost wealth of the shareholders due to divergent behaviour of the managers.

RESIDUAL METHOD. A method allocating the purchase price for the acquisition of another firm among the acquired assets.

RESIDUAL OPTION. An option to renew the lease at the end of the initial lease term. Here, too, care must be taken in granting a renewal option for a fair rental value. If this is not done properly, it may later be ruled that the lease is not a true lease — indemnity clauses activated.

RESIDUAL VALUE. The predicted disposal value of along-lived asset.

RESIDUAL VALUE. The value of equipment at the conclusion of the lease term.

RESIDUALS. Parts of stock returns not explained by the explanatory variable (the market index return). They measure the impact of firm-specific events during a particular period.

RESOURCE-BASED VIEW OF THE FIRM. A perspective that holds that each company has a unique combination of competencies.

RESOURCES. Anything a nation

uses to produce economic goods and services, minerals, labour, etc.

RESPONSIBILITY. The obligation owed by subordinates to their superiors for exercising authority delegated to them in a way to accomplish results expected.

RESPONSIBILITY. The obligations are to perform certain tasks and duties.

RESPONSIBILITY ACCOUNTING. A system of accounting that recognizes various responsibility centres throughout the organization and reflects the plans and actions of each of these centres by allocating particular revenues and costs to those having the pertinent responsibilities. Also called profitability accounting and activity accounting.

RESPONSIBILITY BUDGET. The responsibility budget specifies plan in terms of individual responsibilities.

REST. A little given to the surplus account that appears in the published statement of the Bank of England elsewhere in the English bank accounting, this account is called for 'Reserve fund'.

REST FREQUENCY. The frequency with which the floating rate changes.

RESTRAINT OF TRADE. Actions by business firms that tend to lessen or eliminate competition.

RESTRICTIVE COVENANTS. Provisions that place constraints on the operations of borrowers, such as restrictions on working capital, fixed assets, future borrowing, and payment of dividend.

RETAIL CREDIT. Credit granted by a firm to consumers for the purchase of goods or services.

RETAIL. Individual and institutional customers as opposed to dealers and brokers.

RETAINED EARNINGS. *See* Retained income.

RETAINED EARNINGS. That part of a company's post-tax earnings not distributed to the shareholders, and thus retained by the firm to finance the day-to-day running of the company and any future expansion. Retained earnings are added to reserves and hence appear on the firm's balance sheet.

RETAINED INCOME. Additional owners' equity generated by profits.

RETURN ON INVESTMENT (ROI). A measure of income or profit divided by the investment required to help obtain the income or profit.

RETURN ON CAPITAL. Measure of how well a company's capital

is used, equal to 100 times the trading profit (before tax and interest) divided by the average capital used.

RETURN ON CAPITAL EMPLOYED. The ratio of accounting profit to capital employed.

RETURN ON EQUITY (ROE). It is an indicator of profitability. Determined by dividing net income for the past 12 months by common stock holders' equity (adjusted for stock splits). Result is shown as a percentage. Investors use ROE as a measure of how a company is using its money. ROE may be decomposed into return on assets (ROA) multiplied by financial leverage (total assets/total equity).

RETURN ON INVESTMENT. The yield, the interest rate earned by the lessor in a lease which is measured by the rate which the excess cash flows permit recovery of investment. The rate at which the cash flows not needed for debt service or payment of taxes amortize the investment of the equity participant.

RETURN ON INVESTMENT (ROI). The amount of profit, sometimes measured before and sometimes after the payment of taxes, divided by the amount of investment.

RETURN ON STOCKHOLDERS' EQUITY. The rate of return on the invested capital of the shareholders.

RETURN-ON-INVESTMENT CONTROL. A control technique designed to measure a division or other part of a business enterprise by looking on the profit made as a percentage of the investment in assets in that entity.

REVALUATION. A formal change in an exchange rate by which the foreign-currency value of the reference currency rises, resulting in a strengthening of the reference currency.

REVALUATION EQUITY. That portion of stockholders' equity that shows all accumulated holding gains not otherwise shown in retained income.

REVENUE CONVERSION. Trading strategy that locks in arbitrage profit by selling an asset short, writing a put and buying a call on the asset with the same terms.

REVENUES. Generally, a gross increase in net assets from delivering goods or services. More specifically, revenues are inflows or other enhancements of assets of an enterprise or settlements of its liabilities (or a combination of both) during a period from delivering or producing goods, rendering services, or other activities that constitute the enterprise's ongoing major or central operations.

REVERSE DISCRIMINATION. It may exist when a person is denied an opportunity because of preferences given to protected-group individuals who may be less qualified.

REVOCABLE LETTER OF CREDIT. A letter of credit that can be changed by any of parties involved.

RHO. A measure of the change in an option premium with respect to a percentage-point change in the interest rate.

RI. Symbol for residual income.

RIGHT (HUMAN). A concept used in ethical reasoning that means that a person or group is entitled to something or is entitled to be treated in a certain way.

RIGHT OF PRIVACY. A person's fundamental expectation of protection from organizational invasion of one's private life and unauthorized release of confidential information about the person.

RIGHT TO WORK. Laws passed by individual states to permit workers the right to work without having to join a union.

RIGHTS ISSUE. Rights issues are the shares issued to existing shareholders of a company at a subscription price that may be different from the current share price.

RIO DECLARATION. The result of the Rio Earth summit which sets out fundamental principles of environmentally responsive behaviour.

RIO EARTH SUMMIT. A meeting held in Rio de Janeiro in June 1992 that brought together people from around the world to discuss major environmental issues.

RISK-ADJUSTED RETURN. Return earned on an asset normalized for the amount of risk associated with that asset.

RISK ANALYSIS. An approach to problem analysis which weighs risk in a situation. by introducing probabilities to give a more accurate assessment of the risks involved.

RISK-FREE ASSET. An asset whose future return is known today with certainty.

RISK-FREE RATE. The rate earned on riskless asset.

RISK FREE SECURITY. It is one which has a zero variance or standard deviation. It will have the same return under all possible economic scenarios.

RISK MANAGEMENT. The process of identifying and evaluating risk and selecting and managing techniques to adapt to risk exposures.

RISKY ASSET. An asset whose future return is uncertain.

ROBOT. Any automatic machine that performs work without the direct intervention of a human being.

ROI. *See* Return on investment.

ROL. Symbol for return on investment.

ROLL OVER. Most term loans in the Euro-market are made on a roll over basis, which means that the loan is periodically re-priced at an agreed spread over the appropriate, currently prevailing Libor rate. Reinvest funds received from a maturing security in a new issue of the same or a similar security.

ROLLING SETTLEMENT. Prior to July 18, 1994, purchases and sales of securities were combined during an accounting period (normally ten working days) to arrive at a net settlement figure which was due for payment on the second Monday following that account period. After July 18, 1994, a rolling settlement was introduced which initially commenced on a ten-day basis (known as T + 10) whereby settlement was due ten days after the deal so as to reduce the settlement periods and generally speed up transactions. Thus rolling settlement is one in which trades outstanding at the end of the day have to be settled (payments made for purchases or deliveries in the case of sale of securities) at the end of the settlement period.

ROLL-UP FUND. Offshore investments that reinvest interest so that it becomes a part of the capital thus conferring tax advantages.

ROOM TRADER. A stock exchange, member who does not maintain a commission house for the execution of customers orders, but who trades solely for his own account. He is a speculator who takes out an exchange membership in order to save the commission charges on his voluminous transactions and to have the privilege of trading on the floor of the exchange to take advantage of the price fluctuations as they occur.

ROUND LOT. A trading order typically of 100 shares of a stock or some multiple of 100 related odd lot.

ROUND TURN. It is a complete trading transaction *i.e.*, the sale of a security or a commodity previously purchased, a purchase to cover a previous short sale. Thus it is a procedure by which the long or short position of an individual to offset by an opposite transaction or by accepting or making delivery of the actual financial instrument physical commodity.

ROUND-TRIP TRANSACTIONS COSTS. Costs of completing a transaction, including commissions market impact costs, and taxes.

ROUNDS. Conference held by GATT to establish multilateral agreements to liberalize trade.

ROYALTIES. Payments for the use of intangible assets abroad.

RUBBER CHEQUE. A cheque that has bounced because of insufficient balance in the issuer's account.

RULE OF COST. The idea that all human actions generate costs.

RULES. They are specific guidelines that regulate and restrict the behaviour of individuals.

RULES. Required action of non action, allowing no discretion, *e.g.*, 'positively no smoking'.

RUNNING MARGINS. Difference in the rates of interest on money borrowed and on the same money invested.

S

SADC. *See* Southern African Development Community.

SAFE HARBOUR LEASE. A lease to transfer tax benefits of ownership (depreciation and debt tax shield) from the lessee, if the lessee could not use them, to lessor that could use them.

SAFE HARBOUR PROVISIONS. The provisions in the U.S. economic recovery tax act (1981) defining the basic criteria under which a financing transaction could meet the definition of a lease for which purpose the rules represents a considerable liberalization of former IRS guidelines on true and allowed pure tax benefits transfer.

SAFE KEEP. For a fee, bankers will hold in their vault dip coupons on, and present for payment at maturity bonds and money market instruments.

SAFETY. Refers to protection of the physical health of people.

SAFETY CUSHION. In a contingent immunization strategy, the difference between the initially available immunization level and the safety-net return.

SAFETY STOCK. A minimum inventory that provides a cushion against reasonably expected maximum demand and against variations in lead time.

SALARY. Payments made to workers on a weekly, bi-weekly or monthly basis.

SALE AND LEASE BACK. Sale of an existing asset to a financial institution which then leases it back to the user. Sometimes, a user may sell an asset earned by him to the lessor (leasing company) and takes it back for lease from him. Thus it is a transaction which involves the sale of the properly by the owner and a lease of the property back to the seller.

SALE-LEASE BACK. A transaction which involves the sale of the property by the owner and a lease of the property back to the seller.

SALE-REPURCHASE SPREAD. The difference between the sale and repurchase price expressed as a percentage of the net asset value. The spread indicates the load that the investor has to bear for investing in an open-ended scheme.

SALES AND PURCHASE LOAD. It indicates the premium discount to the NAV at which the investor can enter or exit the scheme.

SALES CHARGE. The fee charged by a mutual fund when purchasing shares, usually payable as a commission to marketing agent, such as financial advisor, who is thus compensated for his assistance to a purchaser. It represents the difference, if any between the share purchase price and the share net asset value.

SALES FINANCE COMPANIES. Financial companies that purchase instalment contracts from retailers.

SALES FORECAST. A key input to a firm's financial planning process. External sales forecasts are based on historical experience, statistical analysis, and consideration of various macro economic factors. Thus it an estimation of a future period's sales.

SALES MIX. The relative combination of the quantities of a variety of company products that compose total sales.

SALES PROMOTION. Marketing activities other than personal selling, advertising and publicity that stimulate consumer purchasing and dealer effectiveness, such as displays, shows, exhibits, and other non-recurring selling efforts.

SALES REPRESENTATIVE (FOREIGN). A representative that usually operates either exclusively or nonexclusively within an assigned market and on a commission basis, without assuming risk or responsibility.

SALES RESPONSE FUNCTION. The amount of sales created at different levels of marketing expenditure.

SALES VOLUME VARIANCE. Difference between the flexible budget amounts and the static budget amounts.

SALES-AID LEASE. A form of lessor to encourage business by offering the customer a package deal including lease facilities known in the US as a vendor lease.

SALES-TYPE LEASE. An arrangement whereby a firm leases its own equipment, such as IBM leasing its own computers, thereby competing with an independent leasing company.

SALVAGE VALUE. The minimum value for a depreciable asset. After sufficient depreciation is taken such that the cost minus accumulated depreciation equals salvage value, no more depreciation may be taken. Not the same as residual value.

SAMPLE. A small part of a whole intended to show the quality or style of the whole.

SAMURAI BOND. A yen denominated bond issued in Tokyo by a non-Japanese borrower related, bull-dog bond and Yankee bond.

SAMURAI LEASE. Japanese source lease design of fund foreign assets in order to reduce the Japanese balance of payments.

SAMURAI MARKET. The foreign market in Japan.

SATISFYING. A term used by Herbert A. Simon to denote the tendencies of manages, normally in instances of bounded rationality, in making decisions to pick a course of action that is deemed 'good enough' under the circumstances. *See* Bounded rationale.

SAVING AND LOAN ASSOCIATION. A depository institution originally designed as a mutual association of depositors designed to convert funds from savings accounts into mortgage loans.

SBIC. Small Business Investment Company.

SCALAR RELATIONSHIPS. Authority relationships are said to be scalar when subordinates report to their immediate superiors and when their superiors report directly, as subordinates, to their superiors. In other words, the chain of command that runs from the top of an organization to its lowest ranks.

SCALE ENHANCING. Described a project that is in the same risk class as the whole firm.

SCALE IN. When a trader or investor gradually takes a position in a security or market overtime.

SCALE. A bank that offers to pay different rates of interest on CDs of varying rates is said to be 'post a scale'. Order to buy or sell one or more lots in future at designated price intervals and contingent grouped orders entered.

SCALP. To trade for small gains, it normally involves establishing and liquidating a position quickly, usually within the same day.

SCATTER DIAGRAM. A graph which plots values of one variable on the vertical axis and values of another variable on the horizontal axis.

SCENARIO ANALYSIS. The use of horizontal analysis to project bond total return under different reinvestment rates and future market yields.

SCHEDULED CASH FLOWS. The mortgage, principal and interest payments due to be paid under the terms of the mortgage not including possible pre-payments.

SCIENCE. Organized knowledge of pertinence to an area, usually an area of practice.

SCIENTIFIC MANAGEMENT. A term originally used as denoting the work and approach of F.W. Taylor and his associates in analyzing management. It implies that the methods of scientific inquiry, analysis, and summary can be applied to the activities of managers. It late implied time study and similar methods used by Taylor and his followers to analyze activities of people in organizations. Basically, it sought to develop (1) ways of increasing productivity by making work easier to perform and (2) methods for motivating people to take advantage of labour-saving techniques it developed. It may be summarized as (1) replacing rules of thumb with rules of science, (2) achieving cooperation rather than chaotic individualism, (3) obtaining harmony rather than discord, (4) working for maximum rather than restricted output, (5) developing workers to the fullest extent possible.

SCORCHED EARTH. The term refers to the defensive tactics for a hostile take over bid in which the target company sells its most attractive assets or initiates adverse publicity about itself in an effort to make it seem a less than desirable acquisition.

SCOREKEEPING. That data accumulation function of the accountant's information-supplying task which enables both internal and external parties to evaluate the financial performance of the firm.

SCRA (SECURITIES CONTRACT REGULATION ACT).

SCRAP VALUE. *See* Residual value.

SCREEN BASED TRADING. When buying or selling of securities is done using computers and matching of trade is done by a stock exchange computer.

SDR. *See* Special drawing right.

SEARCH COSTS. Costs associated with locating a counter party to a trade, including explicit costs (such as advertising) and implicit costs (such as the value of time) related, information costs.

SEASONAL CREDIT. Loans made to depository institutions facing strong seasonal variations in deposits and loans such as banks in agricultural areas.

SEASONAL VARIATION. Regular, recurring fluctuations confined to a one-year time period.

SEASONED DATING. Extended credit for customers who

order goods in periods other than peak seasons.

SEASONED ISSUE. Issue of a security for which there is an existing market.

SEASONED NEW ISSUE. A new issue of stock after the company's securities have previously been issued. A seasoned new issue of common stock can be made by using a cash offer or a rights offer.

SEAT. The membership on a stock exchange.

SEC. Securities and Exchange Commission, the primary federal regulatory agency of the securities industry.

SECOND PASS REGRESSION. A cross-sectional regression of portfolio returns on betas. The estimated slope is the measurement of the reward for bearing systematic risk during the period analyzed.

SECONDARY BOYCOTT. The boycotting of a company that does business with a company being boycotted.

SECONDARY INTERACTIONS OR INVOLVEMENT. The relationship a company has with those social and political groups that feel the impact of the company's main activities and take steps to do something about it. These relationships are derived from the firm's primary interactions.

SECONDARY ISSUE. Procedure for selling blocks of seasoned issues of stocks. More generally, sale of already issued stock.

SECONDARY MARKET. The market where existing financial assets are bought and sold.

SECONDARY NEEDS. Human needs that are behaviour based, such as ego and recognition needs.

SECONDARY PERIOD. Frequently optional, the period in a finance lease which follows the full pay-out of the lessor's investment plus profit.

SECONDARY SOURCE OF DATA. Data republished by an agency other than the original collector and publisher.

SECOND-TIER SUBSIDIARIES. Subsidiaries that report to a tax heaven subsidiary.

SECRECY. A characteristic of an accounting system that implies that companies do not disclose much information about accounting practices; more common in Germanic countries.

SECRET PARTNER. A partner who assumes an active role in the business but is not known to the public as a partner.

SECTION 482. The U.S. department of treasury regulations governing transfer prices.

SECTOR FUND. Such funds invest only in stocks belonging to a specific industry. Sector funds usually aim for growth and while this can be very lucrative if the sector is doing well. The corresponding risk is also higher. Sector funds are generally considered to be among those at the greatest risk among equity funds.

SECULAR TOTALITARIANISM. A dictatorship not affiliated with any religious group or system of beliefs.

SECULAR TREND. Long term growth or decay.

SECURED DEBT. Debt that in the event of default has first claim on specified assets.

SECURED PREMIUM NOTES (SPN). It is a secured debenture redeemable at a premium, *i.e.* at a price higher than the purchase (or face) price. It is a medium to long term debenture, zero interest debenture (ZID) OR zero coupon bonds do not carry an explicit rate of interest. The difference between the face value of the bond and its purchase price is the return or the investor.

SECURITIES ACT OF 1934. Main provisions of this act set up securities and Exchange Commission and gave Federal Reserve Board the authority to set margin requirements for buying stocks.

SECURITIES ANALYSTS. Related financial analysts.

SECURITIES AND EXCHANGE COMMISSION (SEC). A U.S. government agency that regulates securities brokers, dealers and markets.

SECURITIES AND EXCHANGE COMMISSION. The federal agency designated by the U.S. Congress as holding the ultimate responsibility for authorizing the generally accepted accounting principles for companies whose stock is held by the general investing public.

SECURITIZATION. It is the process by which illiquid assets are packaged, converted into tradable securities and sold to the third party investors. Currently securitization transactions in the country cover car receivables truck receivables, receivables from the department of telecommunications and housing loan receivables.

SECURITY AGREEMENT. An agreement between the owner trustee and the indenture trustee whereby the owner trustee assigns title to the equipment, the lease, and rental payments under the lease as security for amounts due to the lenders. The same as an indenture of trust or mortgage.

SECURITY. Price of paper that proves ownership of stocks, bonds and other investments.

SEGMENT. Any line of activity or part of an organization for which separate determination of costs and sales is wanted.

SEGMENT MARGIN. The contribution margin for each segment less all separable fixed costs both discretionary and committed a measure of long run profitability.

SEGMENTED MARKET HYPOTHESIS. The hypothesis that bonds with different maturates are not substitutable for one another, their yields are determined indepen-dently of one another.

SEIGNORAGE. The profit from creating money and a source of revenue to the government.

SELECTION. It is the process of picking individuals who have relevant qualifications to fill jobs in an organization.

SELECTIVE BUYING MOTIVES. The motives which enter into the final determination of the specific product which is purchased.

SELF-ACTUALIZATION. It is the striving of an individual to reach the highest level of potential.

SELF-FUNDING. It occurs when an employer sets aside funds to pay health claims in excess of the amount provided by funding in lieu of insurance coverage.

SELF-INSURANCE. When a firm retains enough funds to cover a specific loss.

SELLING AGENT. Sells the entire output of a manufacturer and represents him on a containing basis.

SELLING HEDGE. Anyone who owns a commodity in the actual market and who is considered long simply sells a contract in the futures market (that it becomes a short).

SEMANTICS. The meaning of words.

SEMICONDUCTOR SILICON CHIP. A small computational device made of silicon material that is a key component of computers and other forms of electronic technology. (*See* Microprocessor.)

SEMI STRONG FROM MARKET EFFICIENCY. Asserts that no publicly available information will help predict future asset prices or returns better than the last known value of the asset.

SENIOR DEBT. It derives its name from its position in the hierarchy of capital structure. In a liquidation scenario, senior debt is repaid in full prior to making any payments to the subordinated debt and/ or equity holders, provided the firm has a strong base of equity to which an appropriate amount of debt can be added, senior debt could be the next source of short and long-term capital.

SENSITIVITY ANALYSIS. Measuring how the basic predicted results will be effected by variations in the critical data inputs that will influence those results.

SENSITIVITY INDEX. An index that measures the relationship between sales of a type of product and changes in disposable personal income.

SENSITIVITY TRAINING. A form of training based on behaviour of persons in groups and, through undirected group interchange, designed to make these persons more aware of the feelings and the feelings of others toward them.

SENSITIVITY TRAINING. (*See* Encounter group training.)

SEPARABLE COST. A cost directly identifiable with a particular segment.

SEPARATE ENTITY APPROACH. A system for taxation of corporate income in which each unit is taxed when it receives income, with the result being double taxation.

SEQUESTRATION. The term refers to the act of seizure of property or other assets by the courts until a dispute has been settled.

SERVICE DEPARTMENTS. Those departments that exist solely to aid the production departments by rendering specialized assistance with certain phases of the work.

SERVICE EXPORTS. International received earnings other than those derived from the exporting of tangible goods.

SERVICE SELLING. The type of selling in which a salesperson assists a consumer in completing a purchase where the consumer has already decided to make purchase.

SERVICE SOCIETY. A society in which the provision of services rather than the production of material goods, dominate work and employs the largest proportion of the labour force.

SERVICES. Activities which are offered for sale or are offered in connection with sale of goods.

SERVICES ACCOUNTS. The part of a country's current account that measures travel and transportation tourism and fees and royalties.

SETTLEMENT. It refers to the scrip-wise settlement of trades by a broker after the trading period is over.

SETTLEMENT DATE. After trade has been executed, securities and money must change hands within five business days (excluding Sundays and holidays). For example, if trade is made on Wednesday, it is settled on the following Wednesday.

SETTLEMENT GUARANTEE. Settlement guarantee is the guarantee provided by the clearing corporation of settlement of all trades even if a party defaults to deliver securities or pay cash.

SETTLEMENT OF TRANSACTION IN NON-SPECIFIED SECURITIES. Transactions in non-specified securities are for delivery, unless they are offset by opposite transaction in the course at the settlement period itself. The exchange issues delivery orders and receives orders for all transactions entered into, during the settlement period which are not offset by opposite.

SETTLEMENT PERIOD. The stock exchanges divided the period of one year into settlement periods. The settlement period in specified shares as well as non-specified shares is generally a week.

SEVERANCE PAY. A special payment made to an employee of a firm to compensate for an unexpected permanent layoff.

SHAREHOLDER. (*See* Stockholder.)

SHAREHOLDER PROPOSAL. A proposal made by a stockholder and included in a corporation's notice of its annual meeting that advocates some course of actions to be taken by the company.

SHAREHOLDER SUIT (INDIVIDUAL). A lawsuit initiated by one or more stockholders that attempts to recover damages they (as stockholders) personally suffered due to alleged actions of the company's management.

SHAREHOLDERS DERIVATIVE SUIT. A lawsuit initiated by one or more stockholders that attempts to recover damages suffered by the company due to alleged action of the company's management.

SHARE SPLIT. A share split is a method to increase the number of outstanding shares through a proportional reduction in the par value of the share. A share split affects only the par value and the number of outstanding shares, the shareholders total fund remains unaltered.

SHIPPER'S EXPORT DECLARATION. A shipping document that controls exports and is used to compile trade statistics.

SHOPPING CENTRE. A group of different kinds of stores located in a single area sharing a common parking lot and usually advertising as a group.

SHOPPING GOOD. A good in which price and quality

comparisons are usually made before its purchase. The price is usually a sizable amount, and purchasing are made infrequently. This good is also widely advertised.

SHORT HEDGE. A futures or option position to protect against a possible decrease in prices.

SHORT SELLING. Selling a stock and then buying it back at a later date in order to make a profit.

SHORT TERM ASSETS. Assets in debt market which mature in one year or less from the date of issue.

SHORT TERM INVESTMENT. A temporary investment in marketable securities of otherwise idle cash.

SHORT TERM LEASE. Generally refers to an operating lease.

SHORTAGE. Situation where quantity demanded exceeds quantity supplied.

SHORT-RUN AGGREGATE SUPPLY (SRAS). Characterizes the supply side of the macro economy in the short-run, *i.e.* summarizes the total quantity of goods and services that an economy will produce at various price levels holding constant such things as the prices of inputs, taxes, the stock of physical capital available to firms, and the level of technology.

SHORT-RUN MACROECONOMIC EQUILIBRIUM. The determination of the equilibrium interest rate price level and level of real GDP corresponding to the intersection of aggregate demand and short-run aggregate supply.

SHORT-RUN PERFORMANCE MARGIN. The contribution margin for each segment less separable.

SIDE EFFECT. (*See* Externally.)

SIGHT DRAFT. A commercial bill of exchange that requires payment to be made as soon as it is presented to the party obligated to pay.

SILENT LANGUAGE. The way variety of cues other than formal language by which messages can be sent.

SILENT PARTNER. A partner who invests in the business but does not take an active part in the operations of the business.

SIMPLE DEPOSIT MULTIPLIER. The multiple by which deposits increase in reserves.

SIMPLE QUANTITY THEORY OF MONEY DEMAND. Views transactions as the primary motive for holding money.

SIMPLE RANDOM SAMPLE. Each item in a business has an equal and known chance of being selected for the sample.

SIMPLY FUND. The clearing house has ample protection against default as a result of its original and variation margin requirements. Margin deposits however form only the foundation for the resources that make it possible for the clearing house to guarantee all cleared contracts for both delivery and payment. As a further safeguard and as a condition at membership a clearing member contributes to the guarantee fund at the clearing-house.

SINGLE EUROPEAN ACT. A 1987 act of the EU (then the EC) allowing all proposals except those relating to taxation workers' rights and immigration to be adopted by a weighted majority of member countries.

SINGLE LINE STORE. A store which carriers a wide variety of one line of merchandise.

SINGLE STEP INCOME STATEMENT. One that groups all revenue together and then lists and deducts all expenses together without drawing any intermediate subtotals.

SINGLE TAXATION. Under this system, shareholders' earnings are taxed only once at the corporate level. Dividends received by shareholders are exempt from tax. India currently follows this system and companies in India pay tax on their profits at 35 per cent and they will have to pay additional tax of 10 per cent on the after-tax profits distributed as dividends to shareholders. Shareholders, both individuals and corporations do not pay taxes on the dividend income. However, they do pay tax on capital gains. The marginal personal tax is 30 per cent and capital gain tax rates 20 per cent. Under this system, an investor will prefer dividends over capital gains.

SINGLE-STEP PROFIT AND LOSS ACCOUNT. It records all the revenue items first and then the expense items are shown. The total expenditure is subtracted from the total revenue to obtain the net income or net profit.

SINKING FUND. It is a fund which is created out of fixed payments each period to accumulate to a future sum after a specified period.

SINKING RATE FUND. The rate of interest allocated to a sinking fund set aside for future payment of taxes (generally applicable only in leveraged leases).

SITUATIONAL APPROACH TO LEADERSHIP. The approach that studies leadership on the premise that it is strongly influenced by the situation from which the leader emerges and in which he or she operates.

SIZED OUT. It occurs when a broker cannot cross stock at a block trader's price because another broker is offering a larger number of shares at the trader's prices, making the other broker's offer more attractive.

SKIMMING PRICES. It is a strategy of putting a high initial price followed by several price drops. Skimming allows the seller to attract as many buyers as possible at the highest price before dropping the price some more, which attracts more buyers at the next level.

SLIPPAGE. Under performance of a start-up company. Slippage may lead Sweet Equity.

SMALL BUSINESS ADMINISTRATION. An agency of the federal government created to assist, encourage and protect.

SMITHSONIAN AGREEMENT. A 1971 agreement among countries that resulted in the devaluation of the U.S. dollar, revaluation of other world currencies a widening of exchange rate flexibility and a commitment on the part of all participating countries to reduce trade.

SNAKE. It is the popular term for the European system that links the following currencies, the Belgian and French francs, the Danish Kroner, the Irish punt, the Dutch guilder, the German Dutch mark and the Italian Lira.

SNAP QUOTE. The snap quote feature allows a trading member participant to get instantaneous market information as any desired security descriptor. This is normally used for descriptors that are not already as displayed in the market watch window. The information presented is the same as that of market watch window.

SOCIAL AUDIT. An audit of the performance of an enterprise in those areas which have a significant social impact and importance.

SOCIAL AUDIT. A systematic study and evaluation of an organization's social performance.

SOCIAL CONTRACT. In international business, an unwritten agreement usually derived from business discussions with government and community leaders that a firm in a host nation will serve the needs of that nation's people in a responsive manner so that mutual interests and benefits will develop from the relationship.

SOCIAL FORECASTING. An attempt to estimate major social and political trends that may affects a company's operations and environment in the future.

SOCIAL INVOLVEMENT. (*See* Corporate social involvement.)

SOCIAL MARKET ECONOMY. An economic system in which there is heavy government spending and high taxation to pay for such social services as health care, education subsidized, housing for the poor, and unemployment benefits but the prices of products are determined by supply and demand rather than by government fiat.

SOCIAL OVERHEAD COSTS. Public and private investments that are necessary to prepare the environment for effective operation of a new business or another major institution.

SOCIAL PARTNERSHIP. A temporary or permanent coalition of pluralistic interest groups who cooperate for the purpose of addressing or resolving some social problem.

SOCIAL REGULATIONS. Regulations intended to accomplish certain social improvements such as equal employment opportunity or on the job safety and health.

SOCIAL REPORT. Information about an organization's social performance, often contained in a company's annual report to stockholders and sometimes prepared as a special report to management or the general public.

SOCIAL RESPONSIBILITY. (*See* Corporate social responsibility.)

SOCIAL RESPONSIBILITY OF MANAGERS. The responsibility of managers, in carrying out their socially approved missions, to be responsive to, to be congruent with, and to interact and live with the forces and elements of their social environment.

SOCIAL RESPONSIVENESS. The ability of an enterprise to relate policies and operations to the environment that are beneficial to both the organization and the society.

SOCIAL RESPONSIVENESS. (*See* Corporate social responsiveness.)

SOCIETY. A broad grouping of people having common traditions, institutions and collective activities and interest; the term nation state is often used in international business to denote a society.

SOCIETY. The people, institutions and technology that make up a recognizable human community.

SOCIO-ECONOMIC SYSTEM. The combined and interrelated social economic and political institution's characteristic of a society.

SOCIO-TECHNICAL SYSTEM. A system viewed as an interconnection of physical (technical) and social elements in an organization.

SOFT ARBITRAGE. The term implies the movement of funds between the money markets and bank deposits to benefit from the difference in interest rates.

SOFT BUDGET. A financial condition in which an enterprise excess of expenditure over earnings is compensated for by some other institution typically a government or a state controlled financial institution.

SOFT CURRENCY. *See* Weak currency.

SOFTWARE. The programmes and all documents associated with a computer.

SOGO SHOSHA. Japanese trading companies that import and export merchandise.

SOLA. A bill of exchange that does not have a duplicate as in bills in a set.

SOLE PROPRIETORSHIP. A form of business ownership which consists of a business with one owner.

SOLID WASTE. Any solid waste materials resulting from human activities such as municipal refuse and sewage industrial wastes and agricultural wastes.

SOLID WASTE POLLUTION. Trash and garbage that are not properly disposed of to avoid pollution.

SOLVENCY. It refers to the firm's ability to meet eventually all its long term and short term debts.

SOURCE DOCUMENTS. The original records of any transaction internal or external, that occurs in the entity's operation.

SOURCING STRATEGY. The strategy that a company pursues in purchasing materials, components and final products; sourcing can be from domestic and foreign locations and from inside and outside the company.

SOUTHERN AFRICAN DEVELOPMENT COMMUNITY (SADC). An organization endeavouring to counter the economic influence of South Africa in the region by focusing on economic objectives, such as regional cooperation in attracting investment.

SOVEREIGNTY. Freedom from external control, especially when applied to a body politic.

SPAN OF MANAGEMENT. The phenomenon that there is a limit to the number of persons a manager can supervise, even though this limit varies depending on situations and the competence of a manager.

SPECIAL DRAWING RIGHT (SDR). A unit of account issued to countries by the International Monetary fund to expand their official reserves bases.

SPECIAL PURPOSE PROPERTY. Property which is uniquely

valuable to the lessee and not valuable to anyone else except as scrap.

SPECIALLY STORE. A store which offers a limited variety of merchandise but an extensive assortment of goods which are stocked.

SPECIALTY GOODS. Goods which have some unique quality or characteristic or have a higher degree of brand identification which causes consumers to make a concerted effort to purchase them.

SPECIFIC DUTY. A duty (tariff) assessed on a per-unit basis.

SPECIFIC IDENTIFICATION. This inventory method concentrates on the physical tracing of the particular items sold.

SPECULATING. The purchase and sale of stock quickly with the intent of making a profit in a short period of time. There is considerable risk in speculation.

SPECULATION. A position in an asset designed to perform well if some random variable such as the assets price achieves a certain value.

SPECULATION. The buying or selling of foreign exchange with the objective of earning a profit.

SPECULATIVE MOTIVE. The part of Keynes' theory of money demand depends on interest rates because of the effects of capital gains and losses on bonds.

SPECULATORS. Those who buy and sell in the forward market. Not to hedge a position but to intentionally take a risky position in the market.

SPEED OF ADJUSTMENT. Determines how quickly expectations adjust to past errors in expectations.

SPENDING VARIANCE. Basically, a price variance applied to variable overhead. However, other factors besides price may influence the amount of the variance.

SPILLOVER EFFECTS. Situations in which the marketing programme in one country results in awareness of the product in other countries.

SPIN-OFF ORGANIZATION. A company now operating almost independently of the parent because its activities do not fit easily with the parent's existing competencies.

SPLINTERED AUTHORITY. The situation where the total authority to accomplish a given result rests in more than one position and must be pooled, or combined to make the required decision.

SPLIT CAPITAL TRUST. Type of trust that is issued by an investment trust company, with fixed winding up date on which the investors are paid the surplus assets. Holders of income shares receive payment throughout the life of the trust.

SPLIT RATING. It occurs when two bond rating services give the same issue two different ratings.

SPLIT-OFF POINT. The juncture of the production where the joint products become individually identifiable.

SPLITTING/CONSOLIDATION. The problem of splitting shares that have a high face value into shares of a lower face value is known as splitting. The reverse process of combining shares that have a low face value into one share of higher value is known as consolidation.

SPONTANEOUS CURRENT LIABILITIES. Accounts payable and bills payable and other types of accruals arise spontaneously out of the firm's operations are therefore called spontaneous current liabilities.

SPOT ADVERTISEMENT. The advertiser can broadcast his message over one or many stations at various times by having the stations send out his message separately.

SPOT EXCHANGE RATE. The current value of one unit of a currency in terms of a second currency.

SPOT MARKET. Spot markets are markets for immediate delivery.

SPOT PRICE. Spot price refers to the contract market price of an item available for immediate delivery.

SPOT PRICE. The price on some asset for immediate delivery.

SPOT RATE. The current exchange rate. The rate at which you can exchange a foreign currency for U.S. dollars at this instant.

SPOT TRADING. Trading by delivery of shares and payment for the same on the date of purchase or in the next day.

SPREAD ORDER. Orders may be good for a specified period at time or they may be open that is, effective until explicitly cancelled by the customer. An order may be entered to be good for a day, a week, a month or a year cancelled.

SPREAD. A spread is a trade involving the purchase of one option and the sale of another, both on the same stock.

SQUARING UP TRANSACTIONS. A client settles his contract of sales by purchase and of purchase by sales and by cross contracts within the settlement period. This is known as (i) squaring up transactions or (ii) complete the contract by delivery of shares or payment of cash, as the case may be.

SSAP 21. The UK accounting standard, "Accounting for leases and hire-purchase transactions," issued by the Accounting Standards Committee. Under the standard finance, leases should be capitalized by the lessee. It also has detailed provisions for lessor accounting.

STABILITY OF DIVIDENDS. Stability of dividends sometimes means regularity in paying some dividend annually.

STAFF. A relationship in an organizational position where an incumbent's task is to give some other person advice or counsel.

STAFF AUTHORITY. The authority to advise but not to command. It may be exerted laterally or upward.

STAFFING. Fill and keeping filled, the positions in the organization structure with competent people. This is done through (1) defining work-force requirements (2) inventorying the people available, (3) recruiting, (4) selecting candidates for positions, (5) placing candidates, (6) promoting, (7) appraising, (8) planning the career of, (9) compensating and (10) training or otherwise developing people.

STAGED EQUITY. A lease financing where the lessor does not put up its full equity investment initially but pays this amount over a period of time in the lease.

STAKEHOLDER. (*See* Corporate stakeholder.)

STAKEHOLDERS. The collection of groups including stockholders, employees, customers, and society at large, that a company must satisfy to survive.

STANDARD ABSORPTION COSTING. That type of product costing in which the cost of the finished unit is calculated as the sum of the costs of the standard allowances for factors of production, including fixed factory overhead, without reference to the costs actually incurred.

STANDARD AND POOR'S 500 STOCK AVERAGE. An index of stock prices comprised of 425 industrials, 50 utilities and 25 rails.

STANDARD AND PRICE 500 INDEX. A stock price index consisting of 500 selected stocks.

STANDARD COST. A carefully predetermined cost that should be attained, usually expressed per unit.

STANDARD DEVIATION. Square root of the mean of the squared deviations from the expected value.

STANDARD DEVIATION. The square root of the variance.

STANDARD DIRECT COSTING. That type of product costing in which the cost of the finished unit is calculated as the sum of the costs of the standard allowances for the factors of production, excluding fixed factory overhead which is treated as a period cost, and without reference to costs actually incurred.

STANDARD LOOKBACK OPTION. At the maturity of the option, the payoff for a call option depends on the difference between the spot price of the underlying asset and the minimum value of the asset price over the life of the option. The payoff for a put option depends on the difference between the maximum value of the asset price over the life of the option and the spot price of the underlying asset.

STANDARD OF DEFERRED PAYMENT. The function that money performs when it is used as the standard for calculating payments deferred to a later date.

STANDARD OF LIVING. A measure of wealth of a nation : total production of the nation divided by total population.

STATE BANKING COMMISSIONS. Control the formation of state banks and examine state banks that are not members of the Federal Reserve or the FDIC. Regulations establish for these commissions vary from state to state.

STATE BANKS. Banks chartered by the appropriate agency in the various states.

STATE CONSTITUTIONS. Documents of the individual states that prescribe the form and power of state government within the limits set by the federal constitution.

STATE STATUTES. Legislation passed by the state legislatures.

STATE WIDE BRANCHING. Practice that allows banks to freely open branches throughout the state.

STATED VALUE. A nominal value of a stock certificate that is usually for below the actual cash invested. *See* Par value.

STATEMENT OF CHANGES IN FINANCIAL POSITION. A formal explanation of the sources and uses of resources, usually sources and uses of working capital.

STATEMENT OF FINANCIAL CONDITION. A synonym for balance sheet.

STATEMENT OF PROFIT AND LOSS. The income statement.

STATEMENT OF RETAINED EARNINGS. A financial statement that analyzes changes in the retained earnings.

STATEMENT OF SOURCES AND APPLICATIONS OF FUNDS. *See* Statement of changes in financial position.

STATES. Synonym for events.

STATES OF NATURE. Synonym for events.

STATEWIDE BRANCHING. Practice that allows banks to freely open branches throughout the state.

STATIC BUDGET. A budget prepared for only one level of activity and, on subsequently, one that does not adjust automatically to changes in the level of volume.

STATIC HEDGE. A hedge that consists of buying/selling securities that are held until the maturity date of the derivative being hedged.

STATISTICAL DISCREPANCY. Measures the amount by which the balance of payments accounts do not really balance.

STATISTICAL MAP. Data presented according to geographic divisions.

STATISTICS. The techniques used for collecting, organizing, summarizing, interpreting, and analyzing numerical data and making predictions and forecasts from the data.

STATUS. It is the relative social ranking an individual has in a group or organization.

STEP DEBT. Debt in connection with a leveraged lease, arranged in tiers with different maturates of amortization to improve the lessor's cash flow and reduce the lessee's costs.

STEP-DOWN METHOD. Allocation of service department costs to other service departments as well as production departments. Once a department's costs are allocated to other departments, no subsequent department costs are allocated back to it.

STEPPED RENTALS. Rental payments which vary from one another in a structured lease. Usually done for specific cash flows and for tax reasons.

STEP-VARIABLE COSTS. Those variable costs that change abruptly at intervals of activity because their acquisition comes in indivisible chunks.

STEREOTYPES. A standardized and oversimplified mental picture of a group.

STIPULATED LOSS VALUE. The same as insured value.

STOCK CERTIFICATE. The evidence of ownership in a corporation.

STOCK DIVIDEND. A distribution to stockholders of additional shares of any class of the distributing company's stock, without any payment to the company by the stockholders.

STOCK DIVIDEND. A dividend paid to a common stock in units of additional share of the stock.

STOCK DIVIDEND. A payment to stockholders in the form of shares of stock instead of in cash.

STOCK EXCHANGE. The marketplace where securities are traded.

STOCK INDEX FUTURES. A futures contract written on a stock market index.

STOCK MARKET. The buying and selling of stock for the purpose of making money for the purchasers and sellers of the stock.

STOCK MARKET BUBBLE. When the stocks defy gravity and reach their peak levels, which do not confirm to the fundamentals, it results in a stock market bubble. The market shows irrational exuberance and stocks move up at an exponential speed. The bubble is supported by a P/E ratio, which is not justifiable in such cases. The dot.com boom in early part of 2000 is the best example. Dot.com companies were valued higher than the established brick and mortar companies off the same field. When such a Stock Market Bubble bursts, it leads to a sharp roller coaster ride in the stock prices, which happened in the later part of the year with most of these dot.com companies plunging 70-80 per cent from their peak in 2000.

STOCK MARKET INDEX. A portfolio of common stocks.

STOCK OPTION. An option on a common stock.

STOCK OPTION. It gives an employee the right to buy stock in the company, usually at the fixed price for a period of time.

STOCK OPTIONS. In order to motivate employees and managers and to build the spirit of ownership in the organization stock options are offered. Key managers and employees are offered shares in the venture depending upon several factors like seniority, participation.

STOCK SPLIT. The issuance of additional shares for no consideration and under conditions indicating that the objective is to increase the number of outstanding shares for the purpose of reducing their unit market price.

STOCK SPLIT. A situation in which a company changes the number of outstanding shares of common stock by issuing to each existing shareholder a multiple number of units of the shares originally held.

STOCKBROKER. Acts as the middleman between buyers and sellers of stocks.

STOCKHOLDER. A person group or organization owning one

or more shares of stack in a corporation.

STOCKHOLDERS. Owners of a corporation. Persons who own common or preferred stock of a corporation.

STOCKHOLDERS' EQUITY. The excess of assets over liabilities of a corporation.

STOCKS. The term is used synonymously with the ordinary shares (or with ordinary shares and fixed interest securities collectively) in the USA, however, where ordinary shares are called common stocks. The term is used quite generally with reference to ordinary shares. In U.K., the term is usually used in reference to a fixed interest security issued and quoted in units of 100 pounds.

STOP TRANSFER. The instruction given by a registered holder of shares to the company to stop the transfer of shares as a result of theft, loss, etc. Shares belonging to A are sold to B who gets them transferred in his name and sells them to C. Now C sends these shares to the company and gets them transferred to his name. Meanwhile A discovers that his share certificates were stolen and fraudulently sold by some one else. He gets a court order restraining the company from further transferring the shares and attaching them (currently in possession OFC). This is known as "Stop transfer".

STORAGE COSTS. The costs of storing a commodity.

STORAGE UNIT. The memory of the computer where data are stored for future reference.

STORE OF VALUE. A means of storing today's purchasing power for use tomorrow. An important function of money.

STRADDLE. An option portfolio consisting of a long call and a long put option with the same exercise price and exercise date.

STRAIGHT DEBENTURES. The non-convertible debenture (NCD) is also known as a straight debenture.

STRAIGHT-LINE DEPRECIATION. A method of allocating the cost of plant assets to periods or products based on units of time (years). The result is an equal amount of depreciation per period.

STRAIGHT-LINE METHOD. An accounting method for depreciating assets that spreads the depreciation equally over the estimated useful life of the asset.

STRANGLE. An option portfolio consisting of a long call and long put option position with the same exercise date and different exercise prices.

STRATEGIC ALLIANCE. An agreement between companies that is of strategic importance to one or both companies competitive viability.

STRATEGIC BUSINESS UNITS (SBUs). A distinct form of organization, usually employed within a larger company, constructed around a product or service, so that it will receive the attention normally given a complete product or project organization structure. These units are expected to be handled as though the units are expected to be handled as though they were independent businesses.

STRATEGIC INTENT. An objective that gives an organization cohesion over the long term while it builds global competitive viability.

STRATEGIC PLAN. A long-term plan involving major commitments.

STRATEGIES. General programmes of action and deployment of resources to attain comprehensive objectives; the programme of objectives of an organization and their changes, resources used to attain these objectives, and policies governing the acquisition, use, and disposition of these resources; the determination of the basic long-term objectives of an enterprise and the adoption of courses of action and allocation of resources necessary to achieve these goals.

STRIKE PRICE. Pre-specified price of an option contact.

STRIKE PRICE. The price at which the underlying asset may be purchased or sold when an option is exercised.

STRIKE. Workers stay off the job, stopping work, to gain their demands, the most effective weapon of labour unions.

STRINGENT CREDIT POLICY. When a firm sells on credit on a highly selective basis only, to those customers who have proven credit worthiness and who are financially strong in the firm is following stringent credit policy.

STRIP DEBT. Debt, in connection with a leveraged lease, arranged with different maturities and amortization to improve the lessor's cash flow and reduce the lessee's costs.

STRONG FORM MARKET EFFICIENCY. Asserts that no current information, either publicly available or not, can improve on using the most recently known value of an asset price to predict the future value of the asset price.

STRUCTURED INTERVIEW is conducted using a set of standardized questions that are asked all applicants for a job.

SUBCONTRACTING. Exists when a contractor enters into another contract with a firm to perform part of the function he has contracted to perform.

SUB-LEASE. A transaction in which leased property is re-leased by the original lessee to a third party and the lease agreement between the two original parties remains in effect.

SUBORDINATED. A creditor claim that is junior to other creditor claims.

SUBORDINATED BOND. A bond whose claim on the assets of the issuer — the borrower — is subordinate to a claim by another bond.

SUBORDINATED DEBENTURE. *See* Subordinated and debenture.

SUBPART OF INCOME. Income of a CFC that comes from sources other than those connected with the active conduct of a trade or business such as holding company income.

SUBSIDIARITY. A principle that implies that EU interference should take place only in areas of common concern and that most policies should be set at the national level.

SUBSIDIARY. A corporation owned or controlled by a parent company, through the ownership of more than 50 per cent of the voting stock.

SUBSIDIARY. A foreign operation that is legally separate from the parent company even if wholly owned by it.

SUBSIDIES. Sum paid (usually by government) to companies in certain industries to enable them to sell their goods or services at a price close to the prevailing market price. It is also used to provide financial support to commercial or quasi-commercial activity that would otherwise not be viable in narrow profit and loss term, usually in order to sustain broader economic or social benefits.

SUBSTITUTES. Goods or services that are related in the sense that when the price of one increases, the demand for the other increases because people substitute toward the one that is relatively cheaper.

SUBSTITUTION DRAWBACKS. A provision allowing domestic merchandise to be substituted for merchandise that is imported for eventual export, thus allowing the U.S. firm to exclude the duty paid on the merchandise in costs and in sales prices.

SUBSTITUTION EFFECT. As the return on an asset increases people will substitute away from other assets and towards the one with the relatively higher returns.

SUBUNIT AUTONOMY. Possession of decision-making power by managers of subunits of an organization.

SUM OF THE DIGITS METHOD. An accounting method for depreciating assets providing for the largest depreciation to be taken at the beginning of the asset's life and the smallest depreciation to be taken in the alter year.

SUM-OF-THE-YEARS'-DIGITS DEPRECIATION (SYD). A popular form of accelerated depreciation where the sum of the digits is the total of the numbers representing the years of life.

SUNK COST. A cost that has already been incurred and, therefore, is irrelevant to the decision-making process. Also called historical cost.

SUPER 301. A clause in U.S. tariff legislation permitting U.S. trade negotiators to threaten more restrictive import regulations to get other countries to lower their restrictions against U.S. made products or services.

SUPERMARKET. A store which emphasizes low prices on fast-moving merchandise and offers some customer services.

SUPERVISORS. Same as managers, but ordinarily used to apply to managers as the lowest level, or first line, of managing.

SUPPLY CURVE. A schedule showing the relationship between the price of a good or services and its quantity supplied.

SUPPORTIVE SELLING. Selling efforts in which salespersons try to generate goodwill and provide specialized service rather than trying to get orders.

SURELY INSURANCE. Insures against loss from one party to a contract not fulfilling its obligation.

SURETY-SHIP. Type of primary insurance that covers loss of money through fraud or dishonesty.

SURPLUS FUND. The clearing house has variation margin, requirements original margin and small fee for clearing the member's trades. These sources of revenue become the surplus fund and helps to cover costs. Money in this fund invested in government securities and interest earned is applied to the operating expenses of the clearing house.

SURPLUS. Situation where the quantity supplied exceeds quantity demanded.

SURVIVAL OF THE FITTEST. A phrase derived from the idea of Charles Darwin and Herbert Spencer meaning that only the strongest and most capable individual are able to survive and excel in life's competitive struggles.

SUSHI BOND. It is a Japanese bond demonstrated in Eurodollars.

SWAP. A financial contract that obligates both counter parties to a series of cash payments for a fixed period of time.

SWAP. A simultaneous spot and forward foreign exchange transactions.

SWAPTION. An option on a swap.

SWEETENING DEBT. Warrants help to make the issue of equity and debentures attractive. If the company is doubtful about the full subscription of the debenture issue, warrants are used to sweeten the issue by giving the investors an opportunity to participate in capital gains when the share price appreciates.

SWEETENING FIXED INCOME SECURITIES. Investors generally prefer fixed interest, convertible debentures over non-convertible, because this enables them to earn a definite and fixed income with the chance of making capital gains. Hence, the convertibility feature 'sweetens' the issue. Also the company may offer relatively low interest rate on convertible debentures because of the value of the conversion feature as compared to non-convertible debenture.

SWITCHING BETWEEN OFFERS. The switching of acceptances between different offers is not possible. The offer once accepted by a shareholder cannot be withdrawn. To enable the shareholders to be in a better position to decide as to which of the substituting offers is better and also not to cause last minute decisions/ confusions, the offer price is effectively frozen for 7 working days up to the closing date of the offers. Shareholders would be advised to wait till the commencement of that period to be aware of upward revision in the offer price of either offers (initial and competitive).

SYMMETRIC INFORMATION. In the loan market, when borrowers and banks have the same information about whether a loan will be repaid.

SYNDICATION. Cooperation by a lead bank and several other banks to make a large loan to a public or private organization.

SYNTHETIC DERIVATIVE. A portfolio of traded securities that duplicates the cash flows and payoffs to a derivative.

SYNTHETIC FUEL (SYNFUEL). Fuel produced by converting naturally occurring hydrogen and carbon compounds such as coal, shale rock, and tar sands, into useful forms of energy, such as coal gas, coal liquid fuel and shale oil.

SYNTHETIC PROCESS. A production process that combines raw materials to produce a product.

SYNTHETIC REPLICATION. The process of forming a synthetic derivative.

SYSTEM. A formal means of gathering data to aid and coordinate the process of making decisions.

SYSTEM, DEFINITION OF. A set or assemblage of thins connected, or interdependent and interacting so as to form a complex unity; a whole composed of parts in orderly arrangement according to some scheme or plan. For any system there must be boundaries that separate it from its environment.

SYSTEM MESSAGES WINDOW. This window is for broadcast of messages from the exchange to all the trading members/participants.

SYSTEMATIC AND RATIONAL ALLOCATION. It deals with those costs which expire to generate revenue during a period but cannot be directly associated with the specific revenue. Depreciation is an example of such costs.

SYSTEMS, BOUNDARIES. The demarcation lines or area definition separating a given system from its environment.

SYSTEMS, CLOSED. Not having interactions with the system's environment.

SYSTEMS, OPEN. Having interaction with the system's environment and exchanging information, energy, or material with that environment.

T

T+5 ROLLING SETTLEMENT SYSTEM. In this system, Monday's trades are settled on Monday.

TABLE. A method of presenting statistical data more clearly.

TACTICS. Action plans by which strategies are implemented.

TAFT-HARTLEY ACT. The labour Management Relation Act of 1947 which among other features, outlines unfair labour practices of labour unions and provides for court injunctions to prevent strikes.

TAG ALONG. This is an agreement between the entire capitalist and key employees. This is a protection offered to important employees in the event of a merger or a takeover. The representative of the fund agrees to a certain employees into the new organization.

TAKEOVER. When an acquirer takes over the control or management of the target company, it is termed as takeover.

TAKING INVENTORY. The action of counting all inventory on hand as of a specific time.

TANGIBLE ASSETS. *See* Fixed assets.

TANGIBLE FIXED ASSETS. Tangible fixed assets include land, building, machinery, furniture, etc. These are normally recorded at cost. Cost of tangible fixed assets are allocated over their useful lives. The amount so allocated each year is called depreciation. Cost of tangible fixed assets are reduced every year by the amount of depreciation.

TANGIBLE REWARDS. Exists in the form of pay, better working conditions, fringe benefits, etc.

TAPE DANCING. Unethical methods of manipulating share prices in the USA in which a dealer reports a deal inclusive of his commission. This seems to make the share prices rise.

TARANIWALLA. The taraniwalla may be a jobber or specialist who specializes in specified stocks. He trades in and out of the market for a small difference in price and as such in an important factor in making a market *i.e.* maintaining a continuous and liquid market in stocks in which he specializes. The taraniwalla who specializes in stocks that are relatively not so active frequently received from.

TARGET. In terms of monetary policy, a goal or variable that the policymaker cannot directly control.

TARGET COMPANY. The target company is a company whose shares are listed on stock exchange(s) and whose shares or voting rights are acquired/being acquired or whose control is taken over/being taken over by the acquirer.

TARGET RATE. Often used in capital budgeting as either the minimum desired rate of return or the budgeted rate of return.

TARIFFS. Charges made in return for goods or services.

TASK. It is a distinct identifiable work activity composed of motions.

TASK OF THE MANAGER. *See* Manager's task of.

TAX ALLOCATION. *See* Interpreted tax allocation.

TAX ASYMMETRIES. Most economies have varieties of taxes and tax incentives which cause tax asymmetries. Tax asymmetries make security transactions more beneficial to some. A number of financial transactions may create additional wealth because of tax differences.

TAX BENEFIT TRANSFERS (TBT). A TBT lease, made possible in the US by the 1981 Tax Act (ERTA), was limited by the 1982 Act (FERA). The transaction is set up so that the lessee is also the lender under a leveraged lease arrangement, and all payments except an initial sum paid by the lessor (tax benefit buyer) cancel each other out. That is, one company effectively pays another a fee for the tax benefits associated with capital investment.

TAX EFFECT OF SALVAGE VALUE. The company will make a profit if the asset's salvage value is more than its book value. Capital gain is equal to salvage value minus original value of the asset, capital gains are generally taxed at a rate lower than the ordinary income.

TAX HAVEN COUNTRIES. Countries with low income taxes or no taxes on foreign sources income.

TAX HAVEN SUBSIDIARY. A subsidiary of a company established in a tax haven country for the purpose of minimizing income tax.

TAX HOLIDAY. The period in which a startup company does not need to pay any taxes.

TAX INDEMNITY CLAUSE. Clause inserted into a tax based lease providing for increases in rentals in the event of legislation which adversely affects the lessor's ability to claim tax benefits on the equipment.

TAX RISK. The risk of changes in the tax treatment of interest income.

TAX SAVING FUND. Such funds allow to claim a rebate u/s 99 of the Income tax act. The maximum allowable rebate in any year in r/s 2000 hence, the maximum that one can invest in a tax saving fund locks investors funds is for a period of three years otherwise the rebate is lost.

TAX SHIELD. Usually defined as non-cash items (*e.g.* depreciation) charged against income, thus protecting that amount from tax.

TAX TREATY. A treaty between two countries that generally results in the reciprocal reduction on dividend withholding taxes and the exemption of taxes or royalties and sometimes interest payments.

TAX VARIATION CLAUSE. A clause in lease agreement in the UK which allows the lessor or vary the rentals if either the rate of tax or the tax system changes.

TAX WRITTEN DOWN VALUE. The value of an asset after deducting the total capital allowances claimed from the cost of the asset.

TECHNICAL ANALYSIS. Charting or plotting historical data and asset prices.

TECHNICAL ELITE. Highly trained and technically specialized members of an organization who may exercise great influence on policies and decisions from a purely technical point of view.

TECHNICAL LEARNING. A stage in the development of social responsiveness within a company during which a person with specialized knowledge helps the organization learn more about some social problem and how to cope with it.

TECHNICAL SALESPERSON. Specialist who provides technical expertise in installing and servicing equipment, such as computers.

TECHNICAL SKILLS. The ability of a manager to work with things.

TECHNOLOGY. The branch of knowledge that deals with applied science and industrial arts. Knowledge in science or industry. The tools, machines, skills, technical operations, and abstract symbols involved in human endeavour.

TECHNOLOGY ABSORBING CAPACITY. The ability of the recipient to work effectively with technology particularly in relation to the need for training and equity in the recipient in order to effect a transfer.

TECHNOLOGY ASSESSMENT. An analytic attempt to understand, beforehand if possible the economic and social effects of new technology, particularly the unintended, indirect, and possibility harmful impacts that may occur.

TECHNOLOGY TRANSFER. A business sharing its advanced technology, including patents and operating know-how with another business or government.

TECHNO-STRUCTURE. Members of an organization who possess and use specialized technical knowledge in a group decision-making process.

TELECOMMUTING. A situation where a person can work at home at the computer terminal instead of commuting to work by car, public transportation, of other means.

TELECOMMUTING. Performance knowledge work and transmitting the results of that work by means of computer terminal to an organization's central data bank and management centre, while the employee works at home or at some other remote location.

TELECONFERENCE. A group of people interacting with each other using audio and video media with moving or sill pictures.

TELECONFERENCE. A meeting of an organization's employees who are in widely separated locations that is made possible by two-way television transmission.

TEMPORAL METHOD. A method of translating foreign currency financial statements used when the functional currency is that of the parent company.

TERM INSURANCE. A form of life insurance in which a person is insured for the life of the policy in exchange for premiums. If he does not die in that period the policy ends.

TERM PREMIUM. The compensation required to induce investors to purchase an asset with a different term to maturity than their preferred one.

TERM STRUCTURE OF INTEREST RATES. The graph of various maturity interest rates versus their maturates.

TERM STRUCTURE OF INTEREST RATES. The relationship between the yields of otherwise identical financial assets and their term to maturity.

TERMINAL CASH FLOWS. Cash flows at the end of the terminal year.

TERMINAL VALUE. *See* Residual value.

TERMINATION. Permanent separation from the company.

TERMINATION SCHEDULE. Leases, sometimes contain provisions permitting a lessee to terminate the lease, during the lease term in the event the leased equipment becomes obsolete and surplus to its needs. The liability of the lessee in the event of such termination is set forth in a termination schedule which values the equipment at various times during the lease term. If the equipment is sold at a price lower than the set forth in the schedule, the lessee pays the difference.

TERMS OF TRADE. The quantity of imports that can be bought by a given quantity of a country's exports.

TEST MARKET. Selling a new product in one city to test sales of the product for projection to the entire market.

TFE. Toronto Futures Exchange, Canada.

THE MONEY OPTION. An option with a strike prices equal to the current market price of the underlying asset.

THEOCRATIC LAW SYSTEM. A legal system based on religious precepts.

THEOCRATIC TOTALITARIANISM. A dictatorship led by a religious group.

THEORY. The systematic grouping of interdependent concepts and principles which give a grime-work to, or tie together, significant knowledge.

THEORY OF COUNTRY SIZE. The theory which holds that countries with large land areas are more apt to have varied climates and natural resources and therefore generally are more nearly self-sufficient than smaller countries.

THEORY X AND THEORY Y. Assumption about the nature of people as suggested by Douglas McGregor. For example, theory X suggests that people dislike work and will avoid it if they can. On the other hand, Theory Y suggests, for instance, that the expenditure of physical and mental effort in work is as natural as play or rest.

THEORY Z. Several authors proposed theories using the letter 'z'. In general, theory Z refers to selected Japanese managerial practices adapted to the environment of the United States as suggested by William Ouchi, for example, one of the characteristics of Type Z organizations is the emphasis on interpersonal skills needed for group decision making.

THETA. A measure of the change in an option premium with respect to a one-day change in time-to-maturity.

THETA. The change in the options value for a unit change in time.

THETA NEUTRAL. A portfolio position that has a theta of zero.

THIRD-COUNTRY NATIONALS. Expatriate employees who are neither citizens of the country in which they are working nor citizens of the country where the company is headquartered.

THIRD WAVE. A period of widespread social change characteristic of high technology, service oriented knowledge based societies.

THIRD-WORLD COUNTRIES. Developing countries or those not considered socialist or non-socialist industrial countries.

THIRD WORLD NATIONS. Developing nations as distinguished from more developed free world nations and communist nations.

TICK SIZE. The smallest price change allowed for trading an asset.

TICKER. The ticker displays information about a trade as and when it takes place.

TIE-IN PROVISIONS. Stipulations in licensing that require the license to purchase or sell products from to the licensor.

TIFFE. Tokyo International Financial Futures Exchanges.

TIGHT CREDIT POLICY. Tight credit policy means rejection of certain types of accounts whose credit worthiness is doubtful. This results into loss of sales consequently, loss of contribution. This is an opportunity loss to the firm. As the firm starts loosening its credit policy, it accepts all or some of those accounts which the firm had earlier rejected. Thus the firm will recapture lost sales and thus, lost contribution. The opportunity cost of lost contribution excludes with the loosening of credit policy.

TIME. Adjusted rate of return. *See* Internal rate of return.

TIME DEPOSITS. Savings accounts in commercial banks or savings and loan association.

TIME DRAFT. A commercial bill of exchange calling for payment to be made at some time after delivery.

TIME PREFERENCE FOR MONEY. An individual preference for possession of a given amount cash know rather than the some amount some further time is called time preference for money.

TIME SERIES. A statistical method of illustrating a pattern over time such as in demand for a particular product.

TIME SERIES ANALYSIS. The easiest way to evaluate the performance of a firm so compare its present ratios with the past ratios when financial ratios over a period of time are compared. It is known as time series analysis. It gives an indication of the direction of change and reflects whether the firm's financial performance has improved, deteriorated or remained constant over time.

TIME SPREAD. Having same exercise price if a trade involves purchase options and sale options both on the same stock but one expires later than the other, it is called time spread.

TIME SPREAD. An option portfolio : write a call (put) and buy another call (put) with a longer time to expiration. The options have the same strike price.

TIME VALUE. The amount of money that option buyers are willing to pay for an option in anticipation that, over time, a change in the underlying asset price will cause the option to increase in value. An option's premium is the sum of time value of intrinsic value. The amount by which an option's premium exceeds the option's intrinsic value is the option time value.

TIME VALUE. The part of the options value above its price if it is exercised for certain at the maturity date.

TIME-AT-THE-DAY ORDER. A time-at-the-day order is one that must be executed at a specific time or at specific intervals during the trading session.

TIME-UTILITY. A goods or service must be available at the time it is demanded to satisfy a want.

TIMING DIFFERENCES. Differences between the periods in which transactions affect pretax income for reporting to income tax authorities and the periods in which they enter into the determination of pretax income for reporting to shareholders.

TIMING OPTION. The right to deliver a bond on any day in the delivery month of treasury bond futures contract.

TITLE V 11. It is that portion of the 1964 Civil Right Act prohibiting discrimination in employment.

TNC. *See* Transnational Corporation.

TOBIN'S Q. Tobin's Q is the ratio of the market value of firm's assets to its assets replacement costs. It is argued that firms will have an incentive to invest when Q is greater than 1. They will be reluctant to invest once Q becomes equal to 1.

TOKEN COINS. Coins such as U.S. pennies nickels dimes, and quarters, which resemble commodity money coins but which are fiat money. The face value of these coins exceeds their value as a commodity.

TOP DOWN INVESTMENT. An investment strategy that first takes a view on the economy and then the industry scenario before looking into the potential performance of a company this is opposite to the bottom up techniques.

TORT. A civil wrong independent of a contract.

TOTAL DEFICIT. The difference between all government spending (both primary spending and interest payments) and tax collections.

TOTAL PRODUCT. The total level of output produced with a given quantity of an input.

TOTAL PROJECT APPROACH. A method of comparing two or more alternative courses of action by computing the total expected inflows and outflows of each alternative and then converting these flows to their present value by applying some predetermined minimum rate of return.

TOTAL QUALITY MANAGEMENT (TQM). The process that a company uses to achieve quality where the goal is elimination of all defects.

TOTAL RESERVES. They include foreign currency reserves, old and SDRs.

TOTALITARIANISM. A political system characterized by the absence of widespread participation in decisions making.

TOXIC CHEMICALS. Any type of chemical that is harmful to marine life animals or humans.

TOXIC SUBSTANCES. Any substance used in production or in consumer products that is poisonous or capable of causing serious health problems for those persons exposed (compare with hazardous waste).

TQM. *See* Total Quality Management.

TRACKER BOND. It is lump sum amount invested in equities that guarantees capital and often guarantees also a minimum return.

TRADE ASSOCIATIONS. An organization that represents the business and professional interest of the firm or persons in a trade, industry, or professions, for example medical doctors, chemical manufacturers, or used car dealers.

TRADE DIVERSION. A situation in which exports shift to a less efficient producing country because of preferential trade barriers.

TRADE GUARANTEE. Trade guarantee is the guarantee provided by the clearing corporation for all trades that are executed on the exchange. In contrast the settlement guarantees the settlement of trade after multilateral netting.

TRADE MARKS AND TRADE NAMES. They are the exclusive rights granted by the government to use certain names, symbols, designs, etc.

TRADE-OFFS ECONOMIC AND SOCIAL. An attempt to balance economic and social gains against economic and social costs when it is impossible to achieve all that is desired in both economic and social terms.

TRADE RELATED ASPECTS OF INTELLECTUAL PROPERTY RIGHTS (TRIPS). A provision from the Uruguay round of trade negotiations requiring countries to agree to enforce procedures under their national laws to protect intellectual property rights.

TRADE SECRET. Private company information not available to others, that is useful to the company business but could be harmful if known by others, especially competitors.

TRADEMARK. A name or logo distinguishing a company or product.

TRADEMARKS. Distinctive identification of a manufactured product or a service.

TRADER WORK STATIONS. Trading is done by members and their authorized representative from their trader work stations installed in their offices through the BSE on line trading system.

TRADING ELECTRONICALLY. Clients who use electronic trading service enter orders on-screen to trade with fund managers, brokers, market makers, and exchange specialists around the world. These clients see live orders coming through Instinet and can then negotiate or execute any order they choose. Regardless of a client's size or location, they have an equal opportunity to respond to each other. In more traditional markets where electronic trading is not available, clients can trade by telephone through transaction desk.

TRADING FOR DELIVERY. Trading conducted with an intention to deliver the shares as opposed to a position that is squared off within the settlement.

TRADING ON THE EQUITY. Using borrowed money at a fixed interest rate and/or using funds provided by preferred stockholders with the aim of enhancing the rate of return on common stockholders' equity.

TRADING STRATEGY. A portfolio position that can change over time.

TRADITIONAL COSTING. *See* Absorption costing.

TRAINING. It is a learning process whereby people acquire skills, concepts, attitudes, or knowledge to aid in the achievements of goals.

TRAIT APPRAISALS. Appraising people, whether managers or non-managers, on the basis of personality traits and work-oriented characteristics.

TRANSACTION. Any event that effects the financial position of any entity and requires recording.

TRANSACTION COSTS. The costs involved in buying or selling an asset.

TRANSACTION EXPOSURE. Foreign exchange risk that occurs because the parent company must translate foreign-currency financial statements into the reporting currency of the parent company.

TRANSACTION MOTIVE. The desire to hold money because it is useful in making purchases.

TRANSACTIONAL. An organization in which different capabilities and contributions among different country operations are shared and integrated; (2) multinational enterprise; (3) company owned and managed by nationals from different countries.

TRANSACTIONAL CORPORATION (TNC). A company owned and managed by nationals in different countries also may be synonymous with multinational enterprise.

TRANSNATIONAL LABOUR RELATIONS. Labour activities conducted across national boundaries by organized labour.

TRANSFER. Horizontal movement to a position which may or may not involve more money or responsibility.

TRANSFER DEED. A transfer deed is a form that is used for effecting transfer of shares or debentures as is valid for a specified period. It should be sent to the company along with the share certificate for registering the transfer. The transfer deed must be duly stamped and signed by on behalf of the transferor and transferee and complete in all perspectives. The transfer deed is an important document of transfer and the form is prescribed by the Companies Act 1956. It has to be date stamped by the prescribed authority. It is valid for 12 months from the date of stamping by the prescribed authority or till the date on which the register of members are closed for the first time after the date stamping by the prescribed authority whichever is later.

TRANSFER PAYMENTS. Funds given to private individuals without a *quid pro quo* exchange.

TRANSFER PRICE. The amounts charged by one submit of an organization for a product or service that it supplies to another submit of the same organization.

TRANSFERRED-IN-COSTS. In process costing, costs incurred in a previous department that have been received by a subsequent department.

TRANSMISSION. It is the lawful process by which the ownership of securities is transferred to the legal heirs of the deceased.

TRANSPARENCY. A characteristic of an accounting system that implies that companies disclose a great deal of information about accounting practices more common in Anglo Saxon countries (United States, United Kingdom).

TREASURY BILLS. Short term debt instruments used by the U.S. government to obtain funds. T-bills are sold at a discount from face value. Pay no explicit interest payments, and have maturates of 3, 6, or 12 months.

TREASURY BILL FUTURES. A futures contract written on treasury bills.

TREASURY BOND. A coupon bond issued by the US government with maturity less than ten years.

TREASURY BOND FUTURES. A futures contract written on treasury bonds.

TREASURY NOTE FUTURES. A futures contract written on treasury notes.

TREASURY STOCK. Outstanding stock that has subsequently been repurchased and not cancelled by the company.

TREASURY STRIPS. A synthetic zero-coupon bond constructed from treasury notes and bonds.

TREE HARVESTING PROBLEM. The maximization of the investment (NPV) would depend on when trees are harvested. The net future value of trees increase when harvesting is postponed; but the opportunity cost of capital is incurred by not realizing the value by harvesting the trees. The NPV will be maximized when the trees are harvested at the point where the percentage increases in value equals the opportunity cost of capital.

TREND ANALYSIS. In financial analysis the direction of changes over a period of time is of crucial importance. Time series or trend analysis of ratios indicate the direction of change.

TRIAD STRATEGY. A strategy proposing that an MNE should have a presence in Europe, the United States and Asia (especially Japan).

TRIANGULAR ARBITRAGE. Taking advantage of discrepancies

between the spot exchange rate between two currencies and the exchange rate that can be obtained by trading one of the two currencies first for a third currency. And then trading that third currency for the other of the two currencies.

TRIPS. *See* Trade Related Aspects of Intellectual Property Rights.

TRUE LEASE. A true lease, in the US, is a transaction which qualifies as a lease under the Internal Revenue Code so the lessee can claim rental payments as tax deductions and the lessor can claim tax benefits of ownership as depreciation and ITC. Since the 1981 Tax Act, alternative "safe harbour" rules have been available regarding what constitutes a lease (now more limited in application).

TRUST CERTIFICATE. Document evidencing the beneficial ownership of a trust estate of an equity participant (or owner participant trust or owner or grantor owner) in an owner trust.

TRUST COMPANIES. Companies that receive money and invest it for the benefit of a third party.

TRUST RECEIPT. A title to goods which remain with a financial institution when it has lent a business money with which to purchase merchandise.

TRUSTEE. A bank or trust company which holds title or a security interest in leased property in trust for the benefit of the lessee, lessor, and/or creditors of the lessor. A leveraged lease often has two trustees — owner trustee and indenture trustee.

TRUSTEE FEE. Fees due either to the owner trustee or the indenture trustee.

TRUSTEE OWNER. The lessor or one of the group of lessors under a leveraged lease holding trust certificates evidencing their beneficial interest as owners under the owner trust. A trust or owner is the same as an equity participant or owner.

TSE. Toronto Stock Exchange, Canada.

TURNKEY OPERATION. An operating facility that is constructed under contract and transferred to the owner when the facility is ready to begin operations.

TURNOVER. It is the process in which employees leave the organization and have to be replaced.

TURTLE BLOOD. It is a stable security with no volatility and a price that is not expected to increase quickly.

TYING CONTACTS. An agreement that require a customer to agree to buy all future needs of a product from the seller as a condition of current purchasing.

U

U.S. CANADA FREE TRADE AGREEMENT. *See* Canada U.S. Free Trade agreement.

U.S. SHAREHOLDER. For U.S. tax purposes a person or company owning at least two per cent of the voting stock of a foreign subsidiary.

U.S. TERMS. The practice of using the direct quote for exchange rates.

UMBRELLA PROSPECTUS. Under an umbrella prospectus the issuing company does not need to seek the approval of the market regulator each time it hits the market.

UNADJUSTED RATE OF RETURN. *See* Accounting rule of return.

UNAMIDABLE COST. The opposite of avoidable cost.

UNANTICIPATED INFLATION. The amount of inflation that is different from the expected inflation rate.

UNBILLED REVENUE. Fees earned in a given period but for which no bills have been sent to the customer.

UNCERTAINTY. A situation in which individuals cannot estimate probabilities over outcomes. Either because they cannot list the possible outcomes or because they cannot estimate the probabilities to assign to the various outcomes.

UNCHANGED ISSUES INDEX. It is useful to examine not only the number of stocks that advance and decline but also the number that remain unchanged. When a higher than normal percentage of stocks remain unchanged in price, the market is likely getting a top. The index is calculated each day by dividing the number of issues which are unchanged in price by the total number of stocks traded.

UNCOVERED OPTION. Writing a call or a put on an underlying asset not owned by the writer.

UNDERAPPLIED FACTORY OVERHEAD. The excess of actual factory overhead over the factory overhead applied to products.

UNDEREMPLOYED. Those people who are working at less than their capacity.

UNDERGROUND ECONOMY. That part of the economy that is unrecorded in official measurements of economic activity because it consists of illegal activities and unrecorded cash transactions.

UNDER-LYING. The specific security/asset, which an option contract is based.

UNDER-WATER OPTION. Stock options offered to the US employees. The shares are normally offered at a discount on the market rate, but when the market price falls below the grant price, the option goes under-water.

UNDISTRIBUTED EARNINGS. *See* Retained income.

UNDUE INFLUENCE. When assent is not voluntary because of the nature of the relationship of the parties to the contract.

UNEARNED REVENUE. *See* Deferred revenue.

UNEXPIRED COSTS. Any expenditures benefiting the future any asset, including prepaid express, normally appearing on a balance sheet.

UNFAIR LABOUR PRACTICE. Management or labour union acts prohibited by federal legislation.

UNFAVOURABLE BALANCE OF TRADE. An indication of a trade deficit that is imports are greater than exports.

UNFOUNDED DEBT. The portion of national debt that is in the form of fixed-term securities. It consists of the floating debt, listed securities and small-scale savings.

UNFOUNDED PLAN. Pays pension benefits out of current income to the organization.

UNIFIED BANKING. System where banks serve both as commercial banks and investment banks.

UNIFORM COMMERCIAL CODE. A group of statutes that are recommended to provide some conformity between states' commercial laws.

UNIFORM RESERVE REQUIREMENTS. Identical reserve requirements for commercial banks savings and loans and credit unions.

UNILATERAL TRANSFER. In the balance of payments accounts, the transfers of funds or goods for which no payment is expected in return.

UN-INSURED PLAN. It is one which the benefits at retirement are determined by the employer based upon calculations that consider the age of the employee and years worked.

UNION. Union is a formal association of workers that promotes the welfare of its members.

UNION SHOP. A worker must join the labour union within a stipulated period of time after his employment in order to continue working in that periods.

UNIT BANKING. Restricting a

bank to have only one office or to service a single location.

UNIT OF ACCOUNT. A measure I which prices or values of goods and services are stated. An important function of money.

UNITED NATIONS CONFERENCE ON TRADE AND DEVELOPMENT. An UN body that has been especially active in dealing with the relationship between developing and industrialized countries with respect to trade.

UNITED NATIONS (UN). An international organization of countries formed in 1945 to promise world peace and security.

UNITY OF COMMAND. Having each subordinate report to only one superior. The principle of unity of command implies only that the more an individual reports to a single superior, the less the problem of conflict in instructions and the greater the feeling of personal responsibility for results.

UNIVERSAL COPYRIGHT CONVENTION. A multilateral agreement to protect copyrights.

UNIVERSALITY OF MANAGEMENT. The concept that essential, or basic, management science, theory, principles, and concepts are applicable in any culture even though application in practice may vary depending on cultural differences, contingencies, or situations.

UNLIMITED LIABILITY. This exists in forms of business ownership that allow judgment against not only what the owner has invested in the business but all the rest of his assets.

UNREQUITED TRANSFER. *See* Unilateral transfer.

UP-AND-IN OPTION. For up-and-in option — for up-and-in options, an upper level (barrier) is specified for the asset price on which the option is written. For a up-and-in call (put) option, the contract becomes a standard call (put) option if the price of the underlying asset never goes above the barrier during the life of the contract, otherwise the contract expires worthless.

UP-AND-OUT OPTION. For up-and-out options, an upper level (barrier) is specified for the asset price on which the option is written. For a up-and-out call (put) option, the contract ceases to exist if the price of the underlying asset goes above the barrier. If the price of the underlying asset never goes above the barrier during the life of the contract, the contract expires as an ordinary call (put) option.

UP-DATE LEASE. Up-date lease is intended to prospect the lessee against the risk of obsolescence. The lessor agrees to replace obsolete asset with new one at a specified rent.

UP-TICK RULE. A rule in the stock market that prohibits short sales except when the last transaction in the stock had a price increase.

USAGE VARIANCE. Efficiency variance pertaining to materials or direct labour.

USURY LAWS. Laws that restrict the interest rate that can be charged on loans and credit card balances.

UTILITY. The power of a good or service to satisfy a human want.

UTILITY (SOCIAL). A concept used in ethical reasoning that refers to the net positive gain or benefit to society of some actions or decision.

UV. Disclosed value orders allow the trading member to place an order which gets activated only when the market place of the relevant security crosses a threshold price, until then the order does not enter the market. In the case of an OS sell order, the order gets triggered if the last traded price is less than or equal to the OS sell order price.

V

VALIDITY. Means that a "test" actually predicts what it says it predicts.

VALUE ADDED TAX. A tax that is a percentage of the value added to a product at each stage of the business process.

VALUE CHAIN. The collective activities that occur as a product moves from raw materials through production to final distribution.

VALUE ENGINEERING. The analysis of the operation of a product or service, estimating the value of each operation, and attempting to improve the operation by trying to keep costs low at each step or part.

VALUE MARGINAL PRODUCT OF DEPOSIT. The marginal product of deposits multiplied by the market interest rate on loans : indicates the additional revenue a purely competitive bank gets from an additional $ 1 of deposits.

VALUE-ADDITIVITY PRINCIPLE. It implies that if we know the NPVs of separate projects, the value off the firm will increase by the sum of their NPVs. The firm's value can simply be found by adding their values.

VALUE-AT-RISK. A measurement of risk in terms of potential future financial loss on current investment portfolio. It represents the worst-case future financial loss one can expect to incur on a portfolio within a given time frame (95 per cent confidence level). In the table below, there is a user portfolio and the S & P 500 portfolio. While both portfolios have equal market value, the use of portfolio's higher VaR Numbers indicate that it carries significantly more risk than the S & P 500 portfolio. For example, one can say with 95 per cent confidence that on any given day in future, the currently-held user portfolio could lose up to $ 1,159, and the S&P 500, up to $ 776. Since the user portfolio's daily VaR is presented "with 95 per cent confidence", the user must understand that on any given day in the future there is a 5 per cent probability of maximum financial loss exceeding $ 1,159.

VALUES

VaR-Parameters	User Portfolio	S&P 500 portfolio
Market value of portfolio (as of latest market closing)	$ 95,910	$ 95,910
Daily value at risk	$ 1,159	$ 776
Monthly value at risk	$ 5,311	$ 3,557
Annual value at risk	$ 18,399	$ 12,322

VALUES. Fundamental and enduring beliefs about the most desirable conditions and purposes of human life.

VARIABLE ANNUITIES. Investment opportunities similar to mutual funds sold by insurance companies.

VARIABLE BUDGET. *See* Flexible budget.

VARIABLE COST. A cost that is uniform per unit but fluctuates in total in direct proportion to changes in the related total activity or volume.

VARIABLE COST PERCENTAGE. The variable expense ratio expressed as a percentage.

VARIABLE COST RATIO. *See* Variable expense ratio.

VARIABLE COSTING. *See* Direct costing.

VARIABLE EXPENSE RATIO. All variable expenses divided by revenues.

VARIABLE PRICE. A method of pricing in which buyers and sellers negotiate the price.

VARIABLE SOCIALIZATION.

VARIABLE WORKING CAPITAL. The extra working capital needed to support the changing production and sales activities is called fluctuating or variable or temporary working capital.

VARIANCE. The deviation of actual results from the expected or budgeted result.

VARIANCE. A probability — weighed sum of the squared deviations of potential outcomes from their mean.

VARIATION CALL. *See* Maintenance Margin.

VARIATION MARGIN. The additional funds the trader must deposit is called the variation margin. The gains or losses on open futures contracts calculated by marking the contracts to the market price at the end of each trading day (or session). These gains or losses are credited or debited by the clearing house to each clearing member's account, and by members to their respective customer's accounts.

VARIETY STORE. This store carrier a wide range of relatively inexpensive goods for the household.

VARYING COST OF CAPITAL. In reality opportunity cost of capital is not constant over time. Hence various opportunity costs are applied to, while taking decisions of investment.

VAT. *See* Value added tax.

VEGA. The change in the option's value for a unit change in the volatility.

VEGA NEUTRAL. A portfolio position that has a vega of zero.

VELOCITY. The number of times the average unit of money changes hands in one year.

VENDING MACHINE. A method of distributing through machines merchandise which has high demand and high frequency of sale.

VENDOR. Manufacturers of equipment, could use a lessor as the third party to market the leasing of the period.

VENTURE CAPITAL. Type of financing sought by early-stage companies seeking to grow rapidly.

VER. *See* Voluntary export restrictions.

VERIFIABILITY. *See* Objectivity.

VERTICAL BEAR SPREAD. Buy a call (put) option and sell a call (put) with a lower strike price. All options have the same maturity.

VERTICAL BULL SPREAD. Buy a call (put) option and sell a call (put) with a higher strike price. All options have the same maturity.

VERTICAL COMPANY. The term refers to a company when buys life assurance policies from people with a long term or terminal illness.

VERTICAL INTEGRATION. The control of the different stages as a product moves from raw materials through production to final distribution.

VERTICAL OPTION SPREAD. Buying and selling call or put options with the same expiration date but different strike prices.

VESTIBULE TRAINING. Training which is given in an area away from the job.

VESTING. It is the right of employees to receive benefits from their pension plans.

VIDEODISC. A disc on which television signals have been recorded for the purposes of storing digital data that may be played back.

VISIBLE EXPORTS. *See* Merchandise exports.

VISIBLE IMPORTS. *See* Merchandise imports.

VOLATILITY. The standard deviation of an asset's return.

VOLUME VARIANCE. *See* Production volume variance and sales volume.

VOLUNTARY CHAIN. A group of retailers who voluntarily associate themselves with a wholesaler to take advantage of volume purchases and discounts.

VOLUNTARY EXPORT RESTRAINTS. A negotiated limitations of exports between an importing and an exporting country.

VOYAGE POLICY. It is related to marine policy that is valid only for a single, specific voyage.

VULNERABLE DERIVATIVE. A derivative for which there is the risk that the writer of the derivative might default.

W

WAGE. Payments made to workers on an hourly rated basis.

WAGE AND SALARY ADMINISTRATION. It is the group of activities involved in the development implementation and maintenance of a base pay system.

WAGE RATE. The level of wages paid employees.

WAGE RIGIDITY. Nominal wage stickiness or slow adjustment, due to formal and informal contracts.

WAGNER ACT. The national labour relations act of 1935 which outlined unfair labour practices of management.

WALL STREET. A customary way of referring to the financial community of banks, investment institutions and stock exchanges centred in the wall street area of New York city.

WALL STREET JOURNAL. The most familiar business newspaper.

WALL STREET RULE. A common practice among corporate stockholders of voting their shares of stock to support the company's management or selling the stock if they disagree seriously with management policies.

WAREHOUSE RECEIPTS. Receipts for goods stored in a warehouse.

WAREHOUSE SHOWROOM. A retailing operation which includes in one building a large warehouse used for storage and a showroom for displaying samples of each piece of brand-name merchandise handled. Furniture and catalogue showrooms are two major users of this retailing method.

WAREHOUSING. On the stock markets, using funds invested in insurance or unit trusts to buy shares that are falling in price, usually as a precursor to a takeover bid.

WASH LEASE. US jargon, particularly under 1981 Tax Act, same as grip lease. This sale of TIC benefits independently of depreciation benefits to lessors requiring specifically short term shelter.

WATER POLLUTION. Low levels of oxygen, low or high pH,

temperature, or toxic chemicals in the water that harm marine life or human.

WATERED STOCK. Stock that has become a smaller percentage of a company's total share capital because of subsequent share issues.

WEAK CURRENCY. A currency that is not fully convertible.

WEAK FORM MARKET EFFICIENCY. Claims that the best prediction of next period's asset price is this period's price.

WEALTH. The value of assets minus the value of debts owned by an individual or institution.

WEALTH EFFECT. During periods of prolonged asset price rise or a bull phase in the stock markets, consumption patterns may also show an increase, this increase is known as the wealth effect. During the boom period, asset holders reap larger returns from their holdings in stocks and property, and hence consume more. Even those who do not hold to many assets tend to jump on the consumerist bandwagon. This also results in a fall in savings.

WEIGHTED-AVERAGE COST. This inventory method assumes that all items available for sale during the period are best represented by their weighed average cost prices.

WEST AFRICAN ECONOMIC COMMUNITY. A regional economic group involving Benin, Burkina Faso, Coted'lvoire Mali Mauritania, Niger and Senegal.

WESTERN HEMISPHERE. Literally the earth's area between the zero and 180th meridian but usually indicates the continents of the American and adjacent islands excluding Greenland.

WHIPSAW. Violent movements (or series of movements) in the prices of any market.

WHISTLE BOWLING. An employee's disclosure to the public of alleged organizational misconduct.

WHITE SQUARE DEFENCE. In a takeover situation a target company may place a significant number of its shares with a friendly party in order to prevent the raider from acquiring them.

WHOLE LIFE INSURANCE. A type of life insurance in which a person is insured as long as he pays premiums and collects only at death.

WHOLESALE PRICE INDEX. The Wholesale Price Index (WPI) covers all commodities : *i.e.*, primary goods, power, fuel, and manufactured goods and services. Each off these is given a different weightage in the index, according to its importance. The WPI is not intended to capture the effect of price rise on the consumer as it takes the wholesale prices.

WHOLESALER. The middleman between the producer and final consumer in the channel of distribution.

WILDCARD OPTION. The right to deliver on a futures contract after the close of trading but before the star of the next trading day.

WILDCAT BANK. Banks in the early 1800s that would purposely issue excessive notes and locate in remote places to make redemption difficult.

WILDCAT SCHEME. It is a speculative investment that is not expected to succeed.

WIPO. *See* World Intellectual Property Organization.

WITH-HOLDING TAX. Payable on the rentals received from many cross border leases, depending on the double taxation arrangements between the countries involved may be prohibitively high.

WORK ETHIC. The belief that human labour and work are inherently worthwhile, admirable and both personally and socially valuable. The work ethic is sometimes called "the protestant ethic" or "the protestant work ethic" due to its origin among early protestant theologians.

WORK GROUP. It is a collection of individuals brought together to perform organizational work.

WORK MEASUREMENT. The careful analysis of a task, its size, the methods used in its performance, and its efficiency.

WORKER'S COMPENSATION. It provides benefits to a person injured on the job.

WORKING CAPITAL. The excess of current assets over current liabilities.

WORKING CAPITAL. Funds used in the daily operations of the business for such purposes as payrolls, raw materials and accounts receivable.

WORKING CAPITAL CYCLE. *See* Operating cycle.

WORKING CAPITAL PROVIDED BY OPERATIONS. Revenues less all operating expenses requiring working capital.

WORLD INTELLECTUAL PROPERTY ORGANIZATION (WIPO). A multilateral agreement to protect patents.

WORLD TRADE ORGANIZATION (WTO). A voluntary organization through which groups of countries negotiate trading agreements and which has authority to oversee trade disputes among countries.

WORLDWIDE TRANSACTION DESKS. Instinet transaction desks are located in eight of the world's key financial centres and staffed by professionals with many years of experience in their local market. Their trading professionals are available around the clock to discuss trading strategies, place orders, check executions, and provide other services that one may require.

WPG. Winnipeg commodity exchange, Canada.

WRITER. A person who issues a derivative security.

WRITTEN DOWN ALLOWANCE. A depreciation allowance where each year's allowance is based on a percentage of the written down value at the end of the previous year. Cars, and asset leased to tax paying bodies are all subject to 25% annual writing down allowances, and those leased abroad, to 10% writing down allowances.

WTO. *See* World Trade Organization.

Y

YELLOW BOOK. Popular term for a publication entitled admission of securities, listing, issued by the London Stock Exchange Council, setting out regulations of admission to the officials list and the obligations of the securities admitted.

YELLOW-DOG CONTRACT. The requirement by an employer that employees agree not to join a union as a condition of employment. This action is prohibited by labour legislation today.

YIELD CURVE. The relationship between interest rates on otherwise — identical financial assets and their term to maturity.

YIELD TO MATURITY. The interest rate at which the amount used to purchase a financial asset, like a bond, would have to be invested in order to grow to the face value paid at maturity.

YIELD. The yield — maturity of a bond.

Z

ZAIBATSU. Large family owned Japanese business that existed before World War II and consisted of a series of financial and manufacturing companies usually held together by a large holding company.

ZAI-TECH. Japanese and the US stock market practice of borrowing money in order to invest in stocks and bonds.

ZBB. Symbol for zero base budgeting.

ZERIAL BOND. It is a stripped treasury bond or other zero-coupon debt instrument issued in serial form.

ZERO DEFECTS. The elimination of defects which results in the reduction of manufacturing costs and an increase in consumer satisfaction.

ZERO DISCHARGE. An abstract unattainable environmental goal that would involve the eliminate of all industrial and agricultural pollution.

ZERO SUM GAIN. A situation in which one party's gain equals another party's loss.

ZERO-BASE BUDGETING. Budgeting from the ground up as though the budget were being initiated for the first time.

ZERO-BASE BUDGETING. Budgeting in which enterprise programmes are divided into 'packages' comprising goals, activities, and needed resources, and costs are calculated for each package from the ground up.

ZERO-COUPON BOND. A bond that makes no interest or coupon payments.

Z-TRENCH : HIGH–PAY-OUT CLIENTELE. Investors who prefer near dividends to future dividends are high pay-out clientele. They prefer dividends than capita gains. They wish firms to pay high dividends than retention of profits.